DENMARK, FINLAND, AND SWEDEN

DENMARK, FINLAND, AND SWEDEN

EDITED BY AMY MCKENNA, SENIOR EDITOR, GEOGRAPHY

Britannica
Educational Publishing
IN ASSOCIATION WITH
ROSEN
EDUCATIONAL SERVICES

Published in 2014 by Britannica Educational Publishing
(a trademark of Encyclopædia Britannica, Inc.)
in association with Rosen Educational Services, LLC
29 East 21st Street, New York, NY 10010.

Distributed exclusively by Rosen Educational Services.
For a listing of additional Britannica Educational Publishing titles, call toll free (800) 237-9932.

First Edition

Britannica Educational Publishing
J.E. Luebering, Director, Core Reference Group
Adam Augustyn, Assistant Manager, Core Reference Group
Marilyn L. Barton: Senior Coordinator, Production Control
Steven Bosco: Director, Editorial Technologies
Lisa S. Braucher: Senior Producer and Data Editor
Yvette Charboneau: Senior Copy Editor
Kathy Nakamura: Manager, Media Acquisition
Edited by: Amy McKenna, Senior Editor, Geography and History

Rosen Educational Services
Jeanne Nagle: Editor
Nelson Sá: Art Director
Cindy Reiman: Photo Researcher
Brian Garvey: Designer, Cover Design
Introduction by Alexandra Hanson-Harding

Library of Congress Cataloging-in-Publication Data

Denmark, Finland, and Sweden/edited by Amy McKenna.
     pages cm.—(The Britannica guide to countries of the European Union)
"In association with Britannica Educational Publishing, Rosen Educational Services."
Includes bibliographical references and index.
ISBN 978-1-61530-969-6 (library binding)
1. Denmark—Juvenile literature. 2. Finland—Juvenile literature. 3. Sweden—Juvenile
literature. I. McKenna, Amy, 1969-
DL109.D434 2014
948—dc23

2012045262

Manufactured in the United States of America

On the cover: A composite of two images showing the new library (built in 2007) and an environmental-art sculpture in Turku, Finland. Turku was named by the European Union as the European Capital of Culture for 2011. *Cavaglia Denis/hemis.fr/Getty Images (sculpture), Allan Baxter/Photographer's Choice/Getty Images (library)*

On page xii: Map of Scandinavia showing Denmark, Finland, and Sweden. *Stasys Eidiejus/ Shutterstock.com*

Cover, p. iii (map and stars), back cover, multiple interior pages (stars) ©iStockphoto.com/ pop_jop; cover, multiple interior pages (background graphic) Mina De La O/Digital Vision/ Getty Images

CONTENTS

31

44

74

118

133

141

164

166

176

191

197

210

Hammerfest

Alta

Kirkenes

Harstad

Kiruna

Rovaniemi

Norwegian Sea

Mo

Lulea

Skelleftea

Gulf of Bothnia

FINLAND

Umea

Ostersund

Vaasa

Trondheim

SWEDEN

NORWAY

Helsinki ★

Bergen

Gavle

Tallinn ★

Oslo ★

ESTONIA

Stockholm ★

Parnu

LATVIA

Goteborg

Riga ★

DENMARK

Liepaja

North Sea

Baltic Sea

Klaipeda **LITHUANIA**

Vejle

Copenhagen ★

Vilni ★

NETH.

Gdansk

Olsztyn

Hamburg

Elbe **GERMANY**

POLAND

0û

10ûE

20ûE

30ûE

B

Denmark, Finland, and Sweden have emerged as three of the world's most thriving nations, with futures as bright as the 24-hour Arctic summer sun. In this volume readers will learn how these countries have become so successful.

Located between the North and Baltic seas and attached to Germany by the Jutland Peninsula, Denmark counts more than 400 islands among its geographic territory, including Zealand, the largest island at 2,715 square miles [7,031 square km]. During the Ice Age, the Nordic lands were crushed below sea level by the weight of glaciers. This left behind rocky soil, peat bogs, marshes, lakes, islands, and jagged coastlines, which are still the predominant geologic features of Denmark today. Travel by bicycle is popular in this relatively flat country; the highest point is only 568 feet (173 metres) above sea level. Two other territories are attached to Denmark, the Faroe Islands and Greenland, though both have home rule.

Denmark's ruler is Queen Margrethe II, but the real governmental power is held by the Folketing, or parliament. High taxes pay for social welfare services Danes value, such as public health programs and pensions. The economy of Denmark revolves around service industries, trade, and manufacturing. Among items produced by the Danes are clothing, furniture, electronics, and even windmills. Culturally, Denmark has made many contributions in the arts and sciences. Fairy tale scribe Hans Christian Andersen is arguably the most famous Danish export in the realm of authorship, while Carl Nielsen and Lars von Trier are among the country's notable composers and film directors, respectively. Denmark is home to physicist Niels Bohr and renowned philosopher Søren Kierkegaard as well.

Signs of human life in the land now known as Denmark date as far back as 12,000 BCE. The early Danes believed in a panoply of Norse gods, such as the thunder god Thor and Freyja, the love goddess. In the 10th century CE, however, King Harald I (Bluetooth) claimed to have unified the country and converted the Danes to Christianity, according to one of the famous inscribed gravestones known as the Jelling Stones. The reign of Harald I occurred during an era known as the Viking Age. In addition to being merchants and explorers, Vikings were notorious for plundering and conquests. Some Danish Vikings settled in a part of eastern England called the Danelaw, as well as in Normandy, France.

In the 1000s, Canute the Great temporarily united Denmark with England and Norway. During the Middle Ages, Danish territory also included Estonia, southern parts of Sweden, and the Duchies of Schleswig and Holstein (now mostly part of Germany).

In 1397, Denmark, Sweden (which then included Finland), and Norway signed the Kalmar Union, uniting under one ruler. The Nordic alliance began to crumble after years of resistance from Sweden, which contended that Denmark held too much power. In 1520, King Christian II of Denmark punished Sweden for its opposition by finally defeating its regent, usurping the crown, and killing more than 80 of the regent's supporters. The last incident, referred to as the "Stockholm Bloodbath," outraged Swedes, who rebelled and in 1523 declared independence, thus tearing the Union asunder. Relations with Sweden continued to be strained into the 17th century and beyond, often resulting in outright warfare.

During the Napoleonic Wars, Britain destroyed Denmark's fleet, blockaded Denmark's sea route to Norway, and destroyed three-fourths of the Danish capital, Copenhagen. As a result of interrupted trade, Denmark declared bankruptcy in 1813. Steps toward economic recovery began with the formation of an independent national bank in 1818.

Although Denmark was able to remain neutral throughout the course of World War I, the country was forced to enter into World War II when German troops invaded the country on April 9, 1940. Danish resistance groups created illegal newspapers, spied, and sabotaged Nazi plans. In one of Denmark's finest hours, when the Germans planned to round up Denmark's 7,000 Jews in 1943, Danes hid most of the Jews and helped them escape to neutral Sweden.

The later portion of the 20th century was something of a mixed bag for Denmark, in terms of progressive political and social reforms. In 1989, Denmark became the first country to allow registered partnerships for same-sex couples. ("Gender-neutral" marriage laws were enacted in 2012.) In the 2011 elections, a centre-left coalition took power, resulting in the election of Helle Thorning-Schmidt as the country's first female prime minister.

As with Denmark, Finland was once covered by massive ice sheets that left behind a landscape dotted with thousands of lakes. Located between Russia and Sweden, Finland is a rich country whose students are among the world's top achievers. Famous Finns include architect Eliel Saarinen and composer Jean Sibelius, whose *Finlandia* still has occasion to stir up feelings of nationalist pride. A republic, Finland is led by a president and a prime minister, and has a 200-member parliament, the Eduskunta.

Nomads arrived in Finland about 9,000 years ago; around 1000 BCE, the ancestors of the present Finns arrived. In 1157 CE, Sweden's King Eric crusaded to bring Catholicism to Finland; by 1249, much of the territory that is now Finland had come under Swedish rule. In the 1500s, Finland turned to Protestantism, a transformation largely bolstered by the efforts of Finnish reformer Mikael Agricola, who had studied under Reformation leaders in Germany. Among his other accomplishments, he is known for having translated the New Testament into Finnish.

During the Second Northern War, Russians occupied Finland from 1713 to

1721, and forced Sweden to give up parts of southeastern Finland. Then, in 1809, Sweden lost Finland completely to the Russians, who made Finland an autonomous grand duchy within Russia. In 1835, a collection of traditional Finnish myths, the epic Kalevala, was created. Finns began to feel a sense of themselves as a separate people. More people started speaking Finnish. This national pride, and the opportunity provided by the Russian Revolution in 1917, led to Finland's independence from Russia later that year.

The Finns ran afoul of Russia (at this point, known as the Soviet Union) once again during the Winter War of 1939–40, and were forced to surrender a large portion of southeastern part of their country. In part to counterbalance increasing demands from the Soviet Union, German troops were allowed to move across Finnish soil in order to stage attacks on the Soviet Union during World War II. This decision launched what is known as the War of Continuation. The Finns won some battles early on, but the Red Army eventually prevailed. The price of peace in that conflict was expulsion of German troops and the payment of land and monetary reparations.

By the mid-1960s, more Finns worked in manufacturing than the traditional farming and forestry. For decades the bulk of Finland's industrial trade was with their former nemesis, the Soviet Union. After the latter's collapse in the early 1990s, Finland had a tough time economically, regrouping as part of the European Union in 1995. Among its successful businesses in the late 20th and early 21st centuries was the cell phone manufacturer Nokia.

The third Nordic country detailed in this book, Sweden is approximately 1,000 miles (1,600 km) long and 310 miles (500 km) wide. The north contains parts of Lappland, homeland of the Sami (Lapp) people. The north can have heavy snowfall for eight months a year, but southern Sweden is milder, thanks to warmer winds from the North Atlantic current. Much of Sweden is covered with birch, fir, and pine forests, and is filled with lingonberries and blueberries that anyone can pick. Preservation of the country's natural environs gave rise to the establishment of Europe's first national park, Sarek National Park, in 1909. The Swedish ecological bent is also evident in its use of hydroelectric power, created by harnessing the currents from Sweden's rivers, which provide about half the country's power needs. Nuclear power provides much of the rest.

Sweden is a constitutional monarchy, but the monarch's powers are ceremonial. The country is run by the 349-member Swedish Parliament (Riksdag), whose members are elected every four years. Nearly one-fifth of all Swedes have at least one parent who was born in another country, pointing to the fact that immigration has contributed to the country's population growth.

Although Sweden's per capita gross national product is high, the country also has high taxes, which pay for generous benefits. The country is a member of the European Union, but it maintains an independent currency, the krona. Popular Swedish exports have included cars (Volvo and Saab), furniture (IKEA), and communication equipment (Ericsson). Culturally, Sweden is famous for author and playwright August Strindberg, actress Ingrid Bergman, director Ingmar Bergmann, author Stieg Larsson (*The Girl with the Dragon Tattoo*), the pop group ABBA, and others.

Archaeologists have found traces of human life in Sweden dating as far back as 9000 BCE. By 850 CE Swedish Viking chieftains had captured parts of Russia and Ukraine. They created a stronghold at the city of Kiev and other river towns, using the Dnieper and Volga rivers to trade slave and furs with Arabic civilizations. Christianity was brought to Sweden, primarily by English missionaries, and a religious stronghold was established in the region by the end of the 11th century.

Beginning in 1397, Sweden was the part of the Kalmar Union, an agreement among Nordic kingdoms (Denmark and Norway, as well as Sweden, which included Finland at the time) to operate under a single monarchy. After a bitter struggle, Sweden left the Union and declared its independence in 1523, naming Gustav I Vasa king. Sweden owed the Hanseatic League a large debt for helping to rid the country of Danish influence, and granted Lübeck, the capital of the Hanseatic League, a monopoly over Swedish trade. But when Denmark got a new king, Christian III, in 1534, the Hanseatic League tried to return the exiled Christian II to power as Denmark's king. Sweden helped young Christian III fight the Hanseatic army, which was defeated, and in 1536 Sweden's debt to the League was wiped out, leaving the country free to trade beyond the Baltic.

In the 17th century, Sweden became a major European power. In 1630, King Gustav II Adolf led Sweden into the Thirty Years' War. He died in battle, but Sweden gained several territorial concessions by the end of the war. In 1655, Charles X Gustav started the First Northern War, during which he conquered most of Poland. Following that, Sweden then wrested four provinces located on the tip of the Swedish Peninsula from Denmark. They have remained under Swedish control ever since. During the Napoleonic Wars that swept across Europe in the early years of the 19th century, Sweden took Norway from Denmark—at least until 1905—although it had lost Finland to Russia (in 1809).

During the 20th century, peace has been an important issue in Sweden. The country stayed neutral in World Wars I and II. Swedish diplomats have played large roles as peacekeepers in the United Nations. One of Sweden's most famous peace and human rights advocates, Prime Minister Olof Palme, was assassinated on

February 28, 1986. The act shocked the country, but in the years that have followed, his accomplishments have been a source of inspiration for many peace and human rights activists.

As this introduction and, indeed, the entire contents of this book show, Denmark, Finland, and Sweden are countries of great physical beauty and abundance. Overall, their people enjoy good health and economic opportunities, and share a strong sense of social justice. They are a tremendous asset to the European Union.

CHAPTER 1

DENMARK: THE LAND AND ITS PEOPLE

Denmark occupies the peninsula of Jutland (Jylland), which extends northward from the centre of continental western Europe, and an archipelago of more than 400 islands

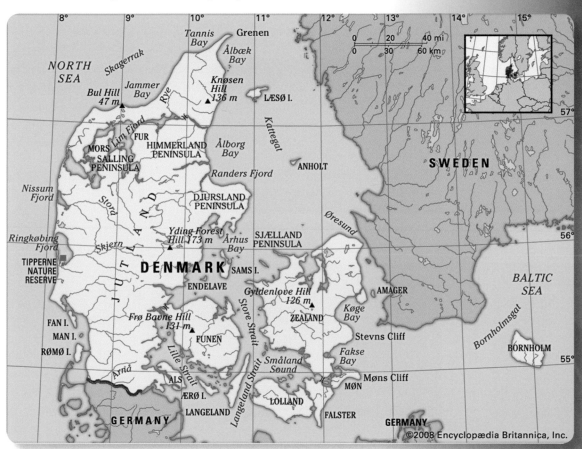

Physical map of Denmark. Encyclopædia Britannica, Inc.

to the east of the peninsula. Jutland makes up more than two-thirds of the country's total land area; at its northern tip is the island of Vendsyssel-Thy (1,809 square miles [4,685 square km]), separated from the mainland by the Lim Fjord. The largest of the country's islands are Zealand (Sjælland; 2,715 square miles [7,031 square km]), Vendsyssel-Thy, and Funen (Fyn; 1,152 square miles [2,984 square km]).

Along with Norway and Sweden, Denmark is a part of the northern European region known as Scandinavia. The country's capital, Copenhagen (København), is located primarily on Zealand; the second largest city, Århus, is the major urban centre of Jutland.

Though small in territory and population, Denmark has nonetheless played a notable role in European history. Denmark has also developed humane governmental institutions and cooperative, nonviolent approaches to problem solving, making an important contribution to world culture.

Denmark is attached directly to continental Europe at Jutland's 42-mile (68-km) boundary with Germany. Other than this connection, all the frontiers with surrounding countries are maritime, including that with the United Kingdom to the west across the North Sea. Norway and Sweden lie to the north, separated from Denmark by sea lanes linking the North Sea to the Baltic Sea. From west to east, these passages are called the Skagerrak, the Kattegat, and The Sound (Øresund). Eastward in the Baltic Sea lies the Danish island of Bornholm.

RELIEF

Denmark proper is a lowland area that lies, on average, not more than 100 feet (30 metres) above sea level. The country's highest point, reaching only 568 feet (173 metres), is Yding

The Danish national flag. Encyclopædia Britannica, Inc.

GREENLAND AND THE FAROE ISLANDS

This volume covers principally the land and people of continental Denmark. However, the Kingdom of Denmark also encompasses the island of Greenland and the Faroe Islands, both located in the North Atlantic Ocean. Each area is distinctive in history, language, and culture. Home rule was granted to the Faroes in 1948 and to Greenland in 1979, though foreign policy and defense remain under Danish control.

With an area of 836,330 sq mi (2,166,086 sq km), Greenland is the world's largest island. Two-thirds of it lie within the Arctic Circle, and it is dominated by the massive Greenland Ice Sheet. The capital, Nuuk, is located in the southwest of the island. Fishing is central to the economy; there are also commercial mineral deposits, including a large gold deposit, as well as offshore oil exploration. About four-fifths of the population are native Greenlanders, principally of Inuit descent, residing in coastal areas. The Inuit probably crossed to northwestern Greenland from mainland North America, along the islands of the Canadian Arctic, from about 2500 BCE to about 1100 CE. The Norwegian Erik the Red visited Greenland in 982; his son Leif Eriksson introduced Christianity in the 11th century. The original Norse settlements became extinct in the 15th century, but Greenland was recolonized by Denmark in 1721. Greenland became part of the Kingdom of Denmark in 1953, with home rule being established in 1979. At the beginning of the 21st century, the movement for full independence began to gain support, as did the belief among many scientists that global warming was responsible for the accelerated melting of the ice sheet.

The Faroe (also spelled Faeroe) Islands lie to the north of the British Isles. There are 17 inhabited islands and many islets and reefs, with a total area of 540 sq mi (1,399 sq km). The largest island, Strømø, holds the capital of Tórshavn. The islands are high and rugged, with coasts that are deeply indented with fjords. The economy is based on fishing and sheep raising. First settled by Irish monks (c. 700), the islands were colonized by the Vikings (c. 800) and were ruled by Norway from the 11th century until 1380, when they passed to Denmark. They unsuccessfully sought independence in 1946 but received self-government in 1948. In the early 21st century they continued discussions with Denmark about full independence.

Forest Hill (Yding Skovhøj) in east-central Jutland.

The basic contours of the Danish landscape were shaped at the end of the Pleistocene Epoch (i.e., about 2,600,000 to 11,700 years ago) by the so-called Weichsel glaciation. This great glacial mass withdrew temporarily during several warmer interstadial periods, but it repeatedly returned to cover the land until it retreated to the Arctic north for the last time about 10,000 years ago. As a result, the barren layers of chalk and limestone that earlier constituted the land surface acquired a covering of soil that built up as the Weichsel retreated, forming low, hilly, and generally fertile moraines that diversify the otherwise flat landscape.

Coast of Bornholm, Den., on the Baltic Sea.
G. Glase-Ostman Agency

Scandinavian and Baltic ice sheets runs from Nissum Fjord on the western coast of Jutland eastward toward Viborg, from there swinging sharply south down the spine of the peninsula toward Åbenrå and the German city of Flensburg, just beyond the Danish frontier. The ice front is clearly marked in the contrast between the flat western Jutland region, composed of sands and gravels strewn by meltwaters that poured west from the shrinking ice sheet, and the fertile loam plains and hills of eastern and northern Denmark, which become markedly sandier toward the prehistoric ice front.

In northern Jutland, where the long Lim Fjord separates the northern tip (Vendsyssel-Thy) from the rest of the peninsula, there are numerous flat areas of sand and gravel, some of

A scenic boundary representing the extreme limit reached by the

THE SOUND

The Sound (Danish: Øresund; Swedish: Öresund), a strait between Zealand (Sjælland), Denmark, and Skåne, Sweden, connects the Kattegat strait in the northwest with the Baltic Sea to the south. It is one of the busiest sea lanes in the world.

Its total length, between the Kullen peninsula in the north and Falsterbo in the south (both in Sweden), is 70 miles (110 km). The more landlocked portion, between Helsingør-Helsingborg in the north (width 3 miles [5 km]) and Copenhagen-Malmö in the south (width 9 miles [14 km]), is 33 miles (53 km) long. The strait has a minimum depth of 23 feet (7 metres) and a surface current flowing up to 3 to 4 miles (5 to 6 km) per hour toward the Kattegat. Ice in the almost tideless strait may impede navigation in severe winters. Three large islands lie in The Sound: Amager (partly embraced by Copenhagen), Ven, and Saltholme. These divide the waters into the channels of Drögden (west) and Flinterenden (east).

The principal ports are Copenhagen and Helsingør (Elsinore) on the Danish side and Malmö and Helsingborg on the Swedish side. In 2000 the Øresund Link, a bridge and tunnel system connecting Malmö and Copenhagen, opened; it has spurred economic growth and cooperation in the region.

The Sound has long been an important commercial sea lane. In the past, political control of The Sound, the shortest route from the Kattegat to the Baltic, conferred great commercial benefits. Between 1429 and 1657, Denmark controlled both shores and exacted tolls from all shipping passing through. Even after Skåne was annexed by Sweden in 1658, the great Danish coastal fortress of Kronborg at Helsingør continued to levy The Sound toll until 1857.

which became stagnant bogs. Burials and ritual deposits interred in these bogs in antiquity—especially during the Bronze Age and the Iron Age—have been recovered by archaeologists. In more recent centuries these bogs were a valued source of peat for fuel. In the 20th century they were drained to serve as grazing areas for livestock.

In places along the northern and southwestern coasts of Jutland, salt marshes were formed by the evaporation of an inland sea that existed during the late Permian Epoch (approximately 260 to 250 million years ago). Senonian chalk, deposited about 100 million years ago, is exposed in southeastern Zealand, at the base of Stevns Cliff (Stevns Klint) and Møns Cliff (Møns Klint), and at Bulbjerg, in northwestern Jutland. Younger limestone of the Danian Age (about 65 million years old) is quarried in southeastern Zealand.

On Bornholm, outcroppings reveal close affinities with geologic formations in southern Sweden. Precambrian granites more than 570 million years old—among the oldest on the Earth's surface—are exposed across extensive areas on the northern half of the island. On the southern half, sandstone and shales of the Cambrian Period (about 540 to 490 million years ago) overlie the older granites.

DRAINAGE

The longest river in Denmark is the Gudenå. It flows a distance of 98 miles (158 km) from its source just northwest of Tørring, in east-central Jutland, through the Silkeborg Lakes (Silkeborg Langsø) and then northeast to empty in the Randers Fjord on the east coast. There are many small lakes; the largest is Arresø on Zealand. Large lagoons have formed behind the coastal dunes in the west, such as at the Ringkøbing and Nissum fjords.

SOILS

In most of Denmark the soil rests on glacially deposited gravel, sand, and clay, under which lie ancient chalk and limestone. The subterranean limestone resulted in a permeation of the soil with calcium, which diminished its value for agriculture when it was first brought under cultivation in the Neolithic Period. Through millennia of cultivation, however, the soil improved greatly, so that more than half of the land surface is excellent for farming.

CLIMATE

Denmark experiences changeable weather because it is located in the temperate zone at the meeting point of diverse air masses from the Atlantic, the Arctic, and eastern Europe. The west coast faces the inhospitable North Sea, but the terminal section of the warm Gulf Stream (the North Atlantic Current) moderates the climate. Lakes may freeze and snow frequently falls during the cold winters, yet the mean temperature in February, the coldest month, is about 32 °F (0 °C), which is roughly 12 °F (7 °C) higher than the worldwide average for that latitude. Summers are mild, featuring episodes of cloudy weather interrupted by sunny days. The mean temperature in July, which is the warmest month, is approximately 60 °F (16 °C).

Rain falls throughout the year but is relatively light in winter and spring and greatest from late summer through autumn. The annual precipitation of approximately 25 inches (635 mm) ranges from about 32 inches (810 mm) in southwestern Jutland to about 16 inches (405 mm) in parts of the archipelago.

PLANT AND ANIMAL LIFE

In prehistoric times, before fields were cleared for cultivation, much of the land was covered with a deciduous forest of oak, elm, lime (linden), and beech trees. The original forest did not survive, but highly valued areas were reforested later to break up the expanses of agricultural fields that dominate the landscape. Denmark borders the coniferous belt and has therefore been receptive to the establishment of plantations of spruce and fir, particularly in parts of Jutland where extensive wastelands of dune vegetation and heather were reclaimed for forestry. In all, about one-tenth of the land is forested.

Abundant postglacial herds of large mammals, including elks, brown bears, wild boars, and aurochs (a now extinct species of wild ox), died out under the pressures of human expansion and an intensive agricultural system. Roe deer, however, occupy the countryside in growing numbers, and large-antlered red deer can be found in the forests of Jutland. The country also is home to smaller mammals, such as hares and hedgehogs. Birds are abundant, numbering more than 300 species, of which about half breed in the country. Storks—common summer residents in the early 20th century—migrate each year from their winter home in Africa, but they are now almost extinct. Fish, particularly cod, herring, and plaice, are abundant in Danish waters and form the basis for a large fishing industry.

ETHNIC GROUPS

Denmark is almost entirely inhabited by ethnic Danes. Few Faroese or

Greenlanders have settled in continental Denmark, despite their status as Danish citizens. Small minorities of Germans and Poles, on the other hand, have been long established and are substantially assimilated. In the early 21st century important ethnic minorities in the country included Turks, Germans, Iraqis, Swedes, Norwegians, Bosniacs (Muslims from Bosnia and Herzegovina), Iranians, and Somalis.

LANGUAGES

Danish, or Dansk, is the official language. It is closely related to Norwegian, with which it is mutually intelligible, especially in the written form. Although the other Scandinavian languages are close relatives, they are sufficiently different to be understood easily only by those schooled or experienced in the effort. Many educated or urban Danes have learned to speak a second language, particularly English. Turkish, Arabic, German, and other minority languages are spoken by members of the country's various ethnic groups.

RELIGION

Religious freedom is an essentially unchallenged value in Denmark. Roman Catholic churches and Jewish synagogues have long existed in the larger cities, and the first mosque in the country was built in 1967. By the early 21st century Islam had become an increasingly important minority religion,

and a significant number of Danes were not religious at all. Nevertheless, the overwhelming majority of Danes remained at least nominally members of the state church, the Evangelical Lutheran People's Church of Denmark (folkekirken).

Lutheranism replaced Roman Catholicism as the country's official religion in 1536, during the Reformation. In the 19th century, at a time when Danish Lutheranism had become very formal and ritualistic, a revitalization movement known as "Grundtvigianism" inspired a new sense of Christian awareness. The founder of the movement, Danish bishop N.F.S. Grundtvig, provided a philosophical, religious, and organizational basis for "educating and awakening" the impoverished peasantry. This was achieved by establishing folk high schools in which Christian belief and peasant culture were taught as a basis for creating pride in the Danish heritage. A separate revival movement also was organized within the framework of the Danish church. Known as the Home Mission (Indre Mission), it was founded by a clergyman, Vilhelm Beck, in the mid-19th century. The Home Mission survives as a contemporary evangelical expression of Lutheran Pietism, which had won converts in the 18th century. Today members of the Home Mission constitute a minority within the church; they place emphasis on the importance of individual Bible study, personal faith, and a sin-free style of living.

N.F.S. GRUNDTVIG

Danish bishop and poet N.F.S. Grundtvig—who was born Nikolai Frederik Severin Grundtvig on September 8, 1783, in Udby, Denmark—was the founder of Grundtvigianism, a theological movement that revitalized the Danish Lutheran church. He was also an outstanding hymn writer, historian, and educator and a pioneer of studies on early Scandinavian literature.

After taking a degree in theology (1803) from the University of Copenhagen, Grundtvig studied the *Edda*s and Icelandic sagas. His *Nordens mythologi* (1808; "Northern Mythology") marked a turning point in this research; like his early poems, it was inspired by Romanticism.

In 1811, after a spiritual and emotional conflict that ended in a "Christian awakening," Grundtvig became his father's curate. His first attempt to write history from a Christian standpoint, *Verdens krønike* (1812; "World Chronicle"), attracted much attention. From 1813 until 1821, his criticism of the rationalist tendencies that were then predominant in Denmark's Lutheran church made it impossible for him to find a pastorate. In poems such as those in *Roskilde-riim* (1814; "The Roskilde Rhymes") and other collections and in *Bibelske prædikener* (1816; "Biblical Sermons"), he called for a renewal of the spirit of Martin Luther, and in his opposition to the Romantic philosophers he foreshadowed Søren Kierkegaard. During these years he also opened the way for research into Anglo-Saxon literature with his version of *Beowulf* (1820).

In 1825 he was the central figure in a church controversy when in his *Kirkens gienmæle* ("The Church's Reply") he accused the theologian H.N. Clausen of treating Christianity as merely a philosophical idea. Grundtvig maintained that Christianity was a historical revelation, handed down by the unbroken chain of a living sacramental tradition at baptism and communion. His writings were placed under censorship, and in 1826 he resigned his pastorate but continued to develop his view of the Christian church in theological writings and in *Christelige prædikener* (1827–30; "Christian Sermons"). He expounded his philosophy in a new and inspired *Nordens mythologi* (1832; "Northern Mythology") and in his *Haandbog i verdenshistorien* (1833–43; "Handbook of World History"). As an educator—e.g., in *Skolen for livet* (1838; "Schools for Life")—he stressed the need for the thorough knowledge of the Danish language and of Danish and biblical history, in opposition to those who favoured the study of the classics in Latin. His criticism of classical schools as elitist inspired the founding, after 1844, of voluntary residential folk high schools, in which young people of every class were encouraged to be educated. These schools spread throughout Scandinavia and inspired adult education in several other countries.

In 1839 Grundtvig was given the position of preacher at Vartov Hospital in Copenhagen, and in 1861 he was given the rank of bishop. His liberal outlook found political expression in his active part in the movement leading to the introduction of parliamentary government in Denmark in 1849.

Particularly lasting is Grundtvig's position as the greatest Scandinavian hymn writer. His *Sang-værk til den danske kirke* (1837–81; "Song Collection for the Danish Church") contains new versions of traditional Christian hymns, as well as numerous original hymns, many of them well known in Norwegian, Swedish, German, and English translations.

N.F. Grundtvig: Selected Writings, in English translation, was published in 1976. Grundtvig died September 2, 1872, in Copenhagen.

SETTLEMENT PATTERNS

The vast majority of the Danish population lives in urban areas. The largest city is Copenhagen (located on the islands of Zealand and Amager), followed by Århus (in eastern Jutland), Odense (on Funen), Ålborg (in northern Jutland), and Esbjerg (in southwestern Jutland). More than one-tenth of Danes continue to inhabit rural areas, but the country's relatively small size and its excellent transportation network mean that no farm or village is truly isolated.

Agriculturalists established a village settlement pattern early in the prehistory of Denmark. From at least the Middle Ages until the 18th century, these settlements were organized under the rules of an open-field system, the dominant feature of which was communalism. Most individual landholders were tenant farmers (fæstebønder), whose farm buildings and

COPENHAGEN

Copenhagen (Danish: København) is the capital and largest city of Denmark. It is located on the islands of Zealand (Sjælland) and Amager, at the southern end of The Sound (Øresund).

The heart of the city is the Rådhuspladsen ("Town Hall Square"). From the square, an old crooked shopping street leads northeast to the former centre of the city, Kongens Nytorv ("King's New Square"), laid out in the 17th century. Buildings there include the Thott Palace (now the French Embassy) and the Charlottenborg Palace (now the Royal Academy of Fine Arts), both of the 17th century, and the Royal Theatre, built in 1874.

Located on the island of Slotsholmen ("Castle Islet") is Christiansborg Palace, built on the site of the old castle founded by Bishop Absalon in 1167. Since 1928 the palace has been occupied by Parliament, the Supreme Court, and the Foreign Office. Nearby buildings house other government offices. Slotsholmen also contains the Bertel Thorvaldsen Museum, the Royal Arsenal Museum, the state archives, and the Royal Library. The Black Diamond, an extension of the library, opened in 1999; a modern structure of steel and glass, it lies on the waterfront.

Other important buildings include the Prinsens Palace, now the National Museum; the Church of Our Lady; the University of Copenhagen, founded in 1479; the Petri Church, used after 1585 as a parish church for the German residents of the city and thoroughly restored (1994–2000); the 17th-century citadel; and the palace of Amalienborg. The botanical gardens laid out in 1874 have an observatory with a statue of the Danish astronomer Tycho Brahe. A more modern attraction named in honour of the 16th-century astronomer is the Tycho Brahe Planetarium, which opened in 1989.

Additional popular sites are the Tivoli amusement park and the Ny Carlsberg Glyptotek, with a fine collection of traditional and modern art. Located at Langelinie Pier is the Little

Statue of the Little Mermaid, a beloved character created by Danish storyteller Hans Christian Andersen, greets visitors to Copenhagen harbour. Andrei Nekrassov/Shutterstock.com

Mermaid statue (1913), which is based on a story by Hans Christian Andersen. A Danish national symbol, it is one of the city's most popular tourist attractions.

The old quarter of Christianshavn is on the harbour to the south. It contains the 17th-century Church of Our Saviour. The western quarter contains the Frederiksberg Park, with its palace and a zoological garden.

For much of the 20th century, Copenhagen and its surrounding areas contained most of Denmark's manufacturing industry. By 2000, however, the city's economy was dominated by public and private services, trade, finance, and education. A number of arterial streets carry traffic toward the centre, across the harbour bridges. There are electric railways (S-baner) for commuters and a network of city bus lines. The last streetcars disappeared in 1972. In the late 1990s construction began on a fully automated subway system in Copenhagen, and the first line opened in 2002. In 2000 the Øresund Link, a combined tunnel-and-bridge system connecting Copenhagen with Malmö, Sweden, opened. It also serves Copenhagen Airport at Kastrup and supports cooperation and regional growth on both sides of The Sound.

In addition to the University of Copenhagen, there are a number of other institutions of higher education. These include the Technical University of Denmark (1829), the Engineering Academy of Denmark (1957), the Royal Danish Academy of Music (1867), the Royal Veterinary and Agricultural College (1856), and the Copenhagen School of Economics and Business Administration (1917).

land belonged to the local manor house (herregård). The scattered plots of tenanted land were located in each of two or three large fields, which were farmed collectively by the tenants; therefore, it was essential that villagers agree on the nature and timing of plowing, harrowing, planting, and harvesting. Meeting at a central place in the village, family heads discussed common problems of field management and agreed on mutual responsibilities and cooperation. Each family received harvests from its own plots but worked with the others to manage the fields. They shared resources in order to assemble large wheeled plows, each drawn by six or eight horses. Livestock were grazed as a single village herd on the stubble of harvested fields. Shared decisions also were made on the use of communal facilities, such as the meadow, commons, village square, pond, and church. Danish peasants cooperated in much of what they did, and a communal spirit was the product.

The open-field system was replaced by the consolidation of fields (udskiftningen) and the purchase of farms (frikøbet) as a result of the great land reforms (de store landboreformer) put into place by reform-minded estate owners. By the beginning of the 19th century, the wheeled plow had been replaced by a lightweight plow that could be pulled by a single horse, which most farmers could afford. The bulk of the economy shifted from subsistence to commercial farming. The result was the dismantlement of the old open-field system and an end to village communalism. As small scattered plots were consolidated into larger individual holdings, some landowners moved their farmsteads away from the village to be closer to their fields, obscuring the pattern of village settlements. Subsequently, an economic shift to light industry and trade was associated with a growth in the size of towns and cities.

DEMOGRAPHIC TRENDS

Denmark's population remained nearly stable during the late 20th century, but in the early 21st century it began growing slowly. As in neighbouring countries, the total fertility rate (average number of births for each childbearing woman) has been under two—below the world average—since the 1970s. The age distribution also has shifted as a consequence of this low level of fertility, with more residents of Denmark over age 60 than under age 15.

However, population losses owing to low fertility and emigration have been offset by slight increases in immigration. In the 1960s an economic expansion required more labour than the country could supply, and "guest workers" (gæstearbejdere) from such countries as Turkey, Pakistan, and Yugoslavia made their way into Denmark. Many of these workers settled permanently in the country. Later in the century, refugees from the former Yugoslavia, Iraq, Somalia, and elsewhere arrived.

Within the country, movement from rural areas to cities has continued, but migration to smaller urban centres grew disproportionately in the late 20th century. Migrants to larger urban areas now commonly settle in suburban residential communities rather than in the cities as such.

CHAPTER 2

THE DANISH ECONOMY

Denmark supports a high standard of living—its per capita gross national product is among the highest in the world—with well-developed social services. The economy is based primarily on service industries, trade, and manufacturing; only a tiny percentage of the population is engaged in agriculture and fishing. Small enterprises are dominant.

The first of the Nordic countries (Denmark, Finland, Iceland, Norway, and Sweden) to do so, Denmark joined the European Economic Community (EEC; ultimately succeeded by the European Union [EU]) in 1973, at the same time as the United Kingdom, then its most important trading partner. Long-standing economic collaboration between Denmark and the other Nordic countries—including those that have not joined the EU—also continues today. Uniform commercial legislation in the Nordic countries dates to the 19th century.

In the Danish mixed welfare-state economy, private sector expenditures account for more than half of the net national income. Public expenditure is directed primarily toward health and social services, education, economic affairs, foreign affairs, and national defense. The government does not have significant commercial or industrial income.

AGRICULTURE AND FISHING

Next to its well-educated labour force, the soil is still Denmark's most important raw material. About half of the land is

Farms surrounding the town of Nørreby, Femø Island, Denmark. Erik Betting/Pressehuset

intensively exploited and extensively fertilized. More than half of the cultivated land is devoted to cereals, with barley and wheat accounting for a large percentage of the total grain harvest. Sugar beets are another leading crop. Oats, rye, turnips, and potatoes are grown in western Jutland, where the soil is less fertile.

Domesticated animals are an important feature of life in Denmark. Dairy cattle, pigs, and poultry are raised in great numbers to supply both the domestic and the foreign markets. Fur farming, especially of minks and foxes, is economically important as well.

At the end of the 19th century, a time of poverty and economic depression, Danish farmers survived by establishing agricultural and dairy cooperatives. Producer cooperatives were partly disbanded after

1950, however, and farms today are generally small or medium-size family-owned enterprises. Fertilization and the application of scientific animal husbandry help to maintain the viability of small farm operations. In addition, the agricultural sector is heavily subsidized by the EU.

The fishing industry remains economically important, and Denmark is among the world's largest exporters of fish products. Herring, cod, and plaice (flatfish) account for most of the total catch; other important species include salmon and eel. Danish commercial fishing also extends into foreign waters in search of Atlantic cod, Norwegian pout, and North Sea sprat (bristling). Aquaculture accounts for a small portion of fish production.

RESOURCES AND POWER

Danish natural resources are limited. The country has a small mining and quarrying industry. Local boulder clays are molded and baked to make bricks and tiles. Moler (marine diatomaceous earth) is mined for use in insulating materials for the building industry, and white chalk is essential for the manufacture of cement.

During the early 1970s the economy suffered from dependence on imported petroleum for the vast majority of its energy needs. The discovery of oil and natural gas fields in the Danish sector of the North Sea later permitted self-sufficiency in this regard. The country also began using coal-fired power plants to produce most of the country's electricity. The switch

from petroleum was accompanied by economies of production: the otherwise-wasted heat that results from the production of electricity began to be used to heat water that is piped to homes and factories. By the early 21st century Denmark was exporting more electricity, oil, and gas than it was importing. (Imports included nuclear and hydroelectric power.) In addition, the Danish government had moved toward more environmentally friendly power sources. The construction of additional coal-burning power plants was banned, and some plants began using biofuels. The government also subsidized wind farms, which now provide a growing portion of the country's electricity.

MANUFACTURING

Though not as important as the service sector, manufacturing still accounts for a significant portion of the gross domestic product. Large manufacturers include the food-processing industry, the pharmaceutical industry, and the producers of metal products, transport equipment, and machinery. Notably, Danish concerns manufacture a substantial portion of the world's windmills. Producers of footwear, clothing, wood and wood products, furniture, and electronic equipment also provide substantial employment. In the second half of the 20th century most of the manufacturing industry moved out of the biggest cities and into thinly populated areas, particularly in Jutland. Many plants are found in small towns.

FINANCE

In 1846 the first commercial bank was established in Denmark. In 1975 commercial and savings banks became equal in status, and foreign banks, which theretofore had maintained representative offices in Copenhagen, were permitted to establish full branches. All banks are under government supervision.

The national currency is the krone; though a member of the EU, Denmark has not adopted the euro, the EU's common currency. (In a 2000 referendum 53 percent of voters rejected adoption of the euro.) The National Bank of Denmark (Danmarks Nationalbank) is responsible for issuing the currency and enjoys a special status as a self-governing institution under government supervision. Profits revert to the state treasury. The national stock exchange, established in 1861, is located in Copenhagen. In the early 21st century the exchange became part of OMX, a Nordic-Baltic common stock exchange, which was subsequently purchased by NASDAQ in 2008.

TRADE

Imports of raw materials and fuel formerly were balanced largely by exports of agricultural products, supplemented by income from shipping and tourism. In the late 20th century the overseas trade pattern shifted to a major reliance on the export of industrial products, including industrial machinery, electronic equipment, and chemical products. These goods—along with fish, dairy products, meat, petroleum, and natural gas—remained important exports into the early 21st century. Denmark also has created an export market for household furniture, toys, silverware, ceramics, plastics, textiles, clothing, and other goods notable for their creative modern design.

As a member of the EU, Denmark relies heavily upon foreign trade within Europe. Germany, Sweden, the Netherlands, the United Kingdom, and Norway are major trading partners.

SERVICES

In the late 20th and early 21st centuries the service sector dominated Denmark's economy. A substantial portion of service jobs are in public administration, education, and health and social services. Tourism is a growing industry, but it is mostly limited to the summer months. The Tivoli park and entertainment complex and the hippie community known as Christiania—both in Copenhagen—attract large numbers of tourists. The capital city's harbour is a major cruise port as well.

LABOUR AND TAXATION

In the early 21st century the vast majority of workers were employed in public and private services, and the unemployment rate remained low. The country's main

Boats docked in Copenhagen harbour. Neil Beer/ Getty Images

association of employees is the National Confederation of Trade Unions (Landsorganisationen); the principal association of employers is the Danish Confederation of Employers (Dansk Arbejdsgiverforening). Membership in unions is normally based upon the particular skills of the workers.

Public income is derived primarily from taxes on real estate, personal income, and capital as well as through customs and excise duties. The heaviest indirect tax, which goes to the national government, is the value-added tax (VAT). Denmark has one of the highest tax burdens in the world; this fact is widely accepted among Danes.

TRANSPORTATION AND TELECOMMUNICATIONS

An extensive road and highway system serves the country. The number of private automobiles in use rose rapidly in the decades after World War II. Bicycles, once a common mode of transport, are still popular. Cities and towns maintain bicycle lanes located parallel to roads and sidewalks.

Bus and coach routes extend throughout the country;

THE GREAT BELT FIXED LINK

The suspension bridge that makes up part of the Great Belt Fixed Link bridge and tunnel system connecting Zealand and Funen. Darren Whitt/Shutterstock.com

In the late 1980s construction began on the Great Belt Fixed Link, a bridge and tunnel system connecting Zealand and Funen via the small island of Sprogø. The largest engineering project in Danish history, it consisted of the East Bridge, a suspension bridge connecting Zealand and Sprogø that has one of the longest spans (5,328 feet [1,624 metres]) in the world; the East Tunnel, a 5-mile (8-km) railway tunnel; and the West Bridge, a rail and road bridge (4.1 miles [6.6 km]) linking Sprogø and Funen. The tunnel opened in 1997 and the bridges the following year.

they are organized regionally by private firms and by local government authorities. A comparatively large railroad network was established during the last half of the 19th century. In the late 1990s work began on a fully automated subway system in Copenhagen, and the first link opened in 2002.

Characteristic features of the Danish transportation system are its many bridges and harbours. Of particular importance are two bridge and tunnel systems: the Great Belt Fixed Link, which conjoins Zealand with Funen (via the small island of Sprogø), and the Øresund Link, which connects Copenhagen with Malmö, Sweden, across The Sound (opened 1997–98 and 2000, respectively). Several bridges also connect Funen and Jutland. Many good harbours provide favourable conditions for both domestic and international shipping.

Kastrup, near Copenhagen, is one of the busiest airports in Europe; it is a centre for international air traffic. The bridge and tunnel link across The Sound lands right by the airport, making Kastrup easily accessible for many Swedes. The Scandinavian Airlines System (SAS), a joint Danish-Norwegian-Swedish enterprise, flies European and intercontinental routes. SAS and smaller airlines also operate services between Copenhagen and other cities on Jutland, Bornholm, the Faroe Islands, and Greenland.

Denmark possesses a highly advanced telecommunications network that features satellite, cable, fibre-optic, and microwave radio links. In the early 21st century cell phones were far more common than traditional telephones; in fact, there was approximately one cell phone subscription for every person in the country. The rate of Internet use, though lower than the rates in other Scandinavian countries, was significantly higher than the overall European average.

CHAPTER 3

DANISH GOVERNMENT AND SOCIETY

The constitution of June 5, 1953, provides for a unicameral legislature, the Folketing, with not more than 179 members (including two from the Faroe Islands and two

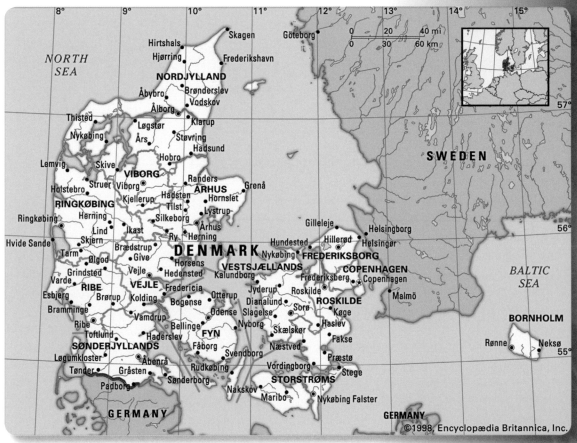

Political map of Denmark. Encyclopædia Britannica, Inc.

from Greenland). The prime minister heads the government, which is composed additionally of cabinet ministers who run the various departments, such as justice, finance, and agriculture. The ceremonial head of state, the monarch, appoints the prime minister (generally the leader of the largest party or coalition in the Folketing) and the cabinet ministers in consultation with the legislature. The monarch also signs acts passed by the Folketing upon the recommendation of the cabinet sitting as the Council of State. To become law, the acts must be countersigned by at least one cabinet member. Faced with a vote of no confidence, the cabinet must resign.

In addition to establishing unicameralism, the 1953 constitution mandates popular referenda (used, for example, to secure public approval for Danish entry into the EEC, now part of the EU) and postulates the creation of an ombudsman office—the first outside Sweden, its country of origin. The Succession to the Throne Act, which accompanied the 1953 constitution, provides for female succession. This allowed the accession of Queen Margrethe II in 1972.

LOCAL GOVERNMENT

Before 1970, local government in Denmark was carried out by a system of county council districts, boroughs, and parishes. A reform in that year reduced the number of counties and replaced the boroughs and parishes with a system of municipalities. In 2007 a further reform replaced the counties with a small number of administrative regions, which encompass the various municipalities. Regions and municipalities are governed by elected councils.

JUSTICE

Most criminal charges and civil disputes fall within the jurisdiction of district courts. Two High Courts hear appeals from the district courts and serve as courts of original jurisdiction in serious criminal cases, in which 12-person juries are impaneled. In some nonjury criminal cases, lay judges sit alongside professional judges and have an equal vote. The Special Court of Indictment and Revision may reopen a criminal case and order a new trial. In Copenhagen there is a Maritime and Commercial Court, which also uses lay judges. The Supreme Court sits at the apex of the legal system.

POLITICAL PROCESS

Denmark has universal adult suffrage by voluntary and secret ballot, with a voting age of 18 for both national and local elections. All voters are eligible to run for office. The voter turnout in national elections historically has been quite high. Elections are held on the basis of proportional representation, in which each political party gains seats in the Folketing in proportion to its strength among the voters. As a result, the national government often has been composed of a coalition of parties that does not enjoy a majority. Members of the Folketing are elected to a four-year term, but the prime minister may dissolve the legislature and call for new elections at any time. Despite the splintering of parties, Denmark has enjoyed stable government, with new elections on an average of once every three years.

The Social Democratic Party (Socialdemokratiet), historically the largest Danish political party, led most Danish governments from the 1930s to the early 1980s. Coalitions of nonsocialist parties headed by the Conservative People's Party (Konservative Folkeparti) and the Liberal Party (Venstre) ruled until 1993, when the Social Democrats regained power. A centre-right Liberal-Conservative coalition held power from 2001 to 2011, when a centre-left coalition led by the Social Democrats took the reins of government. Other prominent parties include the right-wing Danish People's Party (Dansk Folkeparti), which expresses anti-immigration sentiments, and the left-wing Socialist People's Party (Socialistisk Folkeparti), which at first opposed Danish membership in the EU but later modified its hard-line stance. Smaller parties and alliances also maintain seats in the legislature.

HEALTH AND WELFARE

Danes on the whole enjoy excellent health. Aggressive public health programs are directed against the threats of infectious diseases. Public health nurses provide free advice and assistance to mothers, which, with good nutrition and housing, has contributed to a low infant mortality rate. The vast majority of the cost of the health care system is paid for by national and local authorities and employers.

Danish citizens may choose between two primary health care options. Most Danes opt for completely free care that is provided by a general practitioner; some, however, prefer to pay a portion of their medical bills out of pocket for the privilege of choosing any family physician or specialist they wish. Additional, private health insurance also is available.

Denmark's comprehensive social welfare system offers unemployment, disability, old-age, and survivorship benefits at virtually no charge to all Danes. According to the Danish constitution, "Any person unable to support himself or his dependants shall, where no other person is responsible for his or their maintenance, be entitled to receive public assistance." The state welfare programs of Denmark should not be thought of as institutionalized charity, however. They are recognized both legally and in public opinion as morally just social rights that have been paid for by taxes and assessments.

EDUCATION

Education in Denmark is free, and virtually the entire adult population is literate. Nine years of school attendance for children ages 7 to 16 is compulsory. Preschool and kindergarten education is optional but available to all children.

FOLK HIGH SCHOOL

One interesting education option in Denmark is the folk high school, a type of residential school for adults that is standard in Scandinavian countries and has also been adopted elsewhere in Europe. The concept of the folk high school was originated in Denmark by the theologian N.F.S. Grundtvig as a means of providing the common people with a knowledge of their history, religion, and cultural heritage. The model school for the movement was established by the young educator Kristen Kold in 1851 and was soon extensively imitated. Following Denmark's military defeat by Prussia in 1864, these folk high schools served as a powerful instrument of national regeneration. There are no entrance qualifications or leaving examinations; attendance is completely voluntary. The atmosphere is homelike. Students and teachers live, work, and play together. The singing of hymns and folk songs is characteristic. Subjects of general interest in literature and social science predominate. Most students are young adults, originally rural workers, but now urban as well. The schools are private but receive state subsidies, and many folk high schools attract an international body of students.

After reaching the 9th grade, students may leave school to enter the workforce, but the majority continue their education. Some undertake vocational or training programs, while others enroll in a general upper secondary school (gymnasium) or another institution offering a higher preparatory education. While many graduates of these schools subsequently enter the workforce, many others continue on to universities or to schools and academies of university rank that specialize in technical and artistic fields.

Some Danes choose to attend Danish folk high schools, which were first established in the 19th century and continue to offer nonformal educational programs to adults.

At the pinnacle of higher education are the University of Copenhagen (founded in 1479), the University of Aarhus (1928), and the University of Southern Denmark (1966), all state supported. Additional universities were established at Roskilde in 1972 and at Ålborg in 1974.

CHAPTER 4

DANISH CULTURAL LIFE

Danes traditionally faced life from the security of the nuclear family, as has been true throughout Europe, but during the late 20th century, substantial changes took place. For example, marriage lost its status as an almost inevitable social institution. In earlier centuries the Danes easily tolerated sexual relations between individuals who were engaged to be married, and it was not uncommon for marriage to take place after a baby was born—although it was considered immoral and unacceptable not to marry eventually. By the early 21st century, however, cohabitation without the formalities of engagement and wedding was quite common, and nearly half of all live births took place out of wedlock. Consistent with the decline of contracted marriages, the incidence of divorce also rose. In addition, in 1989 Denmark became the first country to establish registered partnerships for same-sex couples, which offered the same rights and duties as marriage.

THE ARTS AND SCIENCES

Although Denmark is a small country, Danes have contributed much to the growth of world civilization, particularly in the humanities. In the late 12th–early 13th centuries Saxo Grammaticus wrote the first major book of Danish history, *Gesta Danorum* ("Story of the Danes"), Denmark's first contribution to world literature. Rasmus Rask founded comparative philology, while N.F.S. Grundtvig founded a theological movement and was a pioneer in education. Søren Kierkegaard helped to shape existentialist philosophy. Bertel Thorvaldsen achieved renown as a sculptor in a Neoclassical style, and Carl Nielsen composed classical music of international fame. Jørn Utzon won world recognition as the architect of the Sydney Opera House in Australia.

In motion pictures, the director Carl Theodor Dreyer became known for his distinctive style, while a number of Danish filmmakers won international renown in the late 20th and early 21st centuries—notably Bille August and Lars von Trier. In the realm of Danish literature, Hans Christian Andersen authored fairy tales that are known throughout the world, and Karen Christence Dinesen, Baroness Blixen-Finecke, achieved world acclaim writing under the name of Isak Dinesen. The Nobel Prize for Literature was awarded to the novelist Henrik Pontoppidan in 1917 and to Johannes V. Jensen, whose works included the novel *The Long Journey*, in 1944.

"Ganymede with the eagle of Zeus," by Danish sculptor Bertel Thorvaldsen. DEA Picture Library/ De Agostini/Getty Images

Many Danes have expanded scientific knowledge as well. Tycho Brahe was a major figure in the early telescopic exploration of the universe; Thomas Bartholin was the first anatomist to describe the human lymphatic system; Nicolaus Steno was instrumental in the establishment of geology as a science; Ole Rømer demonstrated that light travels at a determinable speed; Caspar Thomeson Bartholin, Jr.,

HANS CHRISTIAN ANDERSEN

The stories of Hans Christian Andersen (born April 2, 1805, Odense, Denmark—died August 4, 1875, Copenhagen) are famous throughout the world. Andersen was a unique master of the literary fairy tale as well as being an author of plays, novels, poems, travel books, and several autobiographies. While many of these works are almost unknown outside Denmark, his fairy tales are among the most frequently translated works in all literary history.

Andersen was born in a slum and had a difficult battle breaking through the rigid class structure of his time. The first significant help came from Jonas Collin, one of the directors of the Royal Theatre in Copenhagen, to which Andersen had gone as a youth in the vain hope of winning fame as an actor. Collin raised money to send him to school. Although school was an unhappy experience for Andersen because of an unpleasant headmaster, it allowed him to be admitted to the University of Copenhagen in 1828.

The next year Andersen produced what is considered his first important literary work, *Fodrejse fra Holmens Kanal til Østpynten af Amager i aarene 1828 og 1829* (1829; "A Walk from Holmen's Canal to the East Point of the Island of Amager in the Years 1828 and 1829"), a fantastic tale in the style of the German Romantic writer E.T.A. Hoffmann. This work was an immediate success. He then turned to playwriting. After some unsuccessful attempts, he achieved recognition for *Mulatten* (1840; "The Mulatto"), a play portraying the evils of slavery. The theatre, however, was not to become his field, and for a long time Andersen was regarded primarily as a novelist. Most of his novels are autobiographical; among the best-known are *Improvisatoren* (1835; *The Improvisatore*), *O.T.* (1836; *OT: A Danish Romance*), and *Kun en spillemand* (1837; *Only a Fiddler*).

Andersen's first book of tales, *Eventyr, fortalte for børn* (1835; "Tales, Told for Children"), included stories such as "The Tinderbox," "Little Claus and Big Claus," "The Princess and the Pea," and "Little Ida's Flowers." Two further installments of stories made up the first volume of *Eventyr* (1837); a second volume was completed in 1842, and to these was added *Billedbog uden billeder* (1840; *A Picture-book Without Pictures*). New collections appeared in 1843, 1847, and 1852. The genre was expanded in *Nye eventyr og historier* (1858–72; "New Fairy Tales and Stories").

These collections broke new ground in both style and content. A real innovator in his method of telling tales, Andersen used the idioms and constructions of the spoken language, thus breaking with literary tradition. He combined his natural storytelling abilities and great imaginative power with universal elements of folk legend to produce a body of fairy tales that relates to many cultures.

discovered the ductus sublingualis major and the glandula vestibularis major, both of which bear his name as Bartholin's duct and gland; and Hans Christian Ørsted discovered electromagnetism. In the 20th century, Niels Ryberg Finsen won the Nobel Prize for Physiology or Medicine for his work on the medical uses of ultraviolet rays, and Johannes Fibiger won the same award for his research on cancer; Valdemar Poulsen developed a device for generating radio waves; Niels Bohr won the Nobel Prize for Physics for his achievements in quantum physics, and the same prize was later won by his son, Aage N. Bohr; Henrik Dam won the Nobel Prize for Physiology or Medicine for the discovery of vitamin K; and Jens C. Skou won the Nobel Prize for Chemistry for his discovery of an enzyme that maintains sodium and potassium levels in the cells of animals.

CULTURAL INSTITUTIONS

The first Danish-speaking theatre was opened in Copenhagen in 1722; it was

A performance by the internationally renowned Royal Danish Ballet in Paris, France, 2012. Julien M. Hekimian/Getty Images

followed in 1748 by the Royal Theatre (Det Kongelige Teater), which remained under court patronage for a century. In 1848 it was taken over by the state, and it is now administered by the Danish Ministry of Culture. Besides a relatively large number of classical and modern Danish plays, the repertoire includes much that is current in Britain, the United States, Germany, and France.

A resident ballet company, which also performs in the Royal Theatre, was founded in the 18th century. Only through a young generation of dancers in the style of choreographer August Bournonville (1805–79) did it become internationally acclaimed as the Royal Danish Ballet.

Denmark supports a number of symphony orchestras; two of the more important are the Danish Radio Symphony Orchestra and the Royal Orchestra. Musicians and singers are trained at the Royal Danish Academy of Music in Copenhagen and other conservatories and at the Opera Academy. Several important music festivals take place in the country; among them are the Roskilde Festival of rock music, the Copenhagen Jazz Festival, and the Tønder Festival of folk music.

The Royal Danish Academy of Fine Arts was established in 1754. It produced the 19th-century sculptor Bertel Thorvaldsen and, in the 20th century, the sculptor Robert Jacobsen and the architects Arne Jacobsen and Henning Larsen. Famous craft concerns include the firm of silversmith Georg Jensen, the Royal Copenhagen and Bing and Grøndahl porcelain manufacturers, Holmegaard Glassworks, and the furniture manufacturer Fritz Hansens Eftf.

SPORTS AND RECREATION

The pursuit of sport became popular after defeat in the Danish-Prussian War of 1863–64 as Danes turned to an interest in small arms and physical training. Soon every part of Denmark had established shooting, gymnastics, and athletic clubs. Rowing was organized at a national level as early as 1886. Football (soccer) was introduced to Denmark by British engineers who came to design the railroad system in the 1870s. Football became an organized sport when the Copenhagen Ball Club was established in 1876, and it remains an extremely popular national sport.

The country has competed in every Olympic Games except the 1904 Games in St. Louis, Missouri, U.S. Danish athletes have won Olympic gold medals in such events as canoeing, shooting, swimming, rowing, cycling, and handball. During the 1936 Games 12-year-old Inge Sørensen became the youngest athlete to win an Olympic medal in an individual event when she won a bronze in the 200-metre breaststroke competition. Yachtsman Paul Elvstrøm gained distinction for winning Olympic gold medals in four consecutive Games (1948–60).

These and many other sports appeal to Danes, particularly in the summer months. In addition, Danes and foreign tourists alike often pay visits to the many well-tended parks, forests, and beaches that honeycomb the country. Of particular note are the Baltic Sea resorts on Bornholm, which offer visitors a lively mix of recreational activities such as cycling and kayaking as well as glimpses at Denmark's past.

MEDIA AND PUBLISHING

The publicly held Danish Broadcasting Corporation offers Danish programming on several radio stations and television channels. The owners of radios and televisions pay a license fee, which finances public broadcasting operations. Several commercial television channels, most available via cable or satellite, and a large number of local and commercial radio stations also operate in the country. In addition, in most parts of Denmark it is possible to receive strong radio signals from neighbouring countries, particularly Sweden in the north and Germany in the south.

Complete freedom of the press is guaranteed under the constitution. Dozens of newspapers under private ownership are published throughout the country. Many were once associated with political parties, but now the majority of newspapers are independent. Among the largest dailies are *Ekstra Bladet*, *BT*, *Berlingske Tidende*, and *Politiken*. Free, advertising-funded newspapers have gained importance since the turn of the 21st century.

CHAPTER 5

DENMARK: PAST AND PRESENT

The history of the people of Denmark, like that of all humankind, can be divided into prehistoric and historic eras. Sufficient written historical sources for Danish history do not become available before the establishment of medieval church institutions, notably monasteries, where monks recorded orally transmitted stories from the Viking era and earlier times. To be sure, there are older documents, such as the Roman historian Tacitus's *Germania*, as well as northern European church documents from the 9th and 10th centuries, but these give only incomplete information and nothing about the earliest periods. However, the work of archaeologists and other specialists, especially those of the 19th and 20th centuries, has revealed a good deal about the lives of the earliest peoples of what is now Denmark.

EARLIEST INHABITANTS

By about 12,000 BCE, as the climate warmed and the great glaciers of the Pleistocene Epoch (about 2,600,000 to 11,700 years ago) were receding, the first nomadic hunters moved into what is now Denmark, bringing tools and weapons of the Paleolithic Period (Old Stone Age) with them. Shell mounds (refuse heaps also known as kitchen middens) reveal the gradual development of a nomadic hunter-gatherer society, whose tools and weapons continued to progress in sophistication and complexity. Beginning in the 4th millennium BCE, during the Neolithic Period (New Stone Age), a peasant culture emerged in Denmark as the people living there further developed their stone tools, began keeping livestock, and adopted agriculture. Those first farmers began to clear land in the forests for fields and villages, and after about 3500 BCE they built large, common, megalithic graves. By about 2800 BCE a single-grave culture emerged, but whether this shift indicates a change in local custom or another group moving into the area is not clear. In the last phase of the Stone Age in Denmark, the so-called Dagger period (c. 2400–1700 BCE), flint working reached its apogee with the production of technical masterpieces, including daggers and spearheads modeled after metal weapons that were being imported at the time.

The growing wealth of the region, particularly of the elite portion of society, in the Bronze Age (c. 1700–500 BCE) is illustrated by the fine metalworking skills seen in the spiral decorations on the bronzes of the period—notably the famous Late Bronze Age lurs (long curved, metal horns, often found in pairs), created about 1000–800 BCE. During the same period, increasingly varied and improved tools, such as the bronze sickle, enabled better exploitation of cultivated areas. It was also during the Bronze Age that woolen cloth began to be produced in Denmark. (Sheep raised prior to this period were used for their milk and their meat rather than for their wool.)

After 500 BCE, bronze was gradually replaced by iron, and a more complex village society developed in a landscape of bogs, meadows, and woods with large clearings. Iron Age farm buildings, generally smaller than those of the Bronze Age, appear to have been moved every generation or so, and the empty plots were then cultivated. That buildings might be reerected on former plots suggests that the population remained in a given area. Objects of great value, as well as people, continued to be laid as offerings in the bogs. The so-called Tollund Man, the well-preserved body of an Iron Age man found in 1950 in a bog near Silkeborg, Denmark, is probably the most famous of these discoveries. Along with evidence of human offerings, there are indications that slavery was practiced during this period.

More-or-less-fixed trading connections were established with the Romans during the Iron Age, and by about 200 CE the first runic inscription appeared—likely inspired by the Etruscan alphabet of northern Italy and possibly also influenced by the Latin alphabet. The Late Iron Age (c. 400–800) appears to have been a time of decline and unrest, and, in the 6th century, bubonic plague raged. Toward the very end of the Iron Age, the first trading towns appeared at Hedeby (near what is now Schleswig, Germany) and Ribe.

THE VIKING ERA

Viking society, which had developed by the 9th century, included the peoples that lived in what are now Denmark, Norway, Sweden, and, from the 10th century, Iceland. In the beginning, political power was relatively diffused, but it eventually became centralized in the respective Danish, Norwegian, and Swedish kingdoms—a process that helped to bring about the end of the Viking era. Although a lot more is known about Viking society than about the earlier peoples in Denmark, the society was not a literate one, runic inscriptions notwithstanding. Some information about the era has thus been gleaned from the Vikings' apparently rich oral tradition, portions of which were later recorded in poems such as *Beowulf* and in sagas such as *Heimskringla*.

The Vikings were superb shipbuilders and sailors. Although they are thought of primarily as raiders, they also engaged in a great deal of trade. In both capacities they traveled widely along routes that stretched from Greenland and North America in the west to Novgorod (now in Russia), Kiev (now in Ukraine), and Constantinople (now Istanbul, Turkey) in the east, as well as from north of the Arctic Circle south to the Mediterranean Sea. The Viking trade routes, especially those along the Russian river system, linked northern Europe to both the Arab trading network and the Byzantine Empire. The major goods moving east were slaves, furs, and amber while those traveling west included precious metals, jewels, textiles, and glassware. Danes, for the most part, occupied the centre of this system; they generally traveled west to England and south along the coast of France and the Iberian Peninsula.

In addition to raiding and trading, Vikings established settlements,

The Viking burial ground at Lindholm Høje, near Ålborg, Den. Inga Aistrup Lind

which at first may have served mainly as winter quarters while abroad. The Danes moved primarily to the eastern part of England that came to be called the Danelaw; this region stretched from the River Thames north through what became known as Yorkshire. It appears that a good number of Scandinavian women accompanied their men to England and also settled there. The other major area of Danish Viking settlement was in Normandy, France. In 911 the Viking leader Rollo became the first duke of Normandy, as a vassal of Charles III of France. While the nationality of Rollo is in dispute—some sources say Norwegian and others say Danish—there is no question that most of his followers were Danes, many from the Danelaw area. Unlike the Danes in England, Rollo's men did not bring many Viking women to France; most of the warriors married local women, resulting in a mixed Danish-Celtic culture in Normandy.

In the midst of the Viking era, in the first half of the 10th century, the kingdom of Denmark coalesced in Jutland (Jylland) under King Gorm the Old. Gorm's son and successor, Harald I (Bluetooth), claimed to have unified Denmark, conquered Norway, and Christianized the Danes. His accomplishments are inscribed in runic on a huge gravestone at Jelling, one of the so-called Jelling stones. Harald's conquest of Norway was short-lived, however, and his son Sweyn I (Forkbeard) was forced to rewin the country. Sweyn also exhausted England in annual raids and was finally accepted as king of that country, but he died shortly thereafter. Sweyn's son Canute I (the Great) reconquered Norway, which had been lost around the time of Sweyn's death in 1014, and forged an Anglo-Danish kingdom that lasted until his own death in 1035. Various contenders fought for the throne of England and held it for short periods until the question of the succession was settled in 1066 by one of Rollo's descendants, William I (the Conqueror), who led the Norman forces to victory over the last Anglo-Saxon king of England, Harold II, at the Battle of Hastings.

Throughout the Viking period, Danish social structures evolved. Society was likely divided into three main groups: the elite, free men and women, and thralls (slaves). Over time, differences among members of the elite increased, and by the end of the period the concept of royalty had emerged, the status of the elite was becoming inheritable, and the gap between the elite and the free peasantry had widened. Slavery did not last past the Middle Ages.

There has been much debate among scholars about the role and status of Viking women. Though the society was clearly patriarchal, women could initiate divorce and own property, and some exceptional women assumed leadership roles in their home communities. Women also played important economic roles, as in the production of woolen cloth.

While no clear line can be drawn, the Viking era had ended by the middle of the 11th century. Many have credited the Christianization of the Scandinavians with bringing about the end of Viking depredations, but the centralization of temporal power also contributed significantly to the decline of the Vikings. Canute the Great, for example, gathered relatively large armies under his control rather than allowing small warrior bands to join him at will—as was the Viking tradition. In fact, Canute and other Nordic kings—behaving more like feudal overlords than mere head warriors—worked to inhibit the formation of independent warrior bands in the Scandinavian homelands. The increasing power of the Mongols on the Eurasian Steppe also affected the Vikings' dominance. As the Mongols moved farther west, they closed the Vikings' eastern river routes, which southern and central European merchants increasingly replaced with overland and Mediterranean routes. Nevertheless, there can be no doubt that the Christian church shaped the emerging society and culture of medieval Denmark and of Scandinavia as a whole.

THE HIGH MIDDLE AGES

During the course of what historians have called the High Middle Ages, beginning about the 11th century, the political, social, and economic structures that scholars have associated with medieval European society came to Denmark, as well as to the rest of Viking Scandinavia. By the end of the 13th century, the systems now known as feudalism and manorialism framed many people's lives, and the Christian church had become firmly established. However, defining the powers of the country's rulers was fraught with difficulties. The ensuing battles for the throne, as well as struggles for power between the nobles and the king, would persist for centuries. Defining the kingdom's borders presented problems as well, and Danish kings were forced to defend their territory against various outside forces.

THE MONARCHY

Sweyn II Estridsen (reigned 1047–74?) was on the throne during the transition from Viking to feudal society. When he took power, the royal succession was largely in the hands of the things, or local assemblies of freemen, which also legislated on various issues. Five of Sweyn's sons succeeded each other on the throne: Harald Hén (ruled 1074–80), Canute IV (the Holy; 1080–86), Oluf Hunger (1086–95),

Erik Ejegod (1095–1103), and Niels (1104–34). Their reigns were marked by conflict over the extent of the king's power, and both Canute and Niels were assassinated. By 1146 civil war had divided the kingdom between three contenders.

After protracted struggles, one of these contenders, Valdemar I (the Great), was acknowledged as the sole king in 1157. Valdemar initially recognized Holy Roman Emperor Frederick I (Barbarossa) as his overlord but later rejected the relationship, thereby emphasizing the independence of the Danish kingdom. Valdemar's reign (1157–82) was followed by those of several other strong rulers, including that of his son Valdemar II (the Victorious; 1202–41). During Valdemar II's reign, two essential works appeared: a code of law and the *Jordebog* ("Land Book"), a cadastre, or land register. In addition, a parliament, the hof, was established by the high prelates and aristocrats as a check against royal misuse of power; it met at short intervals and also functioned as the highest court. After Valdemar II's death, peace and stability disintegrated. Power disputes culminated in two instances of regicide: King Erik IV (Plowpenny) was murdered in 1250 and King Erik V (Glipping, or Klipping) in 1286.

During the reign of Erik V, in 1282, the nobility succeeded in formally limiting the king's power. A charter between the great Danish lords and the king recognized the power of the lords in exchange for their support of the monarch. It forbade the king from imprisoning nobles purely on suspicion and also forced the king to call an annual meeting of the hof. This document (the haandfaestning) may be viewed as Denmark's first constitution—albeit, like the Magna Carta in England, a feudal not a democratic one. Indeed, the charter resulted in a loss of power for the peasantry and the local things.

THE KINGDOM

With one notable exception, establishing the frontiers of the Danish realm had proved to be much easier than determining the extent of the king's power. The inclusion of various islands within the Danish kingdom was fairly straightforward. In the southern Scandinavian Peninsula, in what is now the southern tip of Sweden, Denmark's territory also encompassed the regions of Skåne, Halland, and Blekinge; these remained part of the Danish kingdom until their loss to Sweden in the 17th century.

In the peninsula of Jutland, however, the placement of the kingdom's southern border remained problematic until the current boundary was drawn in 1920. At issue was whether the regions of Schleswig (Slesvig) and Holstein (Holsten) should be part of Denmark or of the constellation of German states. To be sure, there was the Danewirk, a rampart in southern Jutland begun in about 808 to protect Denmark from German incursions, but the Danish-German border seldom coincided with this wall. The

DANEWIRK

The Danewirk (Danish: Dannevirke, or Danevirke [Danes' Bulwark] was the ancient frontier rampart of the Danes against the Germans, extending 10.5 miles (17 kilometres) from just south of the town of Schleswig to the marshes of the river Trene near the village of Hollingstedt. The rampart was begun about 808 CE by Godfred (Gudfred), king of Vestfold. In 934 it was penetrated by the German king Henry I, after which it was extended by King Harald I Bluetooth (c. 940–c. 985); but it was again stormed by the German emperor Otto II in 974. After the union of Schleswig and Holstein under the Danish crown in the 15th century, the Danewirk fell into decay; but in 1848 it was hastily strengthened by the Danes, who were, however, unable to hold it in face of the superiority of Prussian artillery, and on April 23 it was stormed.

From 1850 onward, Danewirk was again repaired and strengthened at great cost and was considered impregnable; but in the war of 1864 the Prussians turned it by crossing the Schlei, and it was abandoned by the Danes on February 6 without a blow. It was thereupon destroyed by the Prussians. In spite of this destruction, however, a long line of imposing ruins still remains. The systematic excavation of these, begun in 1900, yielded some notable finds, especially of valuable runic inscriptions.

problem was complicated by two other factors. Because of their importance, not least militarily, the rulers of Schleswig and Holstein, powerful nobles and often members of the Danish royal family, competed for control within Denmark. In addition, the relationship of the Danish king and the rulers of Schleswig and Holstein to the rulers of the German states and especially to the emperors of the Holy Roman Empire, left the issue of sovereignty of the southern parts of Jutland unclear.

Beyond these core areas of the king-dom—Jutland, the Danish islands, and the southern Scandinavian Peninsula—other areas also came under the Danish crown in the High Middle Ages. During this period the Danes' Viking-era orien-tation toward the North Sea and Norway shifted east and south. Strong rulers in both England and Norway, as well as other interests, forced the attention of the Danes toward the Baltic Sea in particular.

In the early 11th century the Wends, pagan Slavic tribes who lived along the Baltic east of the Elbe River, increasingly attacked merchant shipping in the sea and among the southern Danish islands. Not until the 12th-century campaigns of Valdemar I, combined with the often com-peting, sometimes cooperating efforts of the Saxons from west of the Elbe, were the Wends Christianized and the piracy and raiding stopped. Although Valdemar claimed Danish hegemony over Wendish lands, Saxon settlers, not Danish ones, moved into the area.

Valdemar I's sons continued his east-ern policy and conquered north German lands in the western Baltic region, such as Holstein, part of Mecklenburg, and Pomerania. Competing with various German rulers and the Teutonic Order for converts and territory, the Danes also sent missionaries along the trade route from Schleswig to Novgorod.

Valdemar II turned his attention far-ther east. In 1219 he took his army on what was designated as a crusade to what is now Estonia, where the Danes besieged and captured Tallinn and converted many to Christianity. But again, Germans rather than Danes moved into the area—making the Danish hold tenuous. In 1225, after Valdemar had been taken prisoner by one of his north German vassals, he promised to give up all the conquered areas except Estonia and the island of Rügen. A final attempt to win back the lost areas led to his decisive defeat in 1227, and the Danish empire in the west-ern Baltic came to an end.

THE CHURCH

The establishment of the Christian church in Denmark went hand in hand with the consolidation of royal power and the determining of the Danish frontiers. Under German auspices, a few bishoprics subordinate to the arch-diocese of Hamburg-Bremen had been established in Danish territory as early as the 10th century. In the 11th cen-tury Sweyn II worked with the church to strengthen royal authority. During his reign Denmark was divided into eight bishoprics under the archbishop of Hamburg-Bremen: Schleswig, Ribe, Århus, Viborg, Vendsyssel (part of Vendsyssel-Thy), Odense, Roskilde, and Lund (now in Sweden). In 1103, however, the pope established Lund as the seat of a new, Nordic archbishop, thus liberating the church in Denmark from the influences of German prelates.

Subsequently, a great Romanesque cathedral was built in Lund, and a church-building program began in earnest. Small wooden churches had existed in Denmark since the introduction of Christianity, but during the course of the 12th century hundreds of stone and brick churches were constructed. The monastery system came to Denmark during this period as well. Most of the first monasteries were connected to a cathedral. The Cistercians

SAXO GRAMMATICUS

Saxo Grammaticus (flourished 12th century–early 13th century) was a historian known for writing *Gesta Danorum* ("Story of the Danes"), the first important work on the history of Denmark. It was also the first Danish contribution to world literature.

Little is known of Saxo's life except that he was a Zealander belonging to a family of warriors and was probably a clerk in the service of Absalon, archbishop of Lund from 1178 to 1201. Saxo is first mentioned in Svend Aggesen's *Historia Regum Danicae compendiosa* (1185; "Short History of the Danish Kings") as writing the history of Svend Estridsen (died 1076).

The *Gesta Danorum* was written at the suggestion of Archbishop Absalon: its 16 volumes begin with the legendary King Dan and end with the conquest of Pomerania by Canute IV in 1185. The work is written in a brilliant, ornate Latin. It was his Latin eloquence that early in the 14th century caused Saxo to be called "Grammaticus." The first nine books of the *Gesta Danorum* give an account of about 60 legendary Danish kings. For this part Saxo depended on ancient lays, romantic sagas, and the accounts of Icelanders. His legend of *Amleth* is thought to be the source of William Shakespeare's *Hamlet*; his Toke, the archer, the prototype of William Tell. Saxo incorporated also myths of national gods whom tradition claimed as Danish kings, as well as myths of foreign heroes. Three heroic poems are especially noteworthy, translated by Saxo into Latin hexameters. These oldest-known Danish poems are *Bjarkemaalet,* a battle hymn designed to arouse warlike feelings; *Ingjaldskvadet,* a poem stressing the corruptive danger of luxury upon the old Viking spirit; and *Hagbard and Signe,* a tragedy of love and family feuds. The last seven books contain Saxo's account of the historical period, but he achieves independent authority only when writing of events close to his own time. His work is noteworthy for its sense of patriotic purpose based on a belief in the unifying influence of the monarchy. By presenting a 2,000-year-long panorama of Danish history, he aimed to show his country's antiquity and traditions. Saxo's work became a source of inspiration to many of the 19th-century Danish Romantic poets.

founded their first monastery in 1144 in Skåne. Later in the 12th century the Cistercians founded great monasteries at Esrum and Sorø in Zealand (Sjælland) and at Løgum in southern Jutland. In addition, the Cistercians founded three houses for women before 1200, in the bishopric of Roskilde, in Slangerup in northern Zealand, and in Bergen on the island of Rügen (then under the Danish crown and now part of Germany).

A number of notable individuals oversaw the church in Denmark during this era. Eskil became archbishop of Lund in 1138 and as such oversaw the completion of the cathedral; it was also at his behest that the first Cistercians came north. Absalon, bishop of Roskilde from 1134, wrote the church law of Zealand in 1171 and then in 1177 became archbishop of Lund. Absalon also was a key advocate of the Valdemar dynasty. He ruled as coregent during Canute VI's minority (1170–82) and helped lead Denmark's expansionist campaigns. Aside from serving as a royal adviser, he was the patron of Saxo Grammaticus, who wrote *Gesta Danorum*, the first important work on the history of Denmark. These men and others were responsible for the basic structures of the Danish church that endured until the 16th-century Reformation and, in some measure, beyond.

The church in Denmark eventually amassed significant wealth and power. By the end of the 13th century, the crown and the church controlled the vast majority of land in the realm. The church derived a huge income from its lands and farms and drew still greater revenues from the tithes on the entire grain production of the country—one-third going to the bishops, one-third to the parish churches, and one-third to the parish priests.

In the early days, the objectives of church and crown were in alignment. High-level offices such as abbots and bishops were usually held by the younger sons of nobles, appointed by the Danish king or the pope, and there was seldom enough agreement among bishops in order to confront royal power effectively. Occasionally, however, the administrative apparatus of the church came into competition with the government's, and during the latter half of the 13th century, contention between church and state increased sharply. Three serious confrontations ultimately took place.

The first one began during the reign of Erik IV (1241–50), who disagreed with the pope's installation of Jakob Erlandsen as bishop of Roskilde. The conflict lasted through the reign of Christopher I (1252–59) and Erlandsen's appointment as archbishop of Lund. Christopher's imprisonment of the prelate caused several German rulers to attack Denmark, and in the ensuing war the king died.

The second great confrontation between church and state, which took place in the late 13th century, highlights the conflicting sacred and secular duties of the bishops. The root of the conflict lay in Archbishop Jens Grand's refusal to meet his feudal military obligations: instead of supporting the king, the archbishop had sided with several outlawed magnates who were raiding the Danish coasts. The king, Erik VI (Menved), jailed the archbishop, who subsequently escaped and took his case to the papal court. In 1303 Erik reached a settlement with the pope, who decided in favour of the archbishop but moved him to Riga (now in Latvia).

The third conflict began in the early 14th century, when a new archbishop, Esger Juul, who had been appointed jointly by the king and the pope to the see in Lund, issued bulls against the king for the return of properties lost during the fight with Jens Grand. Ultimately, Juul lost his backing from the other Danish bishops, and in 1317 he fled to Hammershus, a castle on the island of Bornholm, and filed suit in the papal court. King Christopher II eventually reached a settlement with Juul out of court.

Thereafter, relations between church and state remained relatively calm until the Reformation. Not only was the papal position weaker, but the king's role in appointing high church officials grew stronger. By the mid-14th century the Danish government essentially chose Denmark's bishops.

THE LATE MIDDLE AGES

The battle between nobles and kings largely defined late medieval politics. The division between social classes also became more pronounced during this period.

DECLINING ROYAL POWER AND HOLSTEIN RULE

Following the murder of King Erik V in 1286, the guardians of Erik's heir, Erik VI, still a minor, consolidated their power around the young prince and established a nearly absolutist regime. Upon reaching his majority, the king became involved in military adventures abroad, particularly in northern Germany, and by his death in 1319 the country was deeply in debt.

The childless Erik VI was succeeded by his brother, Christopher II, who was forced by the nobles to sign a strict coronation charter; he was also the first king to accept the hof as a permanent institution. He did not abide by the charter, however, and was driven into exile after a battle with the magnates and the count of Holstein.

By this point the kingdom's creditors, mostly great lords from Denmark and the north German states, had acquired significant power. From 1326 to 1330 the young duke of South Jutland, Valdemar, ruled under the regency of the count of Holstein. Christopher II returned to the throne during 1330–32, but during his reign the kingdom was split by a peasant uprising, church discord, and the struggle with Holstein, which received almost all of the country in pawn.

After the death of Christopher in 1332, no new king was chosen. The counts of Holstein ruled the country until 1340, when Gerhard of Holstein, to speed up tax collection, moved his army into Jutland, where he was murdered.

Christopher's son then ascended the throne as Valdemar IV Atterdag.

REUNION UNDER VALDEMAR IV

The new king married the sister of the duke of South Jutland, who gave the northern quarter of North Jutland as her dowry; he began his reign with the reunion of Denmark as his first priority. By selling Estonia (1346) and collecting extra taxes, he reclaimed some of the pawned areas and brought others back through negotiations or force of arms. In 1360 he conquered Skåne, which had come under Swedish rule, and, a year later, the Swedish island of Gotland. Denmark was thus reunited.

Royal power was strengthened during Valdemar IV's reign. The king succeeded in quelling a series of revolts by leading magnates, and at a hof in 1360, a "great national peace" was agreed between the monarch and the people. The hof was replaced by the Rigsråd (Council of the Realm)—a national council of the archbishop, the bishops, and the lensmænd (vassals) from the main castles—and the king's Retterting (Court of Law) became the supreme court. Valdemar also attacked major economic problems: after the Black Death pandemic in 1350, he confiscated ownerless estates and regained royal estates that had been lost during the interregnum; additionally, the army was reorganized.

Valdemar's war on Gotland and the fall of the island's wealthy town of Visby brought him into conflict with Sweden and the Hanseatic League, a powerful organization of mostly north German trading towns, which declared war on Denmark. In 1367 the league, the princes of Mecklenburg and Holstein, and some of the Jutland magnates attacked Valdemar at sea and on land. The king went to Germany to find allies in the rear of his powerful German enemies and succeeded in obtaining a rather favourable peace treaty at Stralsund in 1370, which gave the Hanseatic League trading rights in Denmark and pawned parts of Skåne to the league for 15 years. Valdemar returned home and continued his work of stabilizing the crown's hold on the country until he died in 1375.

MARGARET I AND THE KALMAR UNION

Valdemar's heirs brought the kingdom to its medieval apogee. His youngest and only surviving child, Margaret I (Margrethe I), had married a prince of Sweden, Haakon VI Magnusson, then king of Norway. Their son Olaf (Oluf) was chosen as king of Denmark in 1376. Margaret, as guardian and regent, followed a policy of peace abroad and strengthening the crown internally. In 1380, when Haakon died, Olaf, still a minor, was chosen as king of Norway as well. This brought not only Norway but also Iceland, the Faroe Islands, and Greenland under the Danish crown. Margaret also pushed Olaf's claim to the Swedish throne, as he was last in the male line of Swedish kings. Before she could win the crown for him, however, Olaf died in 1387. Margaret was soon acknowledged as regent in Denmark and Norway, and rebellious Swedish nobles, dissatisfied with the rule of Albert of Mecklenburg, hailed her as regent in Sweden as well. War between the supporters of Margaret and Albert continued until 1398, when Albert's forces finally surrendered Stockholm to Margaret.

Margaret's rule was predicated on her control of the succession, and so she had adopted her great-nephew Erik of Pomerania. In 1397 at Kalmar, Sweden, Margaret oversaw the coronation of Erik as king of Denmark, Norway, and Sweden—thus establishing the Kalmar Union of the three Scandinavian states. Although Erik, known as Erik VII in Danish history, was the titular king, Margaret retained actual power until her death in 1412.

The policies of Erik VII and the subsequent rulers of the Kalmar Union aimed to consolidate and hold together this rather disparate collection of territory. In 1434 a rebellion broke out in Sweden, and the spirit of revolt spread to the king's enemies in Denmark and Norway. He was deposed in 1439 by the Danish and Swedish councils of the realm and in 1442 by Norway. The joint crown was offered to Erik's nephew Christopher III, but his reign did little to strengthen the union, which was temporarily dissolved after his death in 1448. Christian I, founder of the Oldenburg dynasty, succeeded to the Danish and Norwegian

thrones, but efforts to bring Sweden back into the union were only intermittently successful, and when Christian died in 1481, he did not rule that country. He was succeeded by his son John (Hans), whose coronation charter of 1483 acknowledged him as king of all three countries, but he actually held the Swedish throne only from 1497 to 1501.

Swedish revolts continued into the reign of Christian II, who succeeded his father, John, as king of Denmark and Norway in 1513. After defeating the army of the Swedish regent in 1520, Christian was crowned king of Sweden. Following his coronation, he executed more than 80 opponents of his regime in what became known as the Stockholm Bloodbath. Outrage over the massacre encouraged a final rebellion by the Swedes, who declared independence in 1523—marking a permanent end to the Kalmar Union. Opposition to the king grew in Denmark as well; the nobles of Jutland deposed him that year and drove him into exile. The Danish and Norwegian crowns then passed to Christian's uncle, Frederick I.

LATE MEDIEVAL SOCIETY

During the Late Middle Ages the Danish people became more sharply divided into social classes. The nobility in particular developed the characteristics of a caste. Prior to the 15th century any Dane could become a noble, provided he could render military services to the king at his own expense, particularly by providing a prescribed number of men-at-arms. In return, he was exempted from all taxes. From the 15th century, however, he had to show that his forefathers had enjoyed tax exemptions for at least three generations. In addition, the king sought to assume the right to issue titles of nobility. These measures helped to limit the number of nobles in the kingdom. During the 15th century the nobility comprised 264 families, but this number fell to 230 in 1500 and to 140 (including at most 3,000 persons) in 1650; the Gyldenstjerne and Rosenkrantz families (whose names are commemorated in William Shakespeare's *Hamlet*) were among the most important.

Agriculture remained the principal industry. The cultivated land, apart from about 1,000 manors, consisted of about 80,000 farms, clustered together in groups of 5 to 20 as villages. These were managed by peasant farmers in common, whether they held their farms as freeholds or as copyholds. In 1500 about 12,000 peasants owned farms, about 18,000 were copyholding peasants on crown lands, and about 30,000 were copyhold tenants of lands belonging to the church or the nobles.

The peasantry suffered a decline during the Late Middle Ages. Such factors as the outbreak of plague in the mid-14th century, the expropriation of peasant lands, and the migration of young people from farms to towns led to a shortage of labour and a drop in agricultural production. A significant number of peasant farms and even whole villages were abandoned. The nobles—especially on Zealand, Funen (Fyn), and the smaller islands—responded to the crisis by establishing vornedskab, an institution that, like serfdom, tied peasant men and women to the estate of their birth.

Meanwhile, under the Kalmar Union, Danish towns prospered, and the influence of the burghers, or townspeople, grew. By 1500 there were approximately 80 towns, most of them fortified but all of them small; Copenhagen had at most 10,000 inhabitants. A monopoly on internal trade granted by King Erik VII improved the economic position of the burghers, and many German merchants took out citizenship in the towns in order to compete.

REFORMATION AND WAR

King Frederick I reigned during the early years of the Reformation, the religious revolution that resulted in the establishment of Protestantism as a major branch of Christianity. Frederick had promised Denmark's Roman Catholic bishops that he would fight heresy, but he in fact invited Lutheran preachers to the country, most probably to expand royal power at the expense of the church. After Frederick died in 1533, the bishops and other members of the predominantly Catholic Rigsråd postponed the election of a new king; they feared that the obvious candidate, Frederick's son Prince Christian (later King Christian III), if chosen, would immediately introduce

Lutheranism. They tried unsuccessfully to sponsor his younger brother Hans.

Civil war broke out in 1534, when the mayors of Malmö (now in Sweden) and Copenhagen accepted help from the north German city of Lübeck, an important member of the Hanseatic League. The Lübeckers, under the pretext of restoring the exiled Christian II, hoped to regain their declining mercantile supremacy and take control of The Sound, the strait between Zealand and Skåne that was controlled by Denmark. The landing of Lübeck troops, led by Count Christopher of Oldenburg, in Zealand in the summer of 1534 roused the Jutland nobility as well as the Catholic bishops, who came out in favour of Christian III. The leader of Christian III's forces, Johan Rantzau, duke of Holstein and a Lutheran, subdued a revolt of the Jutland peasants and then moved across Funen and Zealand to besiege Copenhagen, Count Christopher's last holdout. Finally, in the summer of 1536, Copenhagen capitulated, ending the so-called Count's War.

Following the war, to consolidate his position as king, Christian III arrested the Catholic bishops and confiscated all church property. The latter act brought vast estates to the crown, though in the following years many were sold or given to creditors to reduce the government's debts. In October 1536 the Danish Lutheran Church was established. The following year, new bishops, all of the burgher class, were appointed. They had little political influence, however, as bishops no longer sat in the Rigsråd. The organization of the new state church was finalized in 1539.

The Rigsråd, now made up only of members of the high nobility, soon asserted itself. The coronation charter that it negotiated with Christian III differed only slightly from earlier ones with regard to its constitutional power and the privileges of the nobility. In accordance with the king's wish to make the throne fully hereditary, the charter named Prince Frederick (later Frederick II) as his father's successor and provided that a Danish prince should always be chosen as king. The latter provision, however, was omitted in Frederick II's charter. The Rigsråd thus suffered no permanent loss of elective power.

The central government of Denmark was decisively strengthened by the Count's War, primarily by the elimination of the church as an independent and occasionally competing administrative structure, as well as by the expropriation of church assets. The further development of a central administrative apparatus, which included a chancery and a new finance department (the Rentekammer), also bolstered the strength of the state. The power of the nobility grew as well: membership in the Rigsråd and most leadership positions in the new administrative structures were reserved for nobles, and many new royal manors and estates were created. Although the merchants of Copenhagen and Malmö had fought Christian III, they nonetheless favoured a strong central government that would protect their interests in the Baltic trade. The centralization of power that took place during Christian's peaceful reign prepared the way for the establishment of absolutism a century later.

Denmark's central government remained strong during the reign of Frederick II (1559–88). Frederick aimed to reinstate the Kalmar Union, and in 1563 he was able to convince the Rigsråd to agree to a war with Sweden (Norway was still part of the Danish kingdom). At the conclusion of the so-called Seven Years' War of the North, however, Sweden remained independent, and Denmark was left deeply in debt. The strain on public finances was relieved partly through heavier taxation but mainly through a duty charged on shipping in The Sound, an important passage for the growing trade in the Baltic. Originally a fixed fee per ship, the duty later became a fee based on tonnage; it was at the king's own disposal, out of reach of the council. The process of collecting taxes and duties led to a more efficient financial administration. Meanwhile, Frederick focused his military policies on the navy and on establishing Danish dominance of the Baltic.

Upon the death of Frederick II in 1588, his son Christian IV succeeded to the throne at the age of 10. An aristocratic regency, headed by the aging chancellor Niels Kaas, governed the country and educated the future ruler for seven years.

The first half of Christian's personal reign was in every respect a success, marked by the dynamic king's many initiatives: establishing trading companies, acquiring overseas possessions, investing in a colony in India at Tranquebar, founding new towns, and erecting monumental buildings in the capital and elsewhere. A particularly important focus of his foreign policy was to secure Danish control of the Baltic. When Sweden began expanding its influence into the sea, Christian reacted by intervening in the Thirty Years' War; in addition to securing a broad sphere of interest in Germany as a counterweight to Swedish expansion, he also wished to strengthen the position of Protestantism. After disastrous battle losses and a devastating occupation of Jutland by German Catholics, the Danes signed a separate peace with the Holy Roman Empire in 1629. Despite this reversal, the king's national government, public administration, jurisdiction, and promotion of business and new industries had great importance for Denmark's future.

Christian IV has been regarded as Denmark's Renaissance ruler as well as one of the greatest Danish monarchs; he was a central figure in later drama, poetry, and art. In reality, however, the military catastrophes of his reign weakened the position of the monarchy, so the high nobility of the Rigsråd decided to curtail the power of his son and successor, Frederick III (1648–70).

In 1657, as part of the First Northern War, hostilities with Sweden broke out

Portrait of Christian IV, king of Denmark (1588–1648). Despite foreign policy troubles, Christian's reign was marked by resounding success at home. © Fine Art Images/SuperStock

again. In the exceptionally cold winter of 1657–58, the Swedish king Charles X Gustav attacked Jutland from the south and marched his troops to Zealand over the frozen sounds of Funen, after which the Danes signed the humiliating Treaty of Roskilde (1658). That summer Charles again invaded Denmark. Copenhagen, assisted by the Dutch, held out against the Swedes and defeated them in February 1659, but the war continued until 1660. The resulting Treaty of Copenhagen, imposed on Denmark by the great powers of Europe, led to the permanent loss of Halland, Skåne, and Blekinge to Sweden.

DANISH ABSOLUTISM

The military debacles of the second half of the 17th century were seen as proof that the nobles were unable to handle the central government; their refusal to pay taxes also angered the crown. Exploiting the situation, the king's councillors drafted a new law that eliminated the special political privileges of the nobility and proclaimed the crown fully inheritable, thus giving the king de facto absolute power. This inheritance law—along with the secret King's Law of 1665, among the most absolutist of all European expressions

TREATY OF COPENHAGEN

A generation of warfare between Sweden and Denmark-Norway was ended in 1660 by the Treaty of Copenhagen. Together with the Treaty of Roskilde, the Copenhagen treaty largely fixed the modern boundaries of Denmark, Norway, and Sweden.

In the Roskilde treaty (signed February 26, 1658) Denmark ceded its most fertile corn-growing provinces, Skåne, Blekinge, and Halland, as well as the Baltic Sea island of Bornholm and the Trøndelag region of central Norway to Sweden. Less than six months later, without warning, Sweden's King Charles X Gustav again invaded Denmark, seized Fünen, and attacked Zealand, but a Dutch fleet broke through the Swedish blockade of Copenhagen in October. The war's turning point was the Danish defense of Copenhagen, led by the heroic King Frederick III, in February 1659. A year later Charles X was planning a further attack on Denmark when he died suddenly of an illness, leaving a four-year-old son heir to the throne. Shortly thereafter Sweden and Denmark negotiated peace.

Signed on May 27, 1660, the Treaty of Copenhagen recovered Fünen and Bornholm for Denmark and Trøndelag for Norway. Denmark's former mainland provinces east of The Sound, however, remained part of Sweden. As a consequence of the peace, the Danish nobility, who had not supported the Danish war effort, became the scapegoats for the country's losses; and in a coup d'état, Frederick was named a hereditary and absolute king.

of absolutism—remained in force until 1848 with only minor modifications.

Absolutist Denmark was governed by a bureaucracy that continued to rely on political leaders from the class of great landowners, although wealth, not noble birth, now gave increased access to this class. The government in Copenhagen consisted of colleges—i.e., the chancelleries; the treasury college (descended from the old Rentekammer); and colleges for war, the navy, and, some years later, commerce. All major decisions were made by a secret council consisting of the leaders of the colleges, who could easily influence the king. Local administration remained largely unchanged after 1660, but the government took pains to curtail the military power of the new county governors (amtmænd).

During this period the crown further reduced its properties through sales to its bourgeois creditors, who thus joined the ranks of the large landowners. The state compensated for the loss of income from former crown lands by increasing taxes on the value of peasant land, though the nobles still paid the taxes for the peasants on their estates. Assessments of land values based both on area and on productivity were first made in 1662, and by 1688 surveyors had completed a nationwide register that served as the basis of taxation in both Denmark and Norway until the 19th century. The legal system was overhauled and regularized as well, and already in 1661 a supreme court, with jurisdiction over the entire kingdom, had replaced the old system whereby the king and the Rigsråd heard legal appeals. Each part of the country had had its own law codes, but under Christian V, who succeeded Frederick III, his father, in 1670, national law was codified.

THE 18TH CENTURY

The 18th century brought a measure of balance in Denmark's foreign relations. Important economic gains were also made at this time with regard to agriculture and international trade.

FOREIGN POLICY

The Second Northern War (Great Northern War; 1700–21) demonstrated that, even with alliances, Denmark had no hope of recapturing the territories lost to Sweden in the preceding century. Sweden, moreover, no longer had the strength to invade Denmark from the south in alliance with the dukes of Schleswig or Holstein. King Frederick IV (1699–1730) decided on a foreign policy of keeping a balance of power in the north and safeguarding communications between Denmark and Norway. This necessitated alliances with Russia and the Netherlands and, from time to time, France. This policy succeeded for the rest of the 18th century, probably because of the common European need for free access to the Baltic. Finally, in the 1770s, the Gottorp lands in Schleswig and Holstein were brought under the rule of the Danish crown.

During the 18th century, Denmark-Norway acquired an important merchant marine and a navy. Freedom of the seas had become a vital issue and a difficult problem, complicated especially by the export of Norwegian timber to Great Britain. During wars in the middle of the century, Denmark-Norway had to bow to the British claim of ruling the waves. In 1780, during the American Revolution (1775–83), the Danish foreign minister Andreas Peter, greve (count) af Bernstorff, negotiated an armed neutrality treaty with Russia, the Netherlands, and Sweden, whose King Gustav III had married a Danish princess. However, because Norwegian export interests would have been threatened if Britain had considered these treaties hostile, Bernstorff also concluded a special treaty with Britain, much to the annoyance of Russia. The French revolutionary wars led Denmark and Sweden to extend the treaty in 1794, but Danish neutrality did not last much longer. After 1800 it became impossible for Denmark to maintain its access to world shipping lanes unimpeded, its efforts to placate the British notwithstanding.

THE ECONOMY AND AGRICULTURAL REFORMS

In the 18th century, Denmark, poor in natural resources except for its soil, nonetheless made important economic gains in international trade and agriculture. No important industries, on the other hand, developed during this period.

Following mercantilist theory, the government supported trade, particularly shipping, to the benefit of Copenhagen merchants. Denmark, however, lacked the political strength to exploit the strategic position of Copenhagen. In the 1730s eastern Norway was made an outlet for Danish grain, but the grain was inferior and normally could not compete with Baltic grain on the western European markets. Besides grain, oxen, and meat, Denmark had very little else to export, so transit trade predominated.

At the beginning of the century, Danish agriculture, like peasant agriculture elsewhere in Europe, was not very productive. Some 300 landlords controlled 800 to 900 estates—about 90 percent of the arable land. Danish landlords, like all European elites, wanted to participate in the generally rising standard of living. To do so, they needed to increase the incomes from their estates. A price depression beginning in the 1720s enabled the landlords to use their position to pressure the peasants further by increasing the corvée (obligatory work owed by peasants to their landlords) to an average of three days a week and by eliminating villages and turning peasants into landless cottars who worked the lord's own farmland. While some peasants, especially in western and northern Jutland, continued to own their farms, the vast majority held their farms as copyholds on an estate. So landlords could better control their labour, it became law for male peasants between 4 and 40 years of age to remain on the estate of their birth, unless they had the landlord's permission to move or they had served six years in the army or navy. Because conscription was controlled by the landlord, he could threaten a young peasant with at least six years of military service if he did not accept a copyhold farm or cottage. Peasants had no right to demand a contract when they took over a holding, nor could they demand payment for improvements they might have made on the holding when the copyhold expired, usually at the death or bankruptcy of the peasant. Each landlord also had the right of petty jurisdiction on his estate. Under this system, despite the changes, productivity remained low. Nevertheless, except for the hog and cattle raisers of Jutland, the estates were the only farms to produce an exportable surplus of agricultural goods.

During the course of the century, influenced by the writings of the French physiocrats, who believed that the wealth of a country came from agriculture, not trade, and by the experiences of Dutch farmers, a reform movement took root and flourished in the kingdom. In 1755 freedom of the press regarding economic and agricultural issues led to a lively debate. It became clear that if agriculture were to become productive, both technical changes—i.e., better tools, farming methods, seed, and stock—and social changes would be necessary. Technical change could occur fairly easily on land under the control of one person, but it was quite difficult in areas of joint tillage. As a consequence, agricultural improvements came first to the estates and then to the glebes (church farmlands) of enlightened Lutheran pastors, although they were not unknown in the peasant villages.

In 1759 some of the first enclosures were instituted—i.e., all the land belonging to one farm was enclosed by a more-or-less-permanent fence, hedge, or stone wall—and the peasants' corvée was replaced by a monetary payment. Elsewhere similar experiments were carried out by reform-minded landlords, many of them nobles. In 1769 the Royal Danish Agricultural Society was founded to encourage and disseminate information about technical improvements in a number of fields, including agriculture.

The land reform movement reached its apogee between the years 1784 and 1797. Danish politics of those years were led by the foreign minister Bernstorff; Christian Ditlev, Greve (count) Reventlow; and Ernst Schimmelmann, all from the landlord class. The politics were also led by the Norwegian jurist Christian Colbjørnsen and the crown prince Frederick (later King Frederick VI), whose father, King Christian VII, was incapable of ruling. Between 1784 and 1788 the Great Agricultural Commission studied the Danish agricultural situation, and its recommendations led to a number of sweeping reforms. Its recognition of the importance of peasant ownership of land led to the availability of low-interest, government-backed loans as well as to a

COUNT REVENTLOW

Beginning in the late 18th century, Christian Ditlev Frederik, Greve (count) Reventlow (born March 11, 1748, Copenhagen, Denmark—died October 11, 1827, Lolland), championed agrarian reforms in Denmark. His efforts led to the liberation of the Danish peasantry.

Reventlow traveled to several western European countries in the 1760s to study economic conditions. He returned to Denmark in 1770 and entered state service in 1773. He experimented with agrarian reform on the Lolland estates, which he inherited in 1775. In 1784 he was named head of the Rentekammer (department of finance), with responsibility for agriculture.

On the basis of four earlier experiments he had conducted, Reventlow took measures to ease the lot of peasants who worked on crown land. In 1786 he persuaded Crown Prince Frederick (later Frederick VI) to create an agrarian commission to study the conditions of the peasantry as a whole. The resulting reforms in 1787 and 1788 led to the end of adscription, the legal bond between Danish peasants and the estate of their birth. Later measures of Reventlow led to clearly defined terms of peasant service on the large estates. Reventlow retired from public service in 1813 after being dismissed from his post.

law ending adscription (the tying of the peasants to the estate of their birth). The work of the commission also stimulated a relatively rapid enclosure of farmland in Denmark. Between 1790 and 1814 all but a few villages were surveyed for enclosure, and the majority of the farms became freeholds. (The remaining copyholds were converted later in the 19th century.) Landlords were compensated for the rights they lost, and, together with the new landowning farmers, they were assured a stable labour force by strict legislation of the small tenant farmers.

The land reforms were possible because of a continuous rise in grain prices between 1750 and 1815 and because the politicians of 1784 had carried out successful reforms on their own estates. These leaders also had an insight into the benefits of a mild inflation and a liberal allocation of state credit, with which they guided the transition to peasant landownership. The land reforms ultimately led to an effective agricultural sector that delivered high-quality products for domestic use and for export.

THE 19TH CENTURY

International affairs in the 19th century were dominated by the Napoleonic Wars and their aftermath, which in the case of Denmark included economic crisis. Domestically, the kingdom experienced growing liberalism and nationalism movements during this period.

THE NAPOLEONIC WARS AND THEIR AFTERMATH

The Napoleonic Wars of the early 19th century ended an era of peace for Denmark and Norway that had lasted since the 1720s. The armed neutrality treaty of 1794 between Denmark and Sweden, which Russia and Prussia joined in 1800, was considered hostile by Great Britain. In 1801 British navy ships entered The Sound and destroyed much of the Danish fleet in a battle in the Copenhagen harbour. When the British fleet next proceeded to threaten the Swedish naval port of Karlskrona, Russia started negotiations with Britain. The result was a compromise, which Sweden was forced to adopt in 1802. While the Danish policy of armed neutrality had failed, Denmark nevertheless managed to keep out of the wars until 1807 and to profit from trade with the belligerents.

The Treaty of Tilsit (1807) between France and Russia worsened the situation. In 1805 France had lost its fleet to the British at the Battle of Trafalgar. The British thus feared that the continental powers might force Denmark to join them so that the Danish navy could be used to invade Britain. To eliminate this threat, the British resorted not to diplomacy but to force. In August 1807 British troops invaded and occupied Zealand; in September British ships bombarded Copenhagen with grenades and incendiary bombs, destroying three-fourths of the city and killing thousands. Denmark, not prepared for war, was forced to capitulate, and the British expropriated the Danish fleet

On October 31, 1807, Denmark joined the continental alliance against Britain. In response, Britain blockaded the sea route connecting Denmark and Norway. Grain shipments from Denmark to Norway stopped, and Norwegian exports could not get out. Britain somewhat relaxed its blockade after 1810, but the years of isolation, economic crisis, and hunger in Norway nevertheless convinced leading groups there of the necessity of Norwegian independence.

In 1813 Sweden, which had become an ally of Britain, attacked Denmark from the south, through Schleswig-Holstein. Hostilities between the two countries were ended on January 14, 1814, by the Treaty of Kiel, but Denmark was forced to cede Norway to Sweden. (However, Denmark maintained its rule of the old Norwegian dependencies of Iceland, the Faroe Islands, and Greenland.) Unhappy at the prospect of Swedish rule, leading Norwegians assembled at the Norwegian village of Eidsvoll, where they adopted a constitution and elected the Danish crown prince and governor of Norway, Christian Frederick (later Christian VIII), to the Norwegian throne. Sweden promptly attacked Norway, however, and Christian Frederick stepped down. Compelled to accept Swedish rule,

People in Copenhagen panic as British firebombs set buildings ablaze during the devastating attack of 1807. Painting by Christofer Willem Eckersberg. DEA/A. Dagli Orti/De Agostini/ Getty Images

Norway could not fully implement the Eidsvoll constitution until 1905, when it finally gained independence.

The Napoleonic Wars proved to be economically catastrophic for Denmark. Trade had been seriously affected, and the widespread overseas connections that formerly had played so large a part in the economic life of Denmark could not be resumed. Copenhagen had been devastated, and its role as an international financial and trading centre was soon taken over by Hamburg. Inflation further contributed to the economic crisis. In 1813 the state was forced to make a formal declaration of bankruptcy.

Denmark's considerable economic problems were worsened by low grain prices across Europe. The loss of Norway and the high import duties on grain that Great Britain imposed at this time deprived Denmark of its surest markets for grain export. The agricultural crisis resulted in the compulsory auctioning of many estates and farms; it also brought the implementation of agrarian reforms to a complete standstill.

It was not until 1818, when an independent national bank with the sole right to issue banknotes was established, that economic stability became possible. From 1830, economic life decidedly took a turn for the better. Prices for agricultural goods improved, and the earlier land reforms were beginning to show results. In fact, the 1830s saw a significant expansion in the agricultural sector of the economy.

THE LIBERAL MOVEMENT

Denmark's government under Frederick VI (1808–39) can be described as a patriarchal autocracy. In the Privy Council, which was regularly convened after 1814, Poul Christian Stemann became the leading figure and was responsible for the government's strongly conservative policies until 1848. His close colleague Anders Sandøe Ørsted pleaded for a somewhat more liberal policy, at least on economic questions.

After the July Revolution (1830) in France, leading men, particularly wealthy merchants and professionals, demanded a liberal constitution. The government was forced to make concessions, and in 1834 consultative assemblies were established in the kingdom as well as in Schleswig and Holstein. Being composed only of wealthy men, however, these were not representative bodies, and their function was only advisory. As the liberal movement grew in strength, especially in the academic world and among the middle classes, the liberal press, whose leading journal was *Fædrelandet* ("The Fatherland"; established in 1834), subjected the monarchy and its conservative administration to severe criticism. When the popular Frederick VI died in 1839, the liberals had great hopes for his successor, Christian VIII, who, during his youth as governor in Norway, had appeared as the spokesman for liberal politics. Over the years, however, Christian VIII had become much more conservative and, as king of Denmark, did not consider the time ripe to moderate the absolute monarchy. He confined himself, therefore, to modernizing the administration, especially between 1837 and 1841, through a program of establishing local government and granting some independence to parishes and counties.

As the liberals gained a political voice, so did the farmers. The farmers' movement started as a religious one, but it soon became dominated by social and political ideas, with agitators such as Jens Andersen Hansen leading the way. When the government intervened, the liberals and the farmers joined forces against the common adversary. In 1846 the farmers' case received further support when a group of liberal reformers led by Anton Frederik Tscherning founded the Society of the Friends of the Farmer (Bondevennernes Selskab), which later developed into the Liberal Party (Venstre; "Left").

After the death of Christian VIII in January 1848 and under the influence of the Revolutions of 1848 in France, Germany, and elsewhere, the new king, Frederick VII (1848–63), installed the so-called March Cabinet, in which Orla Lehmann and Ditlev Gothard Monrad, leaders of the newly formed National Liberal Party, were given seats. After a constituent assembly had been summoned, the absolute monarchy was abolished; it was replaced by the so-called June constitution of June 5, 1849. Together with the king and his ministers, there was now also a parliament with two chambers: the Folketing and the Landsting. Both were elected by popular vote, but seats in the Landsting had a relatively high property-owning qualification. The parliament shared legislative power with the king and the cabinet, while the courts independently exercised judicial power. The constitution also secured the freedom of the press, religious freedom, and the right to hold meetings and form associations.

THE SCHLESWIG-HOLSTEIN QUESTION

Alongside liberalism, nationalism was another important movement in 19th-century Denmark. National feelings were particularly inflamed by the Schleswig-Holstein question. After the loss of Norway in 1814, the Danish monarchy consisted of three main parts: the kingdom of Denmark, Schleswig, and Holstein, the last of which was a member of the German Confederation. Whereas Holstein was German, Schleswig was linguistically and culturally divided between a Danish and a German population. When the liberal German-speaking population in Schleswig opposed autocratic rule and demanded a free constitution as well as affiliation with Holstein and the German Confederation, the emerging Danish National Liberal movement called for Schleswig to be incorporated into Denmark. This demand came to be called the Eider Program, named for the Eider River, which formed the southern boundary of Schleswig.

When the National Liberal government officially adopted this policy in 1848, the people of Schleswig and Holstein resorted to arms, with Prussia supplying military aid. Although the Danish army defeated the rebels in 1851, subsequent agreements in 1851 and 1852, supported by the great powers of Europe, compelled Denmark to take no measures to tie Schleswig any closer to itself than Holstein was. The Eider Program was thus abandoned; the June constitution of 1849 applied only to Denmark, not to either of the duchies.

The National Liberal government was succeeded in 1852 by the Conservative (Højre; "Right") government under Christian Albrecht Bluhme. Nevertheless, the influence of Pan-Scandinavianism and the German Confederation's constant interference in constitutional matters in Schleswig and Holstein caused the Eider Program to win ground once again. The replacement of the Conservative government in 1857 by a moderate National Liberal government, led by Carl Christian Hall, further revived the program. In 1863, in the belief that Prussia was preoccupied with a Polish rebellion against Russia and in expectation of support from Sweden, the Danish government separated Holstein from the rest of the kingdom and applied a constitution to both Denmark and Schleswig. This "November constitution" effectively meant that Schleswig was annexed to Denmark, in contravention of the agreements of 1851 and 1852.

Under the leadership of Otto von Bismarck, Prussia reacted immediately: in February 1864, war broke out between Denmark on one side and Prussia and Austria on the other. After the Danish defeat at Dybbøl, in Schleswig, and the consequent occupation of the whole of Jutland, Denmark was forced by the Treaty of Vienna in October to surrender almost all of Schleswig and Holstein to Prussia and Austria.

THE RIGHT AND THE LEFT

Denmark's defeat in 1864 led to the fall of the National Liberal government. Under Christian IX (1863–1906) a Conservative government was appointed, and in 1866 a new constitution was adopted. It introduced electoral rules that gave weighted votes to great landowners and civil servants, thus securing the distinctly conservative leaning of the Landsting. By 1870 the National Liberals had merged with the Conservatives to form the Right (Højre) Party.

To counter Højre, several groups that represented farmers combined in 1870 to form the United Left (Forenede Venstre), which in 1872 secured a majority in the Folketing. The Left demanded a return to the June constitution of 1849 as well as a number of other reforms, such as making the government responsible to the parliament instead of to the king. The Social Democratic Party (Socialdemokratiet), which actually fell further left than the Left on the political spectrum, formed in the 1870s as well.

However, with Jacob Brønnum Scavenius Estrup, a member of Højre and a great landowner, as prime minister (1875–94), a strictly conservative policy was pursued. Despite the opposing parliamentary majority in the Folketing, the government, with a majority in the Landsting, forced its conservative policies through by means of provisory laws and with support from the king. The result was that all reforms came to a standstill. The crisis was not resolved until 1894, when a compromise between the Left and the Right was reached, at which time Estrup himself left the government. The Left's demand for parliamentary democracy was not granted until the 1901 election, however, when the Left Reform Party (Venstrereformparti), an offshoot of the Left, came to power and what has become known in Denmark as the "Change of System" was introduced.

Meanwhile, particularly after Germany emerged from the Franco-German War of 1870–71 as a powerful unified state, Danish foreign policy was developed along neutral lines. Yet the Right and the Left strongly disagreed on how Danish neutrality should be carried out. The Conservatives demanded a strong defense policy while, within the Left itself, the most radical viewpoint was held by Viggo Hørup, who advocated complete disarmament.

The increasing popularity of the Left and the formation of the Social Democratic Party occurred in the context of great economic and social changes. Industrial production began in the capital and in some of the major towns in the provinces, and, in the last quarter of the 19th century, the percentage of the population living in urban areas increased dramatically. The first rail line was built in 1847; in the late 1860s the government took over railroad building, and, by the end of the 1870s, the trunk lines had been completed. The rapid development of harbours, steamships, and foreign trade facilitated the importation of raw materials needed for industry, especially coal and iron. There also was a steady stream of foreign capital into Denmark. By the end of the century, trade unions and employers' associations had spread across the kingdom. As industry grew, agriculture evolved as well. The implementation of the reforms of the 18th century resumed, and new reforms were adopted. As world grain prices dropped beginning in the 1860s, Danish farmers increasingly shifted to the production of dairy products and meat. The organization of cooperative dairies, starting in 1882, made it possible for even smallholders to produce for export. Eventually cooperative slaughterhouses also were established. By the end of the century, a significant percentage of the butter and bacon consumed in England came from Denmark.

The comparative sophistication and flexibility of Danish farmers in assessing and responding to the market was grounded in several factors, especially the folk high schools, open to both men and women, that were established in the 19th century. Such education made it possible for farmers to use more effectively the technical information made available through the Royal Agricultural Association.

THE 20TH CENTURY

Despite its declarations of neutrality, Denmark found itself affected by World War I and embroiled in World War II. The 20th century also saw a number of political reforms in Denmark, especially after World War II.

PARLIAMENTARY DEMOCRACY AND WAR, c. 1900–45

The Left Reform government that came to power under the Change of System in 1901 went swiftly to work on a number of reforms. Parliamentary supremacy, requiring the king to appoint a parliament-approved government, began in that year. A free-trade law that corresponded to the agricultural export interests was passed. In conformity with the ideas of N.F.S. Grundtvig, the state church was transformed into a folk church, with parochial church councils; the educational system was also democratized. In addition, the reformers changed the tax law so that income, not land, was the main criterion for taxation.

Despite the victory over the Conservatives, it soon became apparent that it was impossible for the Left Reformers, led by Jens Christian Christensen, to remain united. In 1905 a radical faction broke away to become the Radical Left Party (Radikale Venstre), the most important members of which were Peter Rochegune Munch and Ove Rode.

Between 1913 and 1920 the Radicals, supported by the Social Democrats, were in power. In 1915 the constitution was revised, and the privileged franchise to the Landsting was revoked, although the electoral qualifying age of 35 was retained. At the same time, the franchise to both the Folketing and the Landsting was extended to women, servants, and farmhands. The right-wing majority in the Landsting agreed to the constitutional reform on condition that the single-member constituency be replaced by proportional representation. There followed a number of reforms, including trial by jury and a land reform bill that aimed to redistribute land from large estates to increase the size of smallholders' farms.

In the years leading up to World War I, it became increasingly important to define Germany's intended attitude toward Denmark in the event of a European conflict. The Germans were well aware that the Schleswig affair had

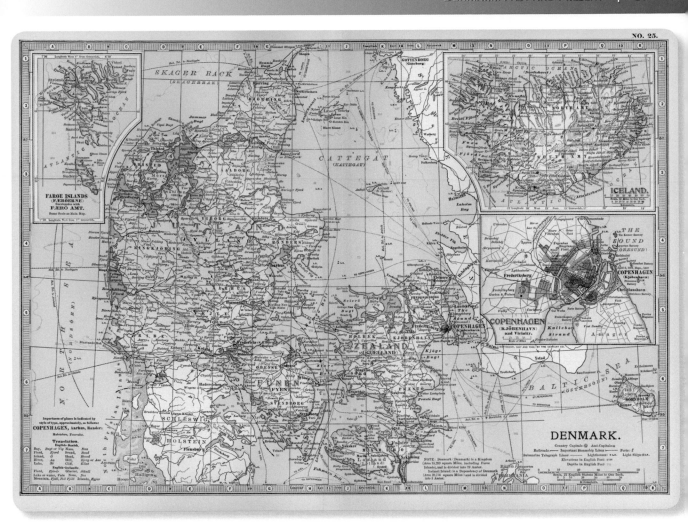

Map of Denmark (c. 1900), from the 10th edition of *Encyclopædia Britannica.*

left a good many Danes with a loathing for everything German, and the constant friction between the Danish minority and the German administration in Schleswig increased the tension between the two countries. Danish governments after 1901 made persistent efforts to assure Germany of Denmark's benevolent neutrality, but the disagreement over this policy's implementation remained unreconciled. At the outbreak of war in 1914, Germany insisted that Denmark lay mines in the Great Belt, a strait between several Danish islands that connects the Baltic Sea with an arm of the North Sea. However, as the British fleet made no serious attempts to break through, neutrality was maintained.

World War I gave Denmark and other neutral countries good export markets in the belligerent countries, but the conflict also led to a shortage of supplies. With a widespread overseas trade, the country's economic life was vulnerable. It became especially so in 1917, after Germany opted for unrestricted submarine warfare. (Some of Denmark's exports to Great Britain were thereby reoriented to Germany.) There was a deficit of raw materials in both agriculture and industry, and the government rationed a number of consumer goods.

The Treaty of Versailles, signed at the end of the war, included a clause stating that part of Schleswig should revert to Denmark in accordance with the principle of self-determination. The boundary was determined by a plebiscite in 1920. The discontent that nonetheless arose as a consequence of the drawing of the boundary, coupled with labour unrest and dissatisfaction with remaining wartime restrictions, led to the fall of the government in the same year. A Left government, supported by the Conservatives, then came to power.

In 1924 the Social Democrats, under Thorvald Stauning, formed a minority government with support from the Radicals. This was the first working-class government in Denmark. The cabinet included the historian Nina Bang as the minister of education; she was the first woman to serve as a minister in a democratically elected Danish government. The years 1926 to 1929 saw the Left, supported by the

Conservatives, in power again; however, the Social Democrats scored another victory at the polls in 1929, and a coalition government under Stauning was formed with the Radical Party.

Critical economic conditions, including the periodic high unemployment rate that followed World War I, were a recurring problem for the governments of the 1920s. In 1922 the country's largest private bank, Landmandsbanken, failed. The subsequent decade was no easier. High rates of unemployment resulted from the Great Depression of the early 1930s: in 1933 about 40 percent of organized industrial workers were affected. When Great Britain abandoned the gold standard in 1931, Denmark had followed suit. The greatest blow to the Danish economy, however, was Britain's establishment in 1932 of a system of preferential tariffs for members of the British Commonwealth.

To cope with the crisis, the government subjected foreign trade to stringent control by the establishment of a "currency centre" and won the support of the Left in the Kanslergade Agreement, by which it was agreed to devalue the Danish currency, the krone, and to freeze existing wage agreements by law. In addition, the Left agreed to support social reforms that included old-age pensions and health, unemployment, and accident insurance. A number of measures also were adopted in support of agriculture.

The general election of 1935 showed broad support for the Social Democrats' program, and they stayed in power. After the elections to the Landsting in 1936, the government coalition of Social Democrats and Radicals held the majority in both the Folketing and the Landsting for the first time since the inception of democracy. Trade improved, and, during the late 1930s, industry again began to expand.

Denmark had joined the League of Nations in 1920 and had worked for a peaceful solution to international problems during the interwar period. In the 1930s, however, foreign policy was complicated by events in Germany. When Adolf Hitler came to power and Germany began to rearm, Denmark's position again became vulnerable. Although Germany had never recognized the alterations in its boundaries as laid down by the Treaty of Versailles, Denmark tried in vain to obtain German recognition of the Schleswig boundary. At the same time, it avoided measures that could offend its powerful neighbour. When in June 1939 Hitler offered nonaggression pacts to those countries that might feel threatened by Germany's expansionist policy, Denmark, in contrast to the other Scandinavian countries, accepted the offer. In September of that year, at the outbreak of World War II, Denmark—this time together with the other Nordic countries—issued a declaration of neutrality.

Denmark was not allowed to remain neutral, however. On April 9, 1940, German troops crossed the border, and after token resistance the Danish government submitted to a military occupation of the country. Unlike other occupied countries, Denmark formally remained a sovereign state until August 29, 1943. The major parties formed a national unity government, with Stauning as leader, and in July 1940 Erik Scavenius became foreign minister. In 1941, when Germany attacked the Soviet Union, the Danish government was forced to allow the formation of a Danish volunteer corps to fight on the Eastern Front and to outlaw all communist activity in the country. In November 1941 Denmark signed the Anti-Comintern Pact.

Denmark's policy of accommodation did not last. After Stauning's successor, Vilhelm Buhl, was forced to resign in November 1942 under pressure from the Germans, Scavenius, who advocated cooperation with the German authorities, became prime minister. However, the elections of 1943 proved that the Danish people supported the democratic parties of Denmark, not Nazism. At the same time, the resistance movement, first organized in 1940, was growing: thousands of Danes—about 50,000 by the end of the war—joined armed resistance groups, and numerous acts of sabotage were carried out.

Germany's military defeats paved the way for demands for an open breach with the powers of occupation. Dissatisfaction caused by consumer shortages and inflation, combined with the growing opposition to German occupation, led to a series of strikes in the summer of 1943 that in August culminated in actions aimed directly at the Germans. When the Danish government refused to introduce the death penalty for sabotage, to allow the persecution of Jews, or to use force against the strikers, the Germans declared a state of emergency. The Danish government, still under Scavenius's leadership, refused further cooperation, and the German Reichskommissar assumed political control. The Danish army and navy were disbanded, but not before many of the ships were scuttled by their own crews to prevent the Germans from using them.

With the end of Danish accommodation, the relationship between the Danes and the occupying Germans deteriorated even further. In September 1943 the Danish Freedom Council was formed; under its leadership the activities of the various resistance groups could be coordinated, and cooperation between the resistance and leading politicians could be maintained. The major activities of the resistance groups included producing illegal newspapers, running a comprehensive intelligence service, smuggling fugitives to Sweden, and committing acts of sabotage. The Danish resistance movement is perhaps best known for its rescue of nearly all the Jews in Denmark, including Danes who were Jewish as well as Jewish refugees. To maintain the goodwill of the Danish people, the German occupiers had not engaged in any overtly anti-Semitic acts, but that attitude changed when accommodation ceased. In the fall of 1943 the Germans prepared to round up the approximately 7,000 Jews in the country, but fewer than 500 were

ultimately arrested. The remainder of the Jewish population had been successfully hidden, and over the following weeks they escaped to Sweden.

During the last year of the war, the Freedom Council and leading Danish politicians cooperated more closely. When the Germans surrendered on May 5, 1945, a new government—half of which consisted of representatives of the Freedom Council and the other half of politicians from the old political parties—was formed. Elections in the autumn of 1945 brought a Left government, led by Knud Kristensen, to power.

POSTWAR DENMARK, 1945–c. 1990

Following the war, the question of Denmark's southern border arose once again as the Danish minority in German-controlled South Schleswig called for incorporation with Denmark. The idea won strong support among the local population, but in Denmark opinion was divided. In the autumn of 1946, after the United Kingdom formally requested the Danish government to state its intentions regarding South Schleswig, all parties agreed to the October Note of 1946, which rejected any alteration of the 1920 boundary between Denmark and Germany. Once the Social Democrats, under the leadership of Hans Hedtoft, returned to power in 1947, all remaining plans to pursue the boundary question were abandoned.

HANS HEDTOFT

Denmark's shift from neutrality to active membership in NATO is largely the result of the efforts of Hans Hedtoft (born Hans Christian Hedtoft-Hansen, April 21, 1903, Århus, Denmark—died January 29, 1955, Stockholm). Hedtoft, a Danish politician and statesman, initiated the change in Danish policy after World War II.

At the age of 25 Hedtoft-Hansen became president of the Social Democratic Party's youth organization. As secretary of the party in 1935 he was elected to Parliament, but he resigned his seat in 1940, during the German occupation of Denmark in World War II. A member of the Danish resistance movement, Hedtoft-Hansen became minister of social affairs in the first postwar government in 1945. He headed a minority Social Democratic government in 1947–50 (thenceforth as Hans Hedtoft). Alarmed by the Communist coup in Czechoslovakia in 1948, he and his finance minister, H.C. Hansen, inaugurated a strong defense policy for Denmark, including membership in NATO (1949) and closer ties with Norway and Sweden. Hedtoft again became prime minister in 1953, continuing his foreign- and defense-policy initiatives. He died in Stockholm while attending a meeting of the Nordic Council.

Meanwhile, the Danish government had made the defense of the realm a top priority in the immediate postwar period. Denmark joined the United Nations in June 1945 and the North Atlantic Treaty Organization (NATO) in April 1949. Its military defenses were considerably strengthened by statutes passed in 1950 and 1951 and were further complemented by armaments from the United States. Denmark nevertheless rejected a request by the United States to establish air bases on Danish territory. With West Germany's admission to NATO, Denmark succeeded in obtaining guarantees—formalized in the Bonn Protocol of 1955—for the rights of the Danish minority in South Schleswig.

POSTWAR POLITICS

A number of political reforms were instituted in the postwar era. In 1953 the constitution was substantially revised. Female succession to the throne was introduced, allowing Margrethe II to assume the throne in 1972 upon the death of her father, King Frederick IX. In addition, the new constitution reduced the national legislature to one chamber, the Folketing, whose membership was increased to 179—including two seats for Greenland and two for the Faroe Islands. All members of the Folketing were to be elected based on proportional representation, thus making a wide spectrum of political parties possible. On the other hand, it became almost impossible for any one party to secure an absolute majority. As a result, subsequent governments have tended to be either minority governments or coalitions of two, three, or even four parties.

The postwar political scene was dominated by the so-called old parties: the Conservative People's Party (Konservative Folkeparti), the Left (known after 1964 as the Liberal Party), the Radical Left, and the Social Democratic Party (which remained more leftist in its outlook than the so-called Left parties). However, a number of smaller parties also gained influence and complicated the political situation.

The Social Democratic Party was the leading party of the 1950s, '60s, and '70s. From 1953 to 1968 it was in power, either alone or in coalition with the Radicals and, for a short period, the Justice Party (Retsforbundet; a party based on the ideas of the economist Henry George), and always with a Social Democrat as prime minister. The major results were new tax laws, particularly the institution of a general value-added consumer tax as well as a new type of income taxation that deducted taxes from income as it was earned rather than at a later date. This kind of income taxation enabled the government to stimulate or restrain spending by lowering or raising the level of taxation.

In the 1968 election, the majority shifted to the right. The Radical Left's leader, Hilmar Baunsgaard, deserted the Social Democrats and headed a coalition with the Conservatives and the Liberals (the Left) until 1971, when Jens Otto Krag again formed a Social Democratic government.

Krag unexpectedly resigned in 1972, leaving the post of prime minister to Anker Jørgensen, who had to call an election in November 1973. An electoral landslide resulted in heavy losses for the four "old" parties and the emergence of three new parties: the Centre Democrats (Centrum-Demokraterne), the Christian People's Party (Kristeligt Folkeparti), and the Progress Party (Fremskridtspartiet), an antitax party. A weak minority government under Poul Hartling of the Liberal Party tried to solve the country's growing economic problems, but his austerity program resulted in protests from trade unions and the opposition. In 1975 Jørgensen again came to power (from 1978 in coalition with the Liberals), rejecting support from the left-wing Socialist People's Party (Socialistisk Folkeparti), which opposed Danish membership in NATO.

The end of the 1970s brought a deteriorating economic situation and the political system's inability to reach a consensus on measures to solve the problems. Increased indirect taxes to reduce the foreign debt and the deficit on the balance of payments met with strong opposition from the trade unions, many of which staged strikes and demonstrations; in 1979 Jørgensen was again forced to resign. After the election in October, however, he formed a Social Democratic minority government, which introduced what was called the most stringent wage-and-price-freeze program since World War II.

After a new general election in December 1981, the voting age having been reduced from 20 to 18 following a referendum, Jørgensen again lost seats in the Folketing, but he continued as leader of a weak minority government that faced many problems, especially high unemployment, which had risen to about 10 percent. He was once more forced to resign—this time, however, without an election—in September 1982. The leader of the Conservative Party, Poul Schlüter, formed a minority government with three other centre-right parties: the Liberals, the Centre Democrats, and the Christian People's Party. Together, they had only 66 seats in the Folketing.

The Conservatives remained in power through the 1980s and into the 1990s. Schlüter, the first Conservative prime minister since 1901, introduced a counterinflationary and economic recovery program that yielded results in 1985–86, but the country's foreign debt and balance-of-payments deficit continued to cause serious concern during the 1980s. Schlüter was consequently forced to call several general elections (1984, 1987, 1988), carry out government reshuffles (1986, 1987, 1988, 1989), and threaten to call elections or resign. He survived 23 no-confidence votes concerning foreign and defense policy, brought by the Social Democrats in tactical attempts to force him from office.

When Schlüter reshuffled the government in 1988, he incorporated the Radical Left and excluded the Christian People's Party and the Centre Democrats. The coalition government came under greater pressure from the left-wing Socialist People's Party and the right-wing Progress Party, both of which gained seats in the Folketing at the end of the 1980s; the Progress Party advocated substantial cuts in the public sector and a more restrictive policy toward the dramatically increased number of refugees. It was a scandal over Tamil refugees that forced Schlüter's resignation in 1993 and brought a coalition government under the leadership of Social Democrat Poul Nyrup Rasmussen to power.

POSTWAR ECONOMICS

While the postwar period saw its share of economic difficulties, it was also a time of an overall rise in the standard of living. During the early 1950s the Danish economy suffered a large deficit in the trade balance, but the situation improved later in the decade as the result of lower import prices for raw materials, a considerable increase in industrial production, and the stabilization of prices for agricultural export products. The period from 1957 to 1965 saw rapidly rising prosperity. Within the framework of the Organisation for European Economic Co-operation, Denmark, during the 1950s, abolished most of the regulations that had restricted its foreign trade, and it was one of the founding members of the European Free Trade Association in 1959.

During the 1960s, however, the balance-of-payments deficit became larger, and the government was forced to intervene in an attempt to control rising consumption. This was done by instituting the value-added tax, by compulsory savings, by intervention in labour conflicts, and by the regulation of wages and prices. Nevertheless, economic problems worsened in the 1970s. The various Danish governments attempted to impose stringent measures, such as harsh savings programs, but strong opposition to some plans led to the dissolution of the Folketing on several occasions. After 1973, rising oil prices and the international recession badly affected the Danish economy and led to a dramatic increase in unemployment.

In 1972 Denmark was offered membership in the European Economic Community (EEC; later the European Community, which was embedded in and ultimately replaced by the European Union). In a referendum that year, 63 percent of Danish voters approved EEC membership, which became effective on January 1, 1973.

Austerity measures introduced by Prime Minister Schlüter in the early 1980s led to lower inflation, recovery in business confidence and investments, growth of employment in the private sector, and increasing economic activity. It proved difficult, however, to eliminate the budget deficit, and in 1986 the government was forced to increase energy and payroll taxes and to impose new austerity measures to curb private consumption, stimulate saving, and make private borrowing less attractive. The early 1990s brought a gradual recovery in the Danish economy, including a balance-of-payments surplus, despite the general European recession.

DENMARK SINCE THE 1990s

During the 1990s, while the economy improved and unemployment dropped, Danes struggled with three key political and economic issues. First, political controversy surrounded the status of immigrants and refugees in Denmark. A violation of refugees' rights led the prime minister to resign in 1993; right-wing parties adopted anti-immigration platforms; and rioting followed the expulsion in 1999 from Denmark of a Danish-born man of Turkish descent. Second, while most Danes supported maintaining the country's strong social welfare programs, some Danes sought to decrease the programs' high cost in taxes while others opposed any cuts in benefits. Third, Danes also were divided during the 1990s over closer economic ties with the European Community (EC). In 1992 Danish voters rejected the Maastricht Treaty, which provided the framework for an expanded European Union (EU) that would subsume the EC. A second referendum in 1993 approved Danish membership in the EU, but only after Denmark had negotiated exemptions from certain provisions of the treaty that many Danes thought might erode Danish social benefits or environmental protections. In a

ANDERS FOGH RASMUSSEN

Danish politician Anders Fogh Rasmussen (born January 26, 1953, Ginnerup, Denmark) has been at the forefront of Danish politics as well as in international relations for years. He was the leader of the country's Liberal Party from 1998 to 2009 and served as prime minister of Denmark from 2001 to 2009. He was named secretary-general of NATO in 2009.

Rasmussen became involved with Denmark's Liberal Party at an early age, founding and leading a Young Liberals group at Vibong Cathedral School (1970–72) and eventually becoming the national chairman of this group (1974–76). In 1978 he received a master's degree in economics from the University of Århus and was elected to the Folketing (the Danish parliament) as a representative for the Liberal Party. He subsequently held various posts within the national party organization, including vice-chairman (1985–98) and political affairs spokesman (1992–98), before becoming chairman in 1998. He served as minister of taxation from 1987 to 1992 and as minister for economic affairs from 1990 to 1992.

Elected prime minister of a minority government in November 2001, Rasmussen lowered taxes and undertook major reforms in local government, welfare, and education. In the same year, the Liberal Party became the largest party in the country, a distinction long enjoyed by the Social Democrats. Following his reelection in 2005 and 2007, Rasmussen focused his efforts on education, research, and job growth. Although he was criticized for supporting the U.S.-led Iraq War (2003), he remained popular among voters. In April 2009, shortly after being selected secretary-general of NATO, Rasmussen resigned as prime minister; he was succeeded by Lars Løkke Rasmussen (no relation) of the Liberal Party. Anders Fogh Rasmussen assumed his post at NATO in August 2009. He has written several books on economic and political topics.

2000 referendum, Danish voters rejected the single European currency, the euro.

These issues remained political touchstones in the early 21st century. A centre-right coalition of the Liberal and Conservative parties assumed power following the defeat of the Social Democrats in the 2001 elections, which also marked the ascendancy of the far-right Danish People's Party (Dansk Folkeparti), a nationalist organization focused on immigration control. The new government immediately instituted policies further restricting immigration, including rules preventing would-be immigrants younger than age 24 from being naturalized as a result of marriage to, or sponsorship by, a Danish citizen. Despite its domestic popularity, this immigration crackdown was criticized by international observers, who noted that immigrants (primarily about 170,000 Muslims) constituted less than 5 percent of Denmark's population. Also indicative of Denmark's new conservatism, social welfare programs were slashed as expenditures overall were curtailed, though political debates on improving social welfare continued. The Liberal-Conservative coalition, under Prime Minister Anders Fogh Rasmussen, was reelected in 2005 and 2007. When Rasmussen was appointed secretary-general of NATO in 2009, he was replaced as prime minister by the foreign minister, Lars Løkke Rasmussen.

In the 2011 parliamentary elections, some 10 years of centre-right rule came to an end when a centre-left coalition led by the Social Democrats took power, with that party's leader, Helle Thorning-Schmidt, becoming the country's first female prime minister. Denmark's economy had weathered the world economic downturn of the previous few years fairly well, but, as the country's economic fortunes began a precipitous decline, voters looked for a solution from Thorning-Schmidt, who had campaigned on a platform of increased public spending, higher taxes, and a reversal of the draconian regulations for immigrants implemented under the previous regime.

In foreign affairs, the country struggled to define its role as a limited member of the EU. Government policy reflected most Danes' continued opposition to the single currency, joint defense, and EU citizenship, yet Denmark showed more enthusiasm than many of its European neighbours in its support of the Iraq War in 2003, though this stance was losing its popular appeal by mid-decade. The country withdrew most of its troops from Iraq in 2007.

Denmark had become the locus of both a domestic and an international controversy following the 2005 publication in a Danish newspaper of cartoon caricatures of the Prophet Muhammad. The images provoked violent protests by Muslims worldwide and death threats against the cartoonists; the controversy also resulted in the recall of several Islamic ambassadors to Denmark and a sharp drop in Danish exports to Islamic countries. Although the newspaper eventually apologized for printing the cartoons, Prime Minister Rasmussen defended the freedom of the press throughout the crisis. By 2010 more than 100 people had died in incidents related to the cartoons, including attacks on Danish embassies and riots in Pakistan, the Middle East, and Africa.

CHAPTER 6

FINLAND: THE LAND AND ITS PEOPLE

Located in northern Europe, Finland is one of the world's most northern and geographically remote countries and is subject to a severe climate. Nearly two-thirds of Finland is blanketed by thick woodlands, making it the most densely forested country in Europe.

The national flag of Finland. Encyclopædia Britannica, Inc.

The notion of nature as the true home of the Finn is expressed again and again in Finnish proverbs and folk wisdom. The harsh climate in the northern part of the country, however, has resulted in the concentration of the population in the southern third of Finland, with about one-fifth of the country's population living in and around Helsinki, Finland's largest city and continental Europe's northernmost capital. Yet, despite the fact that most Finns live in towns and cities, nature—especially the forest—is never far from their minds and hearts.

Finland is bordered to the north by Norway, to the east by Russia, to the south by the Gulf of Finland, to the southwest by the Gulf of Bothnia, and to the northwest by Sweden. Its area includes the autonomous territory of Åland, an archipelago at the entrance to the Gulf of Bothnia. About one-third of the territory of Finland—most of the maakunna (region) of Lappi (Lappland)—lies north of the Arctic Circle.

RELIEF

Finland is heavily forested and contains some 56,000 lakes, numerous rivers, and extensive areas of marshland; viewed from the air, Finland looks like an intricate blue and green jigsaw puzzle. Except in the northwest, relief features do not vary greatly, and travelers on the ground or on the water can rarely see beyond the trees in their immediate vicinity. The landscape nevertheless possesses a striking—if sometimes bleak—beauty.

Finland's underlying structure is a huge worn-down shield composed of ancient rock, mainly granite, dating from Precambrian time (from about 4 billion to 540 million years ago). The land is low-lying in the southern part of the country and higher in the centre and the northeast, while the few mountainous regions are in the extreme northwest, adjacent to Finland's borders with Sweden and Norway. In this area there are several high peaks, including Mount Haltia, which, at 4,357 feet (1,328 metres), is Finland's highest mountain.

The coastline of Finland, some 2,760 miles (4,600 km) in length, is extremely indented and dotted with thousands of islands. The greatest number of these are to be found in the southwest, in the Turun (Turku; Åbo) archipelago, which merges with the Åland (Ahvenanmaa) Islands in the west. The southern islands in the Gulf of Finland are mainly of low elevation, while those lying along the southwest coastline may rise to heights of more than 400 feet (120 metres).

The relief of Finland was greatly affected by Ice Age glaciation. The retreating continental glacier left the bedrock littered with morainic deposits in formations of eskers, remarkable winding ridges of stratified gravel and sand, running northwest to southeast. One of the biggest formations is the Salpausselkä ridges, three parallel

Physical map of Finland. Encyclopædia Britannica, Inc.

SALPAUSSELKÄ RIDGES

Three parallel ridges, known as the Salpausselkä ridges, cut across Finland. They traverse the breadth of the southern portion of the country from Hangö (Hanko), at the mouth of the Gulf of Finland in the west, to Joensuu, on Lake Pyhäselkä, near the Russian border in the east.

The ridges are acuate (needle-shaped) in form and sometimes more than 1.5 miles (as much as 2 kilometres) wide and 320 feet (100 metres) high. They form two distinct arcs termed Salpausselkä I and II. In some regions a third arc, Salpausselkä III, is recognized, although this has a more restricted distribution. Salpausselkä ridges are characteristically narrow with a flat plateau. They consist of glacial till and material carried in streams that probably flowed through the ice.

Some authorities believe that the ridges were built up outside the ice margin at a time of major halts of the glacial ice. The form and structure of the features were modified by the action of waves; this accounts for the flat tops of the ridges. The Salpausselkä ridges thus provide information about the complex changes in sea levels that occurred simultaneously with the process of deglaciation. The Salpausselkä ridges also serve to provide evidence about varve chronologies, the measurement and counting of thin, annual layers of silts and clays deposited in glacially influenced basins.

ridges running across southern Finland in an arc pattern. The weight of the glaciers, sometimes miles thick, depressed the Earth's crust by many hundreds of feet. As a consequence, areas that have been released from the weight of the ice sheets have risen and continue to rise, and Finland is still emerging from the sea. Indeed, land rise of some 0.4 inch (10 mm) annually in the narrow part of the Gulf of Bothnia is gradually turning the old sea bottom into dry land.

DRAINAGE AND SOILS

Finland's inland waters occupy almost one-tenth of the country's total area; there are 10 lakes of more than 100 square miles (250 square km) in area and tens of thousands of smaller ones. The largest lake, Saimaa, in the southeast, covers about 1,700 square miles (4,400 square km). There are many other large lakes near it, including Päijänne and Pielinen, while Oulu is near Kajaani in central Finland, and Inari is in the extreme north. Away from coastal regions, many of Finland's rivers flow into the lakes, which are generally shallow—only three lakes are deeper than about 300 feet (90 metres). Saimaa itself drains into the much larger Lake Ladoga in Russian territory via the Vuoksi (Vuoksa) River. Drainage from

Aerial view of remote lakes and forests in Finland. © Anterovium/Fotolia

Marshland lake in Finland. © Taina Sohlman/Fotolia

Finland's eastern uplands is through the lake system of Russian Karelia to the White Sea.

In the extreme north the Paats River and its tributaries drain large areas into the Arctic. On Finland's western coast a series of rivers flow into the Gulf of Bothnia. These include the Tornio, which forms part of Finland's border with Sweden, and the Kemi, which, at 343 miles (550 km), is Finland's longest river. In the southwest the Kokemäen, one of Finland's largest rivers, flows out past the city of Pori (Björneborg). Other rivers flow southward into the Gulf of Finland.

Soils include those of the gravelly type found in the eskers, as well as extensive marine and lake postglacial deposits in the form of clays and silts, which provide the country's most fertile soils. Almost one-third of Finland was once covered by bogs, fens, peatlands, and other swamplands, but many of these have been drained and are now forested. The northern third of Finland still has thick layers of peat, the humus soil of which continues to be reclaimed. In the Åland Islands the soils are mainly clay and sand.

CLIMATE

The part of Finland north of the Arctic Circle suffers extremely severe and prolonged winters. Temperatures can fall as low as -22 °F (-30 °C). In these latitudes the snow never melts from the north-facing mountain slopes, but in the short summer (Lapland has about two months of the midnight sun), from May to July, temperatures can reach as high as 80 °F (27 °C). Farther south the temperature extremes are slightly less marked, as the Baltic Sea- and Gulf Stream-warmed airflow from the Atlantic keeps temperatures as much as 10 degrees higher than at similar latitudes in Siberia and Greenland. Winter is the longest season in Finland. North of the Arctic Circle the polar night lasts for more than 50 days; in southern Finland the shortest day lasts about six hours. Annual precipitation,

Cloudberries. © Alexandr Blinov/Fotolia

about one-third of which falls as sleet or snow, is about 25 inches (600 mm) in the south and a little less in the north. All Finnish waters are subject to some surface freezing during the winter.

PLANT AND ANIMAL LIFE

Much of Finland is dominated by conifers, but in the extreme south there is a zone of deciduous trees comprising mainly birch, hazel, aspen, maple, elm, linden, and alder. The conifers are mainly pine and spruce. Pine extends to the extreme north, where it can be found among the dwarf arctic birch and pygmy willow. Lichens become increasingly common and varied in kind toward the north. In autumn the woods are rich in edible fungi. More than 1,000 species of flowering plants have been recorded. The sphagnum swamps, which are widespread in the northern tundra or bogland area, yield harvests of cloudberries, as well as plagues of mosquitoes.

Brown bear in Finland. © Kari N/Fotolia

Finland is relatively rich in wildlife. Seabirds, such as the black-backed gull and the arctic tern, nest in great numbers on the coastal islands; waterfowl, such as the black and white velvet scoter duck, nest on inland lakes. Other birds include the Siberian jay, the pied wagtail, and, in the north, the eagle. Many birds migrate southward in winter. Finland is the breeding site for many water and wading birds, including the majority of the world's goldeneyes and broad-billed sandpipers (*Limicola falcinellus*). Native woodland animals include bear, elk, wolf, wolverine, lynx, and Finnish elk. Wild reindeer have almost disappeared; those remaining in the north are domesticated.

Salmon, trout, and the much esteemed siika (whitefish) are relatively abundant in the northern rivers. Baltic herring is the most common sea fish, while crayfish can be caught during the brief summer season. Pike, char, and perch are also found.

The vegetation and wildlife of the Åland Islands is much like that of coastal southern Finland.

ETHNIC GROUPS

Excavations undertaken in 1996 have led to a radical reconsideration of how long people have inhabited Finland. Finds in a cave near Kristinestad in the southwestern part of the country have led some to suggest that habitation of Finland goes back at least 100,000 years. Ancestors of the Sami apparently were present in Finland by about 7000 BCE. As other groups began to enter Finland some 3,000 years later, the proto-Sami probably retreated northward. Archaeological remains suggest that this second wave of settlers came from or had contact with what was to become Russia and also Scandinavia and central Europe. Peoples of Uralic (specifically Finno-Ugric) stock dominated two settlement areas. Those who entered southwestern Finland across the Gulf of Finland were the ancestors of the Hämäläiset (Tavastians, or Tavastlanders), the people of southern and western Finland (especially the historic region of Häme); those who entered from the southeast were the Karelians. Scandinavian peoples occupied the western coast and archipelagoes and the Åland Islands.

Roughly half of Finland's small Sami population live in the area known as the Sami Homeland (Sámiid ruovttuguovlu), which consists of the three northernmost municipalities in the region of Lappi. In 1995 the Finnish constitution was amended to recognize the status of the Sami as an indigenous people and their right to maintain and develop their own language and culture.

LANGUAGES

Finland has two national languages, Finnish and Swedish, and is officially bilingual. Well more than nine-tenths of the population speak Finnish; the language is an important nationalist feature, although it is spoken in strong regional dialects. The Swedish-speaking population is found mainly in the coastal area in the south, south-west, and west and in the Åland Islands (where Swedish is the sole official language). According to the constitution of 2000, public authorities are required to provide for the needs of the Finnish- and Swedish-speaking populations of the country on an equal basis. Rights and obligations concerning the national languages were addressed in greater detail in the Language Act promulgated in 2004.

There is also a tiny minority of Sami speakers in the extreme north of Finland. Of the 11 Sami languages, 3 are spoken in Finland: North Sami, Inari Sami (spoken only in Finland), and Skolt Sami. The Sami languages are related to Finnish, with North Sami being the most widely spoken, by almost four-fifths of the Sami population.

Relationships between the various language groups in Finland are good, and the position of the minority languages is strong compared with that of minority groups in most other multilingual and multicultural countries. Although Sami is not a national language of Finland like Finnish and Swedish, its status as a regional minority language is guaranteed by the Sami Language Act (2004).

RELIGION

Christianity had entered Finland from both the west and the east by the 13th century. Finland is now one of the most homogeneous countries in Europe in terms of Christianity and has the highest percentage of church membership in Scandinavia. The great majority of the people belong to the Evangelical Lutheran Church of Finland, whose status gradually changed from an official state church to a national church beginning in the 19th century. The archbishop has his see at Turku (Åbo). Yet, despite the high proportion of church membership, only a small number of Finns attend church regularly. Nonetheless, the majority of the people are still baptized, married, and buried with the blessing of the Lutheran church.

A small minority of Finns belong to the Orthodox Church of Finland, the only other faith to have the status of a national church. It was granted autonomy from Moscow in 1920, and in 1923 it was transferred to the jurisdiction of the patriarch of Constantinople. It has one archbishop, with his see at Kuopio. Members of the Pentecostal church constitute another relatively small religious group in Finland, and even fewer Finns belong to independent Protestant churches and the Roman Catholic Church. Small Jewish and Muslim communities date from the 19th century, when Finland was one of the few parts of the Russian empire where Jews and Muslims could practice their religion more or less freely; however, Jews were granted full rights as citizens only after Finland became independent in 1918. With the founding of its first Islamic congregation

EVANGELICAL LUTHERAN CHURCH OF FINLAND

One of Finland's national churches is the Evangelical Lutheran Church of Finland (Finnish: Suomen Evankelis-luterilainen-kirkko), or simply the Church of Finland. It has its roots in the Protestant Reformation in the 16th century, during which Finland saw a shift from the Roman Catholic to the Lutheran faith.

Christianity was known in Finland as early as the 11th century, and in the 12th century Henry, bishop of Uppsala (Sweden), began organizing the church there. He suffered a martyr's death and eventually became Finland's patron saint. Through the influence of Sweden (which ruled in Finland from the 13th century until 1809), Finland gradually accepted Christianity.

When Lutheranism was adopted by Sweden, it was also introduced into Finland and was declared the official religion of the country in 1593. The outstanding Finnish reformer was Mikael Agricola, who had studied at Wittenberg, where Martin Luther was a professor. Consecrated the first Lutheran bishop of Turku (1554), Agricola published several religious works, including a Finnish translation of the New Testament (1548).

During the 17th century the Finnish church, like the German and other Scandinavian Lutheran churches, was influenced primarily by Lutheran orthodoxy. In the 18th century the dominating influence was Pietism, the movement that began in Germany and emphasized personal religious experience and reform. Three revival movements during the 19th century caused many Finns to develop a deeper commitment to the church. In the 20th century a larger percentage of the people took part in church activities than was common in other Scandinavian countries.

The Church of Finland is divided into nine dioceses, each headed by a bishop, with the archbishop of Turku as the presiding bishop of the church. The church general synod, which meets twice a year and is composed of both clergy and lay church members, is the church's highest legislative body. There are facilities for theological education at the University of Helsinki and at the Swedish University in Turku.

The church's relationship with the state was defined by a church law in 1869. The state gives financial support to the church, and the president of the republic and the Parliament must approve the church laws proposed by the church assembly. The former policy that bishops be appointed by the president of Finland from candidates proposed by the general synod was changed in 2000 to make the vote of the synod final. Since 1922, a Finnish citizen can legally withdraw from the national church and belong to no church or to another church.

in 1925, Finland became the first European country to officially recognize an Islamic congregation. More than one-tenth of the population have no church affiliation.

SETTLEMENT PATTERNS

Increased industrialization in Finland has steadily raised the proportion of the population living in urban areas; by the early 21st century, about three-fifths of the total population lived in cities and towns. Farms are most commonly located in the meadowland regions of the southwest, where the fertile land is suitable for mixed agriculture. In the north farmers usually concentrate on small dairy herds and forestry. In Finnish Lapland there is some nomadic life based mainly on the reindeer industry.

The major urban settlements are all in the southern third of the country, with a large number of cities and towns concentrated on the coast, either on the Gulf of Finland, as is the capital, Helsinki, or on the Gulf of Bothnia, as are Vaasa and Oulu (Uleåborg). The only town of any size in the north is Rovaniemi, capital of the region of Lappi. Helsinki is the largest city, with a population that is significantly larger than those of Tampere (Tammerfors) and Turku, the country's capital until 1812.

TRADITIONAL REGIONS

There are three principal regions in Finland: a coastal plain, an interior lake district, and an interior tract of higher land that rises to the fells (tunturi) of Lapland.

The coastal plain comprises a narrow tract in the south, sloping from Salpausselkä to the Gulf of Finland; the plains in the southwestern part of the country; and the broad western coastal lowlands of the region of Pohjanmaa (Ostrobothnia) facing the Gulf of Bothnia. The coastal region has the most extensive stretches of farmland; this region also is the site of the longest continuous settlement and has the largest number of urban centres. Associated with it are the offshore islands, which are most numerous in the Turun archipelago off Turku on the southwest coast. Farther to the north in the Gulf of Bothnia another group of islands lies off Vaasa (Vasa).

The lake district, with its inland archipelagoes, is the heart of Finland. It has been less subject to external influences than the coastal region, but since the end of World War II its population has increased, and it has become considerably industrialized.

The higher land in the northeast and north constitutes what may still be called "colonial" Finland. These are the country's areas of expansion and development where many economic and social interests conflict, including, in the far north, the area of saamelaisalue, or Sami territory.

The Åland Islands is a region entirely distinct from Finland, not only because of its geographic separation but also because it is surrounded by the sea. The islands—whose inhabitants are almost entirely Swedish-speaking—are autonomous, have their own parliament, and fly their own flag. On the islands farming is a more usual occupation than fishing; there are mixed

HELSINKI

Finland's capital, Helsinki, is also the country's leading seaport and industrial city. Helsinki lies in the far south of the country, on a peninsula that is fringed by fine natural harbours and that protrudes into the Gulf of Finland. It is the most northerly of continental European capitals. It is often called the "white city of the north" because many of its buildings are constructed of a local light-coloured granite.

Helsinki was founded in 1550 by King Gustav I Vasa of Sweden. The town was originally located at the mouth of the Vantaa River, at a point about 3 mi (4.8 km) north of its present-day location, and was moved down to the latter site in 1640 in order to obtain more open access to the sea. Helsinki was ravaged by a plague in 1710 and burned to the ground in 1713. Its redevelopment was hindered by Russian attacks later in the 18th century, but in 1748 the settlement became more secure when

Helsinki. © Nici Heuke/Fotolia

a fortress, called Sveaborg by the Swedes and Suomenlinna by the Finns, was constructed on a group of small islands outside the harbour.

When Russia invaded Finland in 1808, Helsinki was again burned to the ground. The next year, Finland was ceded to Russia, and in 1812 the Russian tsar Alexander I moved the capital of the grand duchy of Finland from Turku (Åbo) to Helsinki. Meanwhile, the centre of Helsinki had been completely reconstructed under the influence of the German-born architect Carl Ludwig Engel, who designed a number of impressive public buildings in the Neoclassical style. These include the state council building, the main building of Helsinki University, and the Lutheran cathedral, known as the Great Church, completed in 1852. All of these structures surround the broad expanse of Senate Square. Nearby rise the cupolas of the Uspenski Orthodox Cathedral, one of the few recognizable reminders of the period of Russian rule.

Once Helsinki became the capital of Finland, its population increased rapidly. In December 1917 Finland declared independence from Russia. Although independence was achieved peacefully, it was followed by a brief but bloody civil war in Finland. In subsequent decades Helsinki developed into an important centre of trade, industry, and culture, a process interrupted only by World War II.

Helsinki's economic life and development is based on its excellent harbours and on good railway and road connections to the extensive interior of the country. More than half of Finland's total imports consequently pass through the port of Helsinki. Only a small proportion of the national exports, however, pass through Helsinki, as the largest export ports are elsewhere along the Finnish coast. Helsinki's main industries include food, metal and chemical processing, printing, textiles, clothing, and manufacture of electrical equipment. The wares of the Arabia porcelain factory, one of the largest of its kind in Europe, are internationally known.

Helsinki has theatres, an opera and ballet company, and several symphony orchestras. An annual Helsinki festival features world-famous orchestras and artists and a program of rich variety. In addition to museums and galleries, cultural landmarks include a modern city theatre by Timo Penttilä and a concert building by Alvar Aalto. Other architectural features of the city are the Helsinki Stadium, built for the 1952 Olympic Games, and the railway station (1914), designed by Eliel Saarinen. Helsinki University (founded 1640) is the second largest university in Scandinavia.

farms, as in the southwest of Finland, but fruit is also grown. Mariehamn (Maarianhamina) is the capital and only large town.

DEMOGRAPHIC TRENDS

Until the 1990s emigration exceeded immigration, with Sweden being one of the most attractive destinations for Finnish emigrants. Following World War II, hundreds of thousands of Finns emigrated, while immigration was practically nil, owing to government restrictions. Since 1990, however, Finland has become a country of net immigration. As a result of increasing Finnish prosperity, the fall of the Soviet Union, and a liberalization of Finnish asylum and immigration policy, the number of immigrants rose dramatically at the end of the 20th century and the beginning of the 21st, with the largest numbers coming from Russia, Sweden, Estonia, and Somalia. Internal migration since the 1950s has been steadily toward the large towns and cities.

CHAPTER 7

THE FINNISH ECONOMY

Finland's economy is based primarily on private owner-ship and free enterprise; in some sectors, however, the government exercises a monopoly or a leading role. After World War II, Finland was not fully industrialized, and a large portion of the population was still engaged in agricul-ture, mining, and forestry. During the early postwar decades, primary production gave way to industrial development, which in turn yielded to a service- and information-ori-ented economy. The economy grew rapidly in the 1980s as the country exploited its strong trading relations with both eastern and western Europe. By the early 1990s, however, Finland was experiencing economic recession, reflecting both the loss of its principal trading partner with the col-lapse of the Soviet Union in 1991 and a general European economic slump. The economy began a slow recovery in the mid-1990s as Finland continued retooling its industry and refocused its trade primarily toward western Europe.

Unemployment was relatively low in Finland until 1991, when it increased rapidly. After peaking at nearly 20 percent of the workforce in 1994, the unemployment rate gradually began to decline again, falling in line with conti-nental trends by the end of the 20th century.

Finland has subscribed to the General Agreement on Tariffs and Trade since 1949 and to the Organisation for Economic Co-operation and Development since 1969. It became first an associate (1961) and later a full member (1986) of the European Free Trade Association before leaving that organization to join the European Union (EU) in 1995.

AGRICULTURE, FORESTRY, AND FISHING

The steadily decreasing portion of the labour force working in agriculture is indicative of the sector's declining role in Finland's economy. Much land has been taken out of agricultural production, and most farms consist of smallholdings. Finland has been self-supporting in basic foodstuffs since the early 1960s. Meat production roughly equals consumption, while egg and dairy output exceeds domestic needs. Grain production varies considerably; in general, bread grain (mainly wheat) is imported and fodder grain exported. The climate restricts grain farming to the southern and western regions of the country.

Animal husbandry in Finland traditionally concentrated on the raising of dairy cattle, but cuts were made after

Reindeer in Finland. © 3355m/Fotolia

A large forest of conifers stands in the northern European country of Finland. H. Fristedt/Carl E. Ostman ab

years of overproduction. As a result, the number of milk cows has declined. The keeping of pigs, poultry, and reindeer also is important, while sheep farming and beekeeping are of minor economic significance. The number of horses also declined until the late 1970s but then became generally stable, with the subsequent increase in the number of Thoroughbred horses raised.

Since World War II, fur farming has made great strides in Finland. Practically all furs are exported; Finland is one of the world's main producers of farm-raised foxes, and its mink furs also have a very good reputation on international markets.

Finnish agriculture was heavily subsidized before the country entered the EU, and as a result of negotiation, Finland remains among the most subsidized under the EU's Common Agricultural Policy. Finnish farmers rely heavily on direct payments based on the amount of land under cultivation. Those farmers north of the 62nd parallel receive especially generous subsidies.

Despite the abundance of forest resources, the forest industry faces increasing production costs. The private owners of more than four-fifths of Finland's forests effectively control domestic timber prices; nonetheless, forest products (notably paper) are a major source of the country's export earnings.

Commercial fishing has gradually become less significant to the economy. Among the fish in Finland's catch are salmon, sea and rainbow trout, whitefish, pike, and char. River pollution, as well as dams built for hydroelectric works, have adversely affected natural spawning habits, especially those of salmon and sea trout, and Finland has established a large number of fish-breeding stations at which artificial spawning is induced. There is some trawling for Baltic herring, which also are taken in the winter by seine fishing (dragging nets under the ice) around the offshore islands.

RESOURCES AND POWER

Trees are Finland's most important natural resource. Some three-fourths of the total land area is forested, with pine, spruce, and birch being the predominant species. Government cultivation programs, among other measures, have prevented forest depletion; and acid rain, which has devastated forests in central Europe, has not had any serious consequences in Finland.

About one-fifth of all energy consumed in Finland is still derived from wood, though over half this total is waste sludge from pulp mills, and roughly another one-fourth consists of other forest-industry waste (bark, sawdust, etc.) rather than logs.

Peat deposits cover nearly one-third of the country, but only a small fraction of that land is suitable for large-scale peat production. Although expensive to ship and store, peat nevertheless provides a small percentage of Finnish energy and is also used in agriculture.

A diversity of minerals occurs in the Precambrian bedrock, but mining output is modest, owing to the small size of the deposits and the low metal content of the ore. Most mines are located in the north. Iron is the most important of the industrial metals. The main nonferrous metals are nickel and zinc. Chromium, cobalt, and copper are also economically important. Gold, silver, cadmium, and titanium are obtained as by-products. There is no naturally occurring coal or oil in Finland. Some mica is quarried, mostly for export.

Because of the cold climate and the structure of the country's industry, Finland's per capita energy consumption ranks among the highest in the world. Industries account for about half of total energy consumption, a much higher proportion than the European average. Domestic energy sources meet only about one-third of Finland's total energy requirement, and all fossil fuels must be imported.

Much of Finland's power comes from hydroelectric plants, but the low fall of

PEAT

Peat is an organic fuel consisting of spongy material formed by the partial decomposition of organic matter, primarily plant material, in wetlands such as swamps, muskegs, bogs, fens, and moors. The development of peat is favoured by warm, moist climatic conditions; however, peat can develop even in cold regions such as Siberia, Canada, and Scandinavia. Peat is only a minor contributor to the world energy supply, but large deposits occur in Canada, China, Indonesia, Russia, Scandinavia, and the United States. Major users include Finland, Ireland, Russia, and Sweden.

Peat is usually hand-cut, although progress has been made in the excavation and spreading of peat by mechanical methods. Peat may be cut by spade in the form of blocks, which are spread out to dry. When dry, the blocks weigh from 0.75 to 2 pounds (0.34 to 0.91 kg). In one mechanized method, a dredger or excavator digs the peat from the drained bog and delivers it to a macerator (a device that softens and separates a material into its component parts through soaking), which extrudes the peat pulp through a rectangular opening. The pulp is cut into blocks, which are spread to dry. Maceration tends to yield more uniform shrinkage and a denser and tougher fuel. Hydraulic excavating can also be used, particularly in bogs that contain roots and tree trunks. The peat is washed down by a high-pressure water jet, and the pulp runs to a sump. There, after slight maceration, it is pumped to a draining ground in a layer, which, after partial drying, is cut up and dried further.

Dried peat burns readily with a smoky flame and a characteristic odour. The ash is powdery and light, except for varieties that have a high content of inorganic matter. Peat is used for domestic heating purposes and forms a fuel suitable for boiler firing in either briquetted or pulverized form. It also has been used to produce electricity.

water makes dam building necessary. The loss in 1944 of Karelian hydroelectric resources turned attention to the north of the country, where plants were built on the Oulu and Kemi rivers. Thermal-generated power is also important. Wind power is of lesser importance than it is in some other Scandinavian countries, but it is becoming more prevalent in the windier coastal areas. Finland's electricity grids are linked with those of Sweden and Russia, and electricity is imported. Fortum, the predominantly state-owned electric power company, operates a nuclear plant at Loviisa, east of Helsinki; nuclear power now constitutes about one-fourth of all power generated.

MANUFACTURING

Finland's northern location imposes certain limitations on industrial activity;

severe winter conditions make the costs of construction and heating high, and ice and snow are obstacles to transport. Industrialization in Finland began in the 1860s, but the pace was slow, and early in the 20th century only some 10 percent of the population derived its livelihood from manufacturing. It was not until the mid-1960s that manufacturing overtook farming and forestry together as an employer.

Forest products remain a vital sector of the Finnish economy. In the course of development, the traditional manufactures of vegetable tar and pitch have given way to sawn timber and pulp and later to converted paper products, building materials, and furniture.

Reparations payable to the Soviet Union after World War II, at first a desperate burden, eventually proved a boon to Finland; their payment necessitated the development of heavy industry, which later found markets in western as well as eastern Europe. The technology industry is the largest component of the industrial sector in Finland. Biotechnology has also come to play an increasingly important role in the Finnish economy. Metals and engineering constitute another large sector of Finnish industry. Finland holds a leading international position in the building of icebreakers, luxury liners, and other specialized ships and in the manufacture of paper-processing equipment. Finland's chemical industry has also grown rapidly to become a very important part of the economy. An important branch of the chemical industry is oil refining, the production capacity of which currently exceeds domestic oil requirements.

At the end of the 20th century, Finnish industry embraced new technological developments with great enthusiasm. The manufacture of products related to information technology and telecommunications, led by such firms as Nokia, became increasingly important.

Textile factories are located at Turku, Tampere, Vaasa, Forssa, and Hyvinkää. Helsinki has one of Europe's largest porcelain factories, while Karhula (Kotka), Iittala, and Nuutajärvi are known internationally for glass. Leather and pewter goods, beer and vodka, and cement are among other important products. Food and drink, including functional foods (those that are both nutritious and prevent illness), constitute one of the country's largest industries. Liqueurs, soft drinks, and various sweets are made from domestic cloudberries, currants, gooseberries, and lingonberries.

FINANCE

From 1980 the Finnish financial market underwent rapid change. The state's role in the money market declined, and the economy became more and more market-oriented. Foreign banks were first allowed to operate in Finland in the early 1980s and were permitted to open branch offices there in 1991.

The Bank of Finland (Suomen Pankki), established in 1811 and guaranteed and supervised by the parliament since 1868, is the country's central bank and a member of the European System of Central Banks. In 2002, the EU's common currency, the euro, replaced the markka, which had been Finland's national currency since 1860. Compared with other European countries, Finland has relatively little currency in circulation because Finns are accustomed to banking electronically. Deposit banks are organized into three groups: commercial, cooperative, and savings. Securities trading is handled by the Helsinki Stock Exchange; foreign investors were first allowed to trade there in the early 1980s.

TRADE

Because of Finland's relatively small domestic market, specialized production, and lack of energy sources, foreign trade is vital for the economy. The collapse of the Soviet Union in the early 1990s and its loss as Finland's chief trading partner was a severe blow to the Finnish economy. Trade with Russia, while still significant, has been overshadowed by that with the countries of the European Union. In addition to Russia, Finland's chief trading partners are Germany, Sweden, and the United Kingdom. Although the traditional exports of paper and paper products and wood products remain important, heavy machinery and manufactured products now constitute the largest share of Finland's export trade. Imports consist mainly of raw materials for industrial use, consumer goods, and mineral fuels.

SERVICES

By the beginning of the 21st century, government services made up as much as one-third of the service sector in Finland, but private concerns, especially business and information technology (IT) services, grew at a faster rate than public services. Unlike most other European countries, the service sector's share of Finland's gross domestic product (GDP) and employment has not increased as quickly as that of manufacturing. The Finnish government uses indirect methods, such as grants, loans, and investments in equity, as well as employee development and retraining, to promote investment in areas deemed to be in need of development. Founded in 1983, the Technology Development Centre (now the Finnish Funding Agency for Technology) played an important role in the 1980s and '90s in Finnish technological advancement by funding research and development. By the end of the 20th century, the government had earmarked almost one-third of its total spending for research and development.

LABOUR AND TAXATION

By far the majority of Finns (roughly two-thirds) are employed in the

GULF OF FINLAND

The Gulf of Finland (Finnish: Suomen Lahti; Russian: Finsky Zaliv) is an important shipping route for its main ports: Porkkala, Helsinki, and Kotka in Finland; Vyborg, St. Petersburg, and Kronshtadt in Russia; and Tallinn in Estonia. The gulf is the easternmost arm of the Baltic Sea, between Finland (north) and Russia and Estonia (east and south). Covering an area of 11,600 square miles (30,000 square km), the gulf extends for 250 miles (400 km) from east to west but only 12 to 80 miles (19 to 130 km) from north to south. It has a maximum depth of 377 feet (115 m) at its western end. Of low salinity (six parts per thousand), the gulf freezes over for three to five months in winter. It receives the Neva and Narva rivers and the Saimaa Canal. Included within the gulf are the islands of Gogland (Sur-sari, or Högland), Lavansari (Moshchnyy), and Kotlin (Kronshtadt).

service sector. The next largest source of employment and still significant is manufacturing, while the proportion of those involved in the increasingly marginalized agricultural sector is very small. Finland's largest employer organization is the Confederation of Finnish Industry and Employers (formerly called the Finnish Employers' Confederation); the largest trade union groups are the Central Organization of Finnish Trade Unions and the Confederation of Unions for Academic Professionals.

Employment has long been seen as a self-evident right for women in Finland, which has one of the highest rates of employment for women in Europe, with about nine-tenths of Finnish women employed full-time. On the whole, women workers are slightly better educated than their male counterparts and are more unionized; however, Finnish women are still paid only about seven-tenths of what men earn for the same job. To support the participation of women and parents in the workplace, Finland has a comprehensive system of maternal and paternal leave for new parents.

Income taxes in Finland are higher than those for many other industrialized countries, with the taxation of above-average incomes especially heavy. Finland's value-added tax is among the highest in the European Union. Excise duties on liquid fuels, automobiles, alcohol, and tobacco are also high, while those on food, public transportation, books, and medicine are typically reduced.

TRANSPORTATION AND TELECOMMUNICATIONS

Until the mid-20th century the problems posed for internal communications and transport by Finland's difficult terrain and weather conditions had hardly been tackled, and many communities remained isolated. External communications were mainly by sea, which, especially as a result of the period of Swedish rule, accounts for the series of well-developed ports on the Gulf of Bothnia and the Gulf of Finland.

The country also has an extensive network of navigable waterways comprising lakes, rivers, and canals. Many thousands of miles of additional waterways are suitable for the flotage of felled timber, but truck and rail transport is rendering this practice obsolete in many areas. In 1963 the Soviet Union leased to Finland the Soviet end of the canal linking Lake Saimaa with the Gulf of Finland; it was opened in 1968. Most of Finland's overseas cargoes are carried in its own merchant marine. The country has a passenger-liner service, and car ferries operate to Denmark, Sweden, Germany, Estonia, Russia, and Poland.

Finland now has a good system of highways and roads—of which about two-thirds are paved—but the lakes in the southeast tend to make routes indirect there, while north of the Arctic Circle the roads are still few. Bridges and car ferries assist road travel in the lakeland areas and in the island archipelagoes. The bus system is highly developed throughout Finland and is widely utilized.

The railway system is much less adequate than that of the roads; the southwestern part of the country is the best-served area. The railways, which provide connections with Russia, are state-owned; about one-third of the rail lines are electrified. In 1982 Finland's first subway was inaugurated in Helsinki.

In addition to the international air terminal near Helsinki, Finland has domestic airports, the most northerly of which is at Ivalo, at Lake Inari. Finnair, the national airline, offers domestic and international service.

Not only was Finland quick to develop its telecommunications and information technology industry, but Finns also rapidly made new technology part of their lives. At the turn of the 21st century, Finland had the among the largest per capita numbers of mobile telephone and Internet users in the world.

CHAPTER 8

FINNISH GOVERNMENT AND SOCIETY

Finland adopted a republican constitution in 1919; it has been amended several times, notably in the mid-1990s. Legislative power rests in the unicameral parliament (Eduskunta), whose members are elected for four-year terms, and in the president, whose term is six years. Executive power is shared by the president and the Council of State, or cabinet, the meetings of which are chaired by the president. The president appoints the prime minister and the cabinet. A clause in the constitution stresses that government ministers are responsible to the parliament.

The six-year term of office and the possibility of reelection enhance the president's powers and provide the country with an important source of stability, in view of the frequent changes of government caused by the multiparty system. In cases of complete deadlock, the president can appoint a nonpolitical caretaker government. Government bills can be introduced into the parliament in the president's name; the president can

Political map of Finland. Encyclopædia Britannica, Inc.

refuse to sign a bill but must endorse it if it is passed in a subsequent parliament. The president also can dissolve the parliament, has certain decree-making powers, and is the head of the armed forces. Moreover, the president conducts the country's foreign policy, but decisions on major treaties and questions of war and peace must be validated by the parliament.

LOCAL GOVERNMENT

Finland is divided into 19 maakunnat (regions; singular: maakunta), including the autonomous region of Åland (Ahvenamaa). Each regular maakunna is governed by a council. Previously the country had been divided into läänit (provinces) plus the autonomous territory of Åland, all of which were subdivided into maakunnat, but in 2010 the läänit were abolished and the existing maakunnat divisions became the primary administrative units. To aid with the transition, six regional state administrative agencies were established that same year to work with the local authorities. The regional state administrative agencies assisted in such areas as basic public services, health, safety, and environmental protection.

Åland has special status as a demilitarized, self-governing region. The Act on the Autonomy of Åland (1920), settled by a decision of the League of Nations (1921), provided for Finnish sovereignty over Åland, predicated on a division of political power between the islands and the rest of Finland. Åland has its own parliament (Lagtinget), flag, and representative on the Nordic Council.

JUSTICE

The Finnish judiciary is independent of the legislature and executive; judges are removable only by judicial sentence. There are local, municipal, and rural district courts (käräjäoikeus) held in cities and towns by the chief judge (oikeuspormestari) and assistants and in the country by a judge and jurors. Appeal from these courts lies to courts of appeal in Helsinki, Turku, Vaasa, Kuopio, Kouvola, and Rovaniemi. The Supreme Court (Korkein oikeus), in Helsinki, appoints the district judges and those of the appeal courts. The chancellor of justice (oikeuskansleri) is the supreme judicial authority and also acts as public prosecutor. The parliament appoints a solicitor general, who acts as an ombudsman. The Supreme Administrative Court (Korkein hallintooikeus) is the highest tribunal for appeals in administrative cases.

POLITICAL PROCESS

Suffrage is universal in Finland for those age 18 or older. The president is directly elected. To be elected president, a candidate must win a majority of the vote in a first round of balloting; otherwise, a run-off is held between the two candidates receiving the most votes in the first round. Parliamentary elections are conducted by a system of proportional representation.

Proportional representation has led to a proliferation of political parties, including the Social Democratic Party, the Left-Wing Alliance (formed in 1990 from the People's Democratic League and the Finnish Communist Party), the National Coalition Party, and the Centre Party (or Finnish Centre; formerly the Agrarian Union). The People's Democratic League and its successor have been important parts of the government since World War II. Minor parties include the Swedish People's Party, the environmentalist Green League, and the True Finn Party (formerly the Finnish Rural Party, a splinter of the former Agrarian Union).

Women have played a crucial role in Finnish politics since 1906, when they first became eligible not only to vote but to serve in the parliament. In the early 21st century women held some two-fifths of the seats in the parliament, and in 2003 Finland became the first European country to have a woman president (Tarja Halonen) and a woman prime minister (Anneli Jäätteenmäki) hold office at the same time.

SECURITY

By the Treaty of Paris (1947), made with the Allied Powers after World War II, Finland was permitted to maintain an army of 34,400 individuals, an air force of 3,000 individuals and 60 combat aircraft, and a navy of 4,500 individuals, with ships totaling 10,000 tons. The

ÅLAND ISLANDS

Finland's Åland (Ahvenanmaa) autonomous territory consists of the Åland Islands (Swedish: Åland Skärgård: Finnish: Ahvenanmaa), an archipelago southwest of mainland Finland. The islands lie at the entrance to the Gulf of Bothnia, 25 miles (40 km) east of the Swedish coast, at the eastern edge of the Åland Sea. The archipelago has a land area of 599 square miles (1,551 square km) and consists of about 35 inhabited islands, 6,500 uninhabited islands, and many rocky reefs. The bedrock is primarily granite and covered with a soil that, though mainly clay, is rich in certain areas.

Åland, the largest island in the group, accounts for more than 70 percent of the total land area and is known locally as Fasta Åland ("Main Island"). It consists of rugged granite to the north and rich agricultural soil to the southeast. Eckerö and Lemland are the next largest islands. Åland is home to about 90 percent of the archipelago's population and is the site of Mariehamn, the administrative capital, chief seaport, and only town. Also located on Åland is Orrdals Hill, the highest point of the archipelago, rising to a height of 423 feet (129 metres). From the 19th century until World War II, Mariehamn served as the centre of a sailing fleet engaged in grain trade with Australia. Few of these ships still operate, though the colourful history of the fleet is reflected in an excellent maritime museum. Fishing, which originally brought settlement to coastal areas unsuited to agriculture, is a declining source of income.

The archipelago has the highest crop yields in Finland per unit area because of the mild climate and fertile soil. Small, highly mechanized farms produce wheat, oats, barley, rye, cucumbers, sugar beets, potatoes, and onions. The climate also favours apple, plum, and pear orchards. Ayrshire cattle dominate the dairy farms, and sheep are also raised. Tourism, shipping, and commerce and banking account for much of the nonagricultural employment. The islands are linked to Sweden and the Finnish mainland by car and passenger ferries, steamship service, and air service from Mariehamn airport. The islands' tourist industry has expanded greatly in recent decades, with most visitors arriving by ferry from neighbouring Finland or Sweden. The islands' inhabitants speak Swedish, which is the sole official language and the language of instruction in schools.

The archipelago shows evidence of Bronze and Iron Age settlement as well as distinctive Viking graveyards and numerous medieval granite churches. The islands were Christianized during the 12th century by Swedish missionaries. In 1714 they were seized by the Russian tsar Peter I the Great after his naval victory over Sweden. When the grand duchy of Finland was ceded to Russia in 1809, the islands were included with the provision that they would not be fortified. Russia began fortification in the 1830s, however, with the building of the Bomarsund garrison. The fortress was destroyed in 1854 during the Crimean War by Anglo-French troops. The Åland Convention between Britain, France, and Russia (1856) stipulated that the islands would never be fortified again, though the islands remained under Russian rule. Because of their long history of economic and cultural association with Sweden, the Ålanders claimed the right of self-determination and sought to become part of Sweden when Finland declared its independence in 1917. Finland granted the islands autonomy in 1920 but refused to acknowledge their secession. The League of Nations became mediator of the Åland question, granting the islands a unique autonomy while directing that they remain part of Finland.

transformation of Russia, the EU, and the North Atlantic Treaty Organization (NATO) at the end of the 20th century and the beginning of the 21st has affected security and stability in Finland's environs in northern Europe. The NATO membership of the country's Baltic neighbours Estonia, Latvia, and Lithuania is generally viewed by Finns as a stabilizing factor. All male Finns between the ages of 17 and 60 are liable for military service, but civil service duty is available to conscientious objectors.

The police authorities are subordinate to the Ministry of the Interior. The cities pay to the state a part of the expenses for local police forces.

HEALTH AND WELFARE

Health centres, run by local authorities, supply free medical treatment to Finns, but there are also licensed private practitioners. The country is divided into hospital districts, each with a central hospital maintained by intermunicipal corporations. There are also smaller regional hospitals and a few private hospitals. The patient pays only a small daily hospital charge. In addition the state reimburses a large percentage of the patient's expenditures on drugs. The Finns are known as a healthy and vigorous people and are characterized by their penchant for sauna baths. Indeed, the life expectancy for Finns is among the highest in the world.

Social security in Finland comprises a system of pensions and care for the aged, unemployment benefits, health care, and family welfare plans. The state pays disability pensions and old-age pensions to persons age 65 and older. The cost of these pensions is met from premiums originally paid by the beneficiaries and payments by employers and by the central and local governments. The Central Pensions Security Institute administers an additional earnings-related old-age pension, which is also available to farmers and other self-employed people. The National Board of Social Welfare provides care and attention for the elderly, including recreational centres to provide social amenities. Other social programs include unemployment benefits and compensation for industrial accidents, maternity benefits, and family allowances for all children under age 16.

HOUSING

The National Board of Housing addresses problems of housing supply and development. There is a general housing shortage in Helsinki. About three-fifths of Finns own their own houses or flats, and the right to adequate housing was incorporated as an amendment into the Finnish constitution. Low-income families in Finland are eligible to obtain state-subsidized flats, and government loans for mortgages are also obtainable. Brick and concrete are surpassing wood as building materials, although many Finnish families have vacation cottages, typically modest lakeside dwellings of traditional log or timber construction.

EDUCATION

All Finnish municipalities are required to provide preschool instruction for all six-year-old children, but attendance is voluntary; school attendance in Finland is compulsory beginning at age seven. The national and local governments support the schools, and tuition is free. The introduction of a new nine-year comprehensive school system, consisting of a six-year primary stage and a three-year secondary stage, was completed during the 1970s. The English language is taught beginning in the third year, but students can also have the choice of studying other foreign languages. Finland's nine-year comprehensive school system is followed by either a three-year upper secondary school or a vocational school.

The Finnish higher-education system is composed of two parallel sectors: universities and polytechnics. The only higher-education institutions in Finland that were founded before the country achieved independence are the University of Helsinki, founded at Turku in 1640 and transferred to Helsinki in 1828, and the Helsinki University of Technology, founded in 1849. Instruction is offered in Finnish, Swedish, and often in English. State aid for higher education is available. Adult education and continuing education are also popular in Finland, with adult education leading to certification and reemployment education free of charge.

CHAPTER 9

FINNISH CULTURAL LIFE

Finland is one of the most ethnically and culturally homogeneous countries in Europe. Nevertheless, Finns have been quick to incorporate ideas and impulses from Russia, elsewhere in Scandinavia, and continental Europe, particularly in the arts, music, architecture, and the sciences, but in each instance these influences have evolved into a form that is typically Finnish.

Despite their strong neighbours to the east and west, Finns have preserved and developed the Finnish language, while adapting it to new terminology as needed; for example, the word *tietokone* ("knowledge machine") was coined as the Finnish word for "computer" instead of adopting a variant from another language.

Finns also have kept their cultural identity intact despite the powerful outside influences of neighbouring Finnic, Baltic, and Germanic peoples. Indeed, the traditional region of Karelia (now divided between Finland and Russia), where the songs of the Finnish national epic *Kalevala* originated, bears little influence from either Swedish or Russian culture.

The best-known Finnish regional groups are the Savolainen, Karjalainen, Hämäläinen, and Pohjalainen (from the Savo, Karelia, Hame, and Ostrobothnia regions, respectively). These groups are often characterized with standard descriptors; for example, the Karjalainen are frequently referred to as "talkative." Other regional stereotypes exist for those from Kainuu, Finland proper, and the Satakunta region, but these characterizations are not nearly as common in popular media as are those for the first four groups.

DAILY LIFE AND SOCIAL CUSTOMS

Many Finnish customs are closely associated with forests, which Finns have historically seen not as dark foreboding places but rather as offering refuge and shelter. In one of Finland's signature literary works, *Seven Brothers*, 19th-century writer Aleksis Kivi depicts the socially inept brothers' flight to the protection of the woods. Today, on weekends and during holidays, Finns flee from urban stress to their forest summerhouses.

Other customs associated with trees and wood are alive and well in Finland. Bonfires are lit at Midsummer, the doorways of houses are decorated with birches, and leafy birch whisks are still used in the traditional wooden sauna. On Easter, mämmi, a pudding made from malt and rye flour, is traditionally eaten from containers made of (or made to resemble) birch bark. In late winter, while snow covers the ground, birch branches are brought indoors to remind the household of the coming spring.

MIDSUMMER'S EVE

The longest day of the year in the Northern Hemisphere is the summer solstice, which occurs around June 21. It is celebrated in many countries by the holiday known as Midsummer's Eve (Finnish: Juhannus; Swedish: Midsommar; Danish: Sankt Hans Aften).

Midsummer's Eve is a national holiday in Finland and Sweden, and the official holiday is typically observed on the third Friday in June to allow a three-day weekend. During this time many Scandinavians travel to rural parts of the country. Midsummer's Eve activities in Sweden include gathering around a flower-festooned maypole (*majstång*) to sing and dance, an ancient custom probably related to fertility rites. Before the holiday Scandinavians thoroughly clean their houses and decorate them with flowers and other greenery. In Denmark holiday traditions include singing "Vi elsker vort land" ("We Love Our Land") and building a bonfire where a symbolic straw witch is sacrificed in remembrance of church-sanctioned witch burnings in the 16th and 17th centuries. Traditional foods, such as pickled herring, smoked fish, new potatoes, and strawberries, are served, along with beer and schnapps.

The celebration predates Christianity and is likely related to ancient fertility practices and ceremonies performed to ensure a successful harvest. The holiday was later rededicated to honour St. John the Baptist in Christian times. Although the meaning of the holiday has changed, some pagan customs still persist, such as the bonfires, which originally were believed to ward off evil spirits, and the focus on nature, which harkens back to when plants and water were thought to have magical healing powers on Midsummer's Eve.

Although Finns consider Santa Claus to have his permanent home in Korvatunturi, in northern Finland, the spruce Christmas tree is a relative newcomer to the country, having made its first appearance in the 1820s. Now the Christmas tree is a fixture of Finnish Christmas celebrations, which also involve special foods, including rice porridge (made with milk and cinnamon), a baked glazed ham, and a potato and carrot or rutabaga gratin.

The holiday is not complete without a Christmas sauna bath.

Wood is an essential component of the typical Finnish sauna, which is almost universally constructed out of birch or other sturdy wood beams. Bathers sit on wooden benches, splashing water on the hot stones of the stove and whisking each other with birch branches, just as their ancestors would have done millennia earlier. Traditionally, the sauna was a sacred

Wooden sauna, Finland. © 300dpi/Fotolia

place for the Finns, used not only for the weekly sauna bath but also for ritual purposes. This was particularly the case for those rituals performed by women, such as healing the sick and preparing the dead for burial. The sauna was also used for doing laundry and for key farming activities, such as curing meat and fermenting and drying malt. Given its importance to the farm economy, it is logical that the sauna was originally built within the enclosure surrounding the farm's outbuildings. The current placement of most saunas on a lakeside or coastal inlet goes back only to the early 20th century, following the fashion of the gentry's villas.

For a long time the sauna (whose name comes from a Finnish-Sami word) was usually heated only once a week because it took a whole day to prepare it to stand several rounds of bathers (with men and women bathing separately). Many Finns believe sauna baths provide healing for the mind and body, and they are taken with almost religious reverence. Although not playing the central role it does in Finnish culture, the custom of sauna bathing is also widespread among the other Finnic peoples in the Baltic region— the Estonians, Karelians, Veps, and Livonians—as well as among Latvians and Lithuanians.

THE ARTS

Finland's national epic, the *Kalevala*, compiled in the 19th century by the scholar Elias Lönnrot from old Finnish ballads, lyrics, and incantations, played a vital part in fostering Finnish national consciousness and pride. Indeed, the development of almost all Finland's cultural institutions and activities has been involved with and motivated by nationalist enthusiasm. This theme can be demonstrated in the growth and development of Finnish theatre and opera, in literature and music, in art and architecture, and also in sports. The festivals of various arts, held annually at places such as Helsinki, Vaasa, and Kaustinen, and Finland's many museums, show an awareness of the individuality and importance of Finland's contribution to world culture. Savonlinna, in particular, is celebrated for its annual opera festivals.

THEATRE, OPERA, AND MUSIC

Drama in Finland is truly popular in the sense that vast numbers act in, as well as watch, theatrical productions. Besides the dozens of theatre companies in which all the actors are professionals, there are some in which a few professionals or even the producer alone are supplemented by amateur performers. And there are amateur theatrical companies in almost every commune.

The country's most important theatre is the National Theatre of Finland, established in 1872 with Kaarlo Bergbom as producer and manager; its granite building in Helsinki was built in 1902. There are also several other municipal theatres. One of the most exciting in the country is the Pyynikki Open Air Theatre of Tampere, the revolving auditorium of which can be moved to face any of the natural sets. There are innumerable institutions connected with the theatre in Finland, including the Central Federation of Finnish Theatrical Organizations. There is a wide repertory of Finnish as well as international plays. The Finnish theatre receives some degree of government assistance.

The main centre for opera is the Finnish National Opera in Helsinki; the Savonlinna Opera Festival takes place every summer. The international success of Finnish singers such as Karita Mattila, Jorma Hynninen, and Soile Isokoski has added to the continuing national enthusiasm for opera. Several Finnish operas, including *The Last Temptations* by Joonas Kokkonen and *The Horseman* by Aulis Sallinen, gained notoriety in the late 20th and early 21st century.

The dominant figure in Finnish music during the first half of the 20th century was Jean Sibelius, the country's best-known composer, who brought Finnish music into the repertoire of concert halls worldwide. Other renowned composers include Magnus Lindberg, Kaija Saariaho, and Einojuhani Rautavaara. The Sibelius Academy in Helsinki is a world-famous centre of musical study. The city is also the location of the Helsinki Philharmonic Orchestra and the Finnish Radio Symphony Orchestra. The Sibelius violin competition and Mirjam Helin song competition are held there every five years. There are annual music festivals in Helsinki and several other cities. Internationally known Finnish conductors include Paavo Berglund, Esa-Pekka Salonen, Jukka-Pekka Saraste, and Osmo Vänskä.

LITERATURE

Epic prose has played and continues to play an important role in Finnish

KALEVALA

The *Kalevala*—the Finnish national epic compiled from old Finnish ballads, lyrical songs, and incantations that were a part of Finnish oral tradition—was published by its compiler, Elias Lönnrot, in two editions (32 cantos, 1835; enlarged into 50 cantos, 1849).

Kalevala, the dwelling place of the poem's chief characters, is a poetic name for Finland, meaning "land of heroes." The leader of the "sons of Kaleva" is the old and wise Väinämöinen, a powerful seer with supernatural origins, who is a master of the kantele, the Finnish harplike stringed instrument. Other characters include the skilled smith Ilmarinen, one of those who forged the "lids of heaven" when the world was created; Lemminkäinen, the carefree adventurer-warrior and charmer of women; Louhi, the female ruler of Pohjola, a powerful land in the north; and the tragic hero Kullervo, who is forced by fate to be a slave from childhood.

Among the main dramas of the poem are the creation of the world and the adventurous journeys of Väinämöinen, Ilmarinen, and Lemminkäinen to Pohjola to woo the beautiful daughter of Louhi, during which the miraculous *sampo,* a mill that produces salt, meal, and gold and is a talisman of happiness and prosperity, is forged and recovered for the people of Kalevala. Although the *Kalevala* depicts the conditions and ideas of the pre-Christian period, the last canto seems to predict the decline of paganism: the maid Marjatta gives birth to a son who is baptized king of Karelia, and the pagan Väinämöinen makes way for him, departing from Finland without his kantele and songs.

The *Kalevala* is written in unrhymed octosyllabic trochees and dactyls (the *Kalevala* metre) and its style is characterized by alliteration, parallelism, and repetition. Besides fostering the Finnish national spirit, the poem has been translated into at least 20 languages; it has inspired many outstanding works of art, e.g., the paintings of Akseli Gallén-Kallela and the musical compositions of Jean Sibelius. The epic style and metre of the poem *The Song of Hiawatha* by Henry Wadsworth Longfellow also reflect the influence of the *Kalevala.*

literature. *Seitsemän veljestä* (1870; *Seven Brothers*) by Aleksis Kivi is considered to be the first novel written in Finnish. Other early leading prose writers include Frans Eemil Sillanpää, the winner of the Nobel Prize for Literature in 1939. Although Mika Waltari represented newer trends in literature, it was his historical novels, among them *Sinuhe, egyptiläinen* (1945; *The Egyptian*), that brought him fame. Väinö Linna, a leading postwar writer, became known for his war novel *Tuntematon soltilas* (1954; *The Unknown Soldier*) and for the trilogy *Täällä Pohjantähden alla* (1959–62; *Under the North Star*). Other novelists have written in shorter forms, but the broad epic has remained popular, particularly among writers describing the contradictions in Finnish life from the turn of the century to modern times. One of the central figures in the Finnish modernist movement of the 1950s was poet and playwright Eeva Liisa Manner, perhaps best remembered for her poetry collection *Tämä matka* ("This Journey," 1956). Other well-known Finnish authors include Kari Hotakainen, Leena Lehtolainen, Rosa Liksom, Asko Sahlberg, and Johanna Sinisalo.

Literature written in Swedish has had a long tradition in Finland. Among 19th-century writers, Johan Ludvig Runeberg, the national poet, and Zacharias Topelius played leading roles. Later 20th-century poets such as Edith Södergran had a strong influence on the modern poetry of both Finland and Scandinavia. One of Finland's most beloved and widely translated authors, Tove Jansson, wrote her many books about the Moomin family in Swedish. The Swedish language continues to be used in Finnish literature, and writers such as Kjell Westö, Märta Tikkanen, Monika Fagerholm, and Jörn Donner are widely read in Finland and abroad.

ART, ARCHITECTURE, AND DESIGN

From the time that the *Kalevala* inspired the paintings of Die Brücke Expressionist Akseli Gallén-Kallela, there has been a distinctive school of Finnish painters, but the Finnish artistic genius has been continually drawn to three-dimensional work. Sculpture is important, highly abstract, and experimental; Eila Hiltanen's monument to

Sibelius in Helsinki is composed of chrome, metal, and steel tubes.

Modern Finnish architecture is among the most imaginative and exciting in the world. Its development was closely allied to the nationalist movement, and among its pioneers were the internationally renowned Eliel Saarinen, whose work is exemplified by the National Museum and the Helsinki railway station, and Lars Sonck, whose churches in Helsinki and Tampere are particularly notable. Finnish women were also early innovators as architects, including Wiwi Lönn and Signe Hornborg, the latter one of the first formally trained female architects in the world.

In the 20th century the idea of functionalism was developed by Gustaf

ALEKSIS KIVI

Aleksis Kivi (born Aleksis Stenvall, October 10, 1834, Nurmijarvi, Russian Finland [now in Finland]—died December 31, 1872, Tuusula) is referred to as the father of the Finnish novel and drama. He is also credited with being the creator of Finland's modern literary language.

Though Kivi grew up in rural poverty, he entered the University of Helsinki in 1857. In 1860 he won the Finnish Literary Society's drama competition with his tragedy *Kullervo,* based on a theme taken from the Finnish national epic *Kalevala.* His most famous plays are the rural comedies *Nummisuutarit* (1864; "Shoemakers of the Heath"), the story of the unsuccessful courting of a simple-minded and gullible youth, and *Kihlaus* (1867; "Fugitives"). Kivi's *Seitsemän veljestä* (1870; *Seven Brothers*), the first novel written in Finnish, tells the story of some freedom-loving village youths who take to the woods and live a life of adventure but gradually mature and finally accept the responsibilities of sober citizens in a farming community. It contains elements of realism and Romanticism and a great deal of humour. As Finland's first professional writer, Kivi struggled throughout his life against poverty and hostile criticism. In his last years he was psychotic. Though his works are now regarded as classics, a collection of his poems, *Kanervala* (1866; "Land of the Heathen"), which departed from contemporary poetic conventions, did not begin to be fully appreciated until almost a century after his death.

Helsinki railway station. © Zygimantas. Cepaitis/Fotolia

Chapel of the cemetery at Turku, Fin., by Erik Bryggman, 1938–41. Courtesy of the Museum of Finnish Architecture, Helsinki. Courtesy of the Museum of Finnish Architecture, Helskinki.

Double-cased glass vases designed by Timo Sarpaneva, Iittala glassworks, Finland, 1957. In Die Neue Sammlung, Munich. Courtesy of Die Neue Sammlung, Munich

Strengell. In the 1920s Alvar Aalto and Erik Bryggman began experimenting with regional variations on the International Style. Among the most striking examples of Aalto's work are the Paimio Sanatorium, the library at Viipuri, and Finlandia Hall, a concert and congress hall in Helsinki. There is general experimentation, using concrete and metals, in Finnish industrial buildings and flats and in environmental design, as at the garden town of Tapiola outside Helsinki. The new generation of architects has continued these standards. Architects such as Juha Ilmari Leiviskä, known for his innovative churches, and Pekka Helin and Tuomo Siitonen, whose flexible and adaptive working spaces are intended to encourage creative thinking, have been lauded at home and abroad.

Finnish design—especially in glass, porcelain, and textiles—became internationally known during the postwar period. Factories such as the well-known Arabia and Marimekko in Helsinki have given artists a free hand to develop their ideas and skills. Tapio Wirkkala, Kaj Franck, and Timo Sarpaneva in glassware, Marjatta Metsovaara in textiles, and Dora Ljung in ryijy, a type of knotted pile-weave rug, are among the best-known designers.

CULTURAL INSTITUTIONS

Finland's public cultural institutions are made up of a big, varied, and comprehensive network. The institutions are largely supported, planned, and organized by national and local authorities. The planning of cultural policies is in the purview of the Finnish Ministry of Education. Finnish arts and cultural activities are considered important not only to a strong national identity but as a valuable export and source of international interest. Since 1969, Finland has administered a system of artists' grants that allocate a tax-free monthly stipend (for a variety of periods) to artists working in architecture, motion pictures, crafts and design, dance, literature, music, theatre, photography, and other visual arts. Public support for artists is also made available through grants and subsidies for "high-quality productions"—including films, photographic art books, and crafts and design—and by purchasing works of art for public buildings and spaces.

Finns are also active in creating culture on an amateur basis. People participate eagerly in cultural clubs and organizations, local choirs and orchestras, and local dance, theatre, and dramatic societies, along with other similar groups. These groups organize a wide variety of year-round local and regional cultural events throughout the country.

Of Finland's more than 1,000 museums, about 200 are dedicated to the arts. The national art museum is the Finnish National Gallery, composed of the Ateneum Art Museum, the Museum of Contemporary Art Kiasma, the Sinebrychoff Art Museum, and the Central Art Archives. There are also a number of regional art museums.

Libraries are especially important cultural institutions in Finland, and Finns are among the world's most avid library users. Since the founding of its first library, in 1794 in Vaasa, Finland has developed a comprehensive network of tens of millions of books and other items in its plentiful public libraries, including a seagoing library to serve the needs of islanders. Because of their important role in public education and service, especially in their use as civic meeting places and cultural centres, libraries are highly regarded and well funded by the Finns. The Helsinki University Library is also the National Library of Finland.

SPORTS AND RECREATION

In Finland the basic national sport—which originally was a necessary means of winter transportation—is cross-country skiing. Nationalism also encouraged the development of special proficiency, which was fostered by ski fairs and competitions held at Oulu beginning in the late 1890s. A century later, Finns were still making their mark on the sport, not least being Marja-Liisa Hämäläinen, who won seven Olympic medals in the 1980s and '90s.

An interest in other athletics developed from the time that the Finns took part in the interim Olympic Games

MARJA-LIISA HÄMÄLÄINEN

Finland's foremost female cross-country skier, Marja-Liisa Hämäläinen (born September 10, 1955, Simpele, Finland), captured three Olympic gold medals and a bronze at the 1984 Games in Sarajevo, Yugoslavia (now in Bosnia and Herzegovina), en route to winning seven Olympic medals between 1984 and 1994.

Tall, with an athletic build, Hämäläinen was born into a family of cross-country skiers and as a young girl practiced skiing on the hills of her father's farm. In 1971 she began to ski competitively and five years later made her first appearance at the Winter Olympics. Competing in Innsbruck, Austria, she placed 22nd in the 10-km event. After finishing no better than 18th at the 1980 Games in Lake Placid, Hämäläinen contemplated quitting the sport. After nearly 10 years of competition, she had never won a world championship. Her fiancé, Olympic skier Harri Kirvesniemi, however, encouraged her to continue, and in 1983 she captured her first World Cup. She successfully defended her title the following year.

Hämäläinen entered the 1984 Winter Olympics in Sarajevo as Finland's top female cross-country skier, having won the national championships in the 5-, 10-, and 20-km events (1983). At Sarajevo she swept the individual events to become the first Finn in 60 years to win three gold medals. She dominated the field in both the 5- and 10-km races. She also triumphed in the grueling 20-km event, a contest that was newly added for women that year, defeating her Soviet rival, Raisa Smetanina, by 41.7 seconds. Hämäläinen, who added a bronze in the 4×5-km relay, was the most successful performer at Sarajevo.

Following the 1984 Games, Hämäläinen married Kirvesniemi, who was also a medalist at Sarajevo, capturing a bronze in the 15-km event. She competed at the 1988 Olympics in Calgary, Alberta, Canada, and won a bronze medal in the 4×5-km relay. She failed to medal at the 1992 Olympics in Albertville, France, but she won two bronze medals (5- and 30-km events) at the 1994 Games in Lillehammer, Norway. Outside of cross-country skiing, she pursued a career as a physiotherapist.

held in Athens in 1906. Finland has excelled in Olympic track and field as well as winter sports, especially in distance running, in which the tradition of "Flying Finns" includes Hannes Kolehmainen, Ville Ritola, Lasse Virén, and Paavo Nurmi, who won nine gold medals in Olympic middle- and long-distance running events in the 1920s, becoming a national hero. Other popular sports are waterskiing, riding, fishing, shooting, ice hockey, and pesä-pallo, a Finnish version of baseball.

MEDIA AND PUBLISHING

Freedom of the press is guaranteed by the 1919 constitution and the Freedom of the Press Act (also 1919); both contain provisions safeguarding editorial rights and outlining press responsibilities. The Supreme Court can suppress publications under certain circumstances, but in general there are few restrictions apart from those governing libel and copyright.

Newspaper publication began in Finland in 1771 by the learned Aurora Society, and the *Åbo Underrättelser*, published in Swedish, has been in operation since 1824. Finns are among the world's most voracious newspaper readers, and the country ranks near the top of newspapers sold per capita. Most of Finland's many newspapers are independently owned and operated. The national Finnish News Agency (Oy Suomen Tietotoimisto; founded 1887) is independent and owned by the press.

The state-run Finnish Broadcasting Company (Yleisradio Oy [YLE]; established 1926) operates a number of nationwide television networks—both public service and commercial—along with several digital channels and offers programming in Swedish. YLE also owns Radio Finland, which broadcasts in Finnish, Swedish, English, and Russian. Jointly owned by Finland, Sweden, and Norway, Sámi Radio provides radio service to the Sami areas in northern Lapland.

CHAPTER 10

FINLAND: PAST AND PRESENT

The first people arrived in Finland about 9,000 years ago. They probably represented several groups and tribes, including the ancestors of the present Sami. Lured by the plenitude of game, particularly fur-bearing animals and fish, they followed the melting ice northward. The first people perhaps came to hunt only for the summer, but gradually more and more of them stayed over the winter. Apparently berries played a significant role in their diet.

Another group probably arrived some 3,000 years later from the southeast. They possibly spoke a Finno-Ugric language and may have been related to the ancestors of the present Finns, if they were not actually of the same group. Other peoples—including the ancestors of the Tavastians—followed from the southwest and central Europe, eventually adopting the Finno-Ugric tongue.

During the 1st millennium BCE several more groups arrived, among them the ancestors of the present Finns. The nomadic Sami, who had been scattered over the greater part of Finland, withdrew to the north. Most other groups intermarried and assimilated with the newcomers, and settlement spread across the south of Finland. The population was still extremely sparse, but three loose unities seem to have crystallized: the Finns proper, the Tavastians, and the Karelians. These each had their own chiefs, and they waged war on one another.

Even before the beginning of the Viking Age (8th–11th century CE), Swedes had settled on the southwestern coast. During the Viking Age, Finland lay along the northern boundary of the trade routes to Russia, and the inhabitants of the area served as suppliers of furs. The Finns apparently did not take part in the Viking expeditions. The end of the Viking Age was a time of unrest in Finland, and Swedish and Danish raids were made on the area, where Russians and Germans also traded.

COMPETITION FOR TRADE AND CONVERTS

From the 12th century, Finland became a battleground between Russia and Sweden. The economic rivalry of the powers in the Baltic was turned into a religious rivalry, and the Swedish expeditions took on the character of crusades. Finland is mentioned together with Estonia in a list of Swedish provinces drawn up for the pope in 1120, apparently as a Swedish missionary area. The first crusade, according to tradition, was undertaken in about 1157 by King Erik, who was accompanied by an English bishop named Henry. The bishop remained in Finland to organize the affairs of the church and was murdered by a Finnish yeoman. By the end of the 12th century, he was revered as a saint, and he later became Finland's patron. In a papal bull (c. 1172), the Swedes were advised to force the Finns into submission by permanently manning the Finnish fortresses in order to protect the Christianization effort from attacks from the east.

By the end of the 12th century, competition for influence in the Gulf of Finland had intensified: German traders had regular contacts with Novgorod via Gotland, and Denmark tried to establish bases on the gulf. The Danes reportedly invaded Finland in 1191 and again in 1202; in 1209 the pope authorized the archbishop of Lund to appoint a minister stationed in Finland. The Swedish king counterattacked, and in 1216 he received confirmation from the pope of his title to the lands won by himself and his predecessors from the heathens. He was also authorized to establish a seat for one or two bishops in the Finnish missionary territory. In eastern Finland the Russian church attempted to win converts, and in 1227 Duke Jaroslav undertook a program of forced baptisms, designed to tie Karelia closer to Novgorod. In response the pope placed Finland under apostolic protection and invoked a commercial blockade against Russia (1229). A large force, led by Birger, a Swedish jarl (a noble ranking immediately below the king), and including Swedes, Finns, and crusaders from various countries, was defeated in 1240 by a duke of Novgorod, and the advance of Western Christendom into Russia was halted, while the religious division of Finland was sealed, with the Karelians in the Eastern sphere. The bishop of Finland, Thomas, resigned in 1245, and the mission territory was left without leadership until 1249, when the Dominicans founded a monastery in Turku.

FINLAND UNDER SWEDISH RULE

Birger Jarl decided that a full effort was necessary to bring Finland into the Swedish sphere; in 1249 he led an expedition to Tavastia (now Häme), an area already Christianized. Birger built a fortress in Tavastia and some fortifications along the northern coast of the Gulf of Finland, where Swedish settlement on a mass scale began. Swedes also moved to the eastern coast of the Gulf of Bothnia. In 1293 Torgils Knutsson launched an expedition in an attempt to conquer all of Karelia and built a fortress in Viipuri. The war lasted until 1323, when the Treaty of Pähkinäsaari (Nöteborg; now Petrokrepost) drew the boundary between the Russian and Swedish spheres of influence in a vague line from the eastern part of the Gulf of Finland through the middle of Karelia northwest to the Gulf of Bothnia, and the crusades were ended, with Finland a part of the Swedish realm.

The Swedes began to administer Finland in accordance with Swedish traditions. Castles were built and taxes were collected, mainly in furs and, later, in grain, butter, and money. During the early Middle Ages, Finland was often given to members of the royal family as a duchy. Two new estates, the clergy and the nobility, evolved, with the nobility increased by transplantation from Sweden and the clergy containing a large native element. The first native bishop was appointed in 1291.

In 1362 King Haakon of Sweden established the right of the Finns to participate in royal elections and the equal status of Finland with the other parts of the kingdom. Several years later Haakon was overthrown and Albert of Mecklenburg was crowned. Albert was unpopular with the Finns, and by 1374 a Swedish nobleman, Bo Jonsson Grip, had gained title to all of Finland. Grip died in 1386, and Finland soon after became part of the Kalmar Union.

THE 15TH, 16TH, AND 17TH CENTURIES

Under Swedish sovereignty the Finnish tribes gradually developed a sense of unity, which was encouraged by the bishops of Turku. Study in universities brought Finnish scholars into direct touch with the cultural centres of Europe, and Mikael Agricola (c. 1510–57), the creator of the Finnish literary language, brought the Lutheran faith from Germany. As part of medieval Sweden, Finland was drawn into the many wars and domestic battles of the Swedish nobility. In 1581 King John III raised Finland to the level of a grand duchy to irritate his Russian rival, Tsar Ivan IV the Terrible. Dispute over the Swedish crown, combined with quarrels over social conditions, foreign policy, and religion (Roman Catholic versus Lutheran), led to the last peasant revolt in Europe, the so-called Club War, in 1596–97. The hopes of the Finnish peasants were crushed, and, even when

Charles IX, whom the peasants had supported, became king (1604–11), the social conditions did not improve. In the course of the administrative reforms of Gustav II Adolf (1611–32), Finland became an integral part of the kingdom, and the educated classes thereafter came increasingly to speak Swedish.

On its eastern frontier Finland was harassed by constant warfare, and the danger became more serious when Novgorod, at the end of the medieval period, was succeeded by a more powerful neighbour, the Grand Duchy of Moscow. In 1595, however, by the Peace of Täysinä, the existing de facto boundary, up to the Arctic Ocean, was granted official recognition by the Russians. By the Peace of Stolbovo (Stolbova; 1617), Russia ceded Ingermanland and part of Karelia to the kingdom of Sweden-Finland. The population of the ceded territories was of the Greek Orthodox faith, and when the Swedish government began forceful conversion to Lutheranism many fled to Russia and were replaced by Lutheran Finns. After Stolbovo, Sweden found new outlets for expansion in the south and west and developed into one of the leading powers of Europe. Though Finnish conscripts played their part in making Sweden a great power, the role of Finland in the kingdom steadily decreased in importance.

THE 18TH CENTURY

In Charles XII's reign, Sweden lost its position as a great power. During the Great Northern War, Russians occupied Finland for eight years (1713–21), and, under the Peace of Uusikaupunki (Nystad) in 1721, Sweden had to cede the southeastern part of Finland with Viipuri as well as the Baltic provinces. Sweden's capacity to defend Finland had weakened, and the years of hostile occupation had given the Finns a permanent feeling of insecurity.

In the course of the next Russo-Swedish War (1741–43), the Russian empress Elizabeth declared to the Finnish people her intention of making Finland a separate state under Russian suzerainty, but she failed to follow up the idea and at the peace settlement of Turku in 1743 contented herself with annexing a piece of Finland. Meanwhile, however, her original idea had found favour with some Finns. During the next bout of hostilities (1788–90), a number of Finnish officers involved themselves in the activities of Göran Magnus Sprengtporten, a Finnish colonel who had fled to Russia and who wanted to detach Finland from Sweden; this movement won little general support, however.

AUTONOMOUS GRAND DUCHY

As a part of the Swedish monarchy, Finland had been accorded practically no institutions of its own, but from the middle of the 18th century the majority of officials and intellectuals were of Finnish origin. In those circles there was a growing feeling that Finland had to bear the

GÖRAN MAGNUS SPRENGTPORTEN

Soldier and politician G.M. Sprengtporten (born Georg Magnus Sprengtporten [also known as Göran Magnus Sprengtporten], August 16, 1740, Gammelbacka, Finland—died October 13, 1819, St. Petersburg, Russia) spent many years conspiring to bring Sweden's grand duchy, Finland, into the Russian Empire. His hopes were realized when Sweden ceded the grand duchy to Russia in 1809.

Sprengtporten first achieved prominence in August 1772, when, as a major in the Swedish Army in Finland, he joined his half brother, Baron J.M. Sprengtporten, in leading a successful coup d'etat, which secured absolute power for King Gustav III. Feeling ill-rewarded for his part in the coup, and dissatisfied with the inadequacy of defense fortifications in Finland, Sprengtporten, now a colonel, resigned his commission in 1777.

For the next few years Sprengtporten was in contact with Russian diplomats in various European capitals to promote schemes for affiliating Finland with Russia. In 1786 he entered Russian service as a major general. During the Russo-Swedish War of 1788–90, he led Russian forces against the Swedes and negotiated with the traitorous Swedish officers of the Anjala League. When the two powers again went to war in 1808, the complete occupation of Finland by Russia soon became inevitable, and Sprengtporten urged Tsar Alexander I to grant Finland complete independence under a member of the Romanov dynasty. Although his suggestion was not accepted, he undoubtedly influenced the Tsar's decision to honour Finland's constitution after Sweden ceded the grand duchy to Russia in September 1809. Sprengtporten served briefly (1808–09) as Finland's only non-Russian governor general during the union of the two states. He was made a count in 1809.

cost of Swedish extravagances in foreign policy. The feeling was not unfounded. Swedish strategic directives of 1785 implied that, in case of Russian attack, Swedish forces should retire from the frontier, leaving Finnish detachments behind, and that under extreme danger the whole of Finland should be evacuated. This strategy was put into effect in 1808–09. Even the treachery of the Anjala association in 1788 was repeated in 1808, when Sveaborg (Viapori; now Suomenlinna) near Helsinki capitulated to the Russians. In 1809 the Finns themselves had to carry the responsibility of coming to terms with Russia. Alexander I offered to recognize constitutional developments in Finland and to give it autonomy as a grand duchy under his throne.

THE ERA OF BUREAUCRACY

The political framework of Finland under Russia was laid down by the Porvoo (Borgå) Diet in 1809. Finland was still formally a part of Sweden until the peace treaty of Hamina (Fredrikshamn) later that year, but most of the Finnish leaders had already grown tired of Swedish control and wanted to acquire as much self-government as possible under Russian protection. In Porvoo, Finland as a whole was for the first time established as a united political entity—a nation.

In recognition of Finnish autonomy, Alexander I promised to respect the religion and fundamental laws of Finland, as well as the privileges and rights of the inhabitants (that is to say, the Swedish constitution of 1772 as amended in 1789, by which the regent alone had the executive power while the consent of the Diet was required for legislation and the imposition of new taxes). The grand duke (the emperor) was not obliged to convene the Diet at regular intervals, and as a result it did not meet until 1863. From 1809 to 1863 Finland was ruled by a bureaucracy chosen by the Russian emperor, who was represented in Finland by a governor-general. Some holders of this office were Finns in the early period of the Russian regime. The highest administrative organ during the period was the Senate, which consisted of a judicial department and an economic department. The former was the country's supreme court, while the latter became a sort of ministry. A ministerial state secretary in St. Petersburg represented Finnish affairs to the emperor.

REFORMS OF THE RUSSIAN PERIOD

For most Finns the "era of bureaucracy" was a time of growing prosperity, favourable economic conditions, and no warfare except during the Crimean War (in Finland, the War of Åland). At that time an Anglo-French fleet attacked the Åland Islands, the fortress of Viapori in Helsinki, and some coastal towns on the Gulf of Bothnia. On its separation from Sweden in accordance with the Treaty of Hamina, Finland had a population of more than 900,000. As elsewhere in the Nordic countries, population growth was rapid, and by 1908 the figure had exceeded 2 million. Most of the population lived off the land. Manufacture of wooden articles, export of timber, shipbuilding, and merchant shipping were practiced in the small coastal towns.

Despite the strongly authoritarian and bureaucratic form of government, a number of important reforms were implemented. In 1812 the Emperor was induced to restore those areas of Finnish territory that Sweden had ceded to Russia by the treaties of Uusikaupunki (1721) and Turku (1743). Furthermore, in 1812 Helsinki was chosen as the capital, and the monumental buildings in its centre stem from this period. But the vast rural population and purely agrarian structure prevented the spread of liberal and national ideas to any great extent during the first part of the 19th century.

THE LANGUAGE PROBLEM

The reaction reached its climax with the Finnish language ordinance of 1850, which forbade the publication in Finnish of books other than those that aimed at religious edification or economic benefit. Since Finnish was the only language understood by the majority of the population, the ordinance smacked of an attempt to maintain class differences and was well suited to preserve the existing bureaucracy.

As late as the mid-19th century, Swedish was the only language allowed within the Finnish administration. There was an almost total lack of literature in Finnish, and teaching at both the secondary and university levels was in Swedish. The division between the two languages became not only of national and cultural significance but also a social distinction. This is one of the reasons why the language controversy in Finland created such bitterness. To begin with, the advocates of a Finnish-speaking Finland, or Fennomans, were successful. By recording folk songs and writings, a Finnish literature was developed during the latter part of the 19th century. The first purely Finnish-speaking grammar school appeared in 1858. In 1863 Alexander II (ruled 1855–81) issued a decree stating that, after a 20-year interim period, Finnish was to be placed on an equal footing with Swedish in the administration and in the law courts, as far as their relations with the public were concerned. Swedish, however, remained the language of internal administration, and it was not until 1902 that Swedish and Finnish were placed on an equal footing as official languages.

REFORM OF THE DIET AND OTHER REFORMS

During the reign of Alexander II other reforms were begun. The most important was his convening of the Diet in 1863, and the promulgation of a new act in 1869 providing that it thereafter should be convened regularly. The next great reform period came after the Russian defeat in the war against Japan (1904–05).

Until the 1890s, Russia respected Finland's special position within the Russian Empire in all essentials. In addition to the Diet ordinance of 1869, the country acquired its own monetary system (1865), and a law on conscription, which laid the foundations for the Finnish Army, was passed in 1878.

THE STRUGGLE FOR INDEPENDENCE

Nationalism had already begun to raise its head in Russia before the end of Alexander II's reign, but his strong-minded successor, Alexander III, who had a personal liking for Finland, was able to resist the demands of the Russian nationalists for the abolition of Finnish autonomy and the absorption of the Finns into the Russian nation. The emergence of a united Germany south of the Baltic also worried the Russians, who wanted to secure the loyalty of Finland. Russian jurists took the line that, though Alexander I in virtue of his supreme powers had granted Finland autonomous rights, any Russian emperor exercising the same supreme powers was entitled to take them back whenever he wished. Applying this principle, Nicholas II issued a manifesto on February 15, 1899, according to which he was entitled, without the Finnish Diet's consent, to enact laws enforceable in Finland if such laws affected Russian interests. Direct attempts at Russification were then made. The gradual imposition of Russian as the third official language was ordered in 1900, and in 1901 it was decreed that Finns should serve in Russian units and that Finland's own army should be disbanded. Increasing executive power was conferred on the ultranationalist governor-general, General Nikolay Bobrikov. Faced with this situation, two opposing factions crystallized out of Finland's political parties: the Constitutionalists (the Swedish Party and the Young Finnish Party), who demanded that no one observe the illegal enactments; and the Compliers (the Old Finnish Party), who were ready to give way in everything that did not, in their opinion, affect Finland's vital interest. The Constitutionalists were dismissed from their offices and their leaders were exiled. Young men of Constitutionalist views refused to report for service when called, and at last the Emperor had to give in: the Finnish Army remained disbanded, but no Finns were drafted into the Russian Army. A more extreme group, known as the Activists, was prepared to endorse even acts of violence, and Bobrikov was assassinated by them.

RESISTANCE AND REFORM

Further opposition came from the Labour Party, which was founded in 1899 and which in 1903 adopted Marxist tenets, changing its name to the Social Democratic Party. Unwilling to compromise with tsarist Russia, the party was developing along revolutionary lines. When the Constitutionalists, availing themselves of Russia's momentary weakness, combined with the Social Democrats to organize a national strike, the Emperor restored the situation that had prevailed before 1899 (November 4, 1905)—but not for long. Another result of the strike was a complete reform of the parliamentary system (July 20, 1906). This had been the Social Democrats' most insistent demand. The old four-chamber Diet was changed to a unicameral Parliament elected by equal and universal suffrage. Thus, from having one of Europe's most unrepresentative political systems, Finland had, at one stroke, acquired the most modern. The parliamentary reform polarized the political factions, and the ground was laid for the modern party system. The introduction of universal and equal suffrage meant that the farmers and workers potentially commanded a great majority. The Social Democrats became the largest party in Parliament, obtaining 80 seats out of 200 in the very first elections (1907). Nevertheless, the importance of Parliament remained very small, as it was constantly being dissolved by the Emperor; thus the assault on Finnish autonomy soon began afresh. The Constitutionalists resigned from the government, and the Compliers soon followed their example, since even in their opinion the extreme limit had been overstepped. In the end an illegal Senate composed of Russians was formed. In 1910 the responsibility for all important legislation was transferred to the Russian Duma.

RETURN TO AUTONOMY

During World War I the Finnish liberation movement sought support from Germany, and a number of young volunteers received military training and formed the Jägar Battalion. After the Russian Revolution in March 1917, Finland obtained its autonomy again, and a Senate, or coalition government, assumed rule of the country. By a law of July 1917 it was decided that all the authority previously wielded by the emperor (apart from defense and foreign policy) should be exercised by the Finnish Parliament. After Russia was taken over by the Bolsheviks in November 1917 Parliament issued a declaration of independence for Finland on December 6, 1917, which was recognized by Lenin and his government on the last day of the year.

EARLY INDEPENDENCE

Although the liberation from Russia occurred peacefully, Finland was unable to avert a violent internal conflict. After the revolutionary Reds had won control of the Social Democratic Party, they went into action and on January 28, 1918, seized Helsinki and the larger industrial towns in southern Finland. The right-wing government led by the Conservative Pehr Evind Svinhufvud fled to the western part of the country, where a counterattack was organized under the leadership of Gen. Carl Gustaf Mannerheim. At the beginning of April the White Army under his command won the Battle of Tampere. German troops came to the aid of the White forces in securing Helsinki; by May the rebellion had been suppressed, bringing to an end the Finnish Civil War. It was followed by trials in which harsh sentences were passed.

During the summer and fall of 1918 some 20,000 former revolutionaries either were executed or died in prison camps, bringing the total losses of the war to more than 30,000 lives. A few of the revolutionary leaders, however, managed to escape to Soviet Russia, where a small contingent founded the Finnish Communist Party in Moscow; others continued their flight to the United States and western Europe, some gradually returning to Finland.

POLITICAL CHANGE

When the Civil War ended, it was decided, during the summer of 1918, to

Gen. Carl Gustaf Mannerheim, in full military regalia. Mannerheim led the Finnish government's troops against revolutionary forces inside the country during the 1918 Finnish Civil War. © AP Images

PEHR EVIND SVINHUFVUD

The first chief of state of independent Finland was Pehr Evind Svinhufvud (born December 15, 1861, Sääksmäki, Finland—died February 29, 1944, Luumäki). He headed the Finnish government during his country's civil war and in the early 1930s. He was instrumental in suppressing Finland's Communist Party and maintaining a rightist regime.

Svinhufvud entered the Finnish Parliament in 1894, while Finland was still part of the Russian Empire. His anti-Russian position earned him exile in Siberia from 1914 to 1917. Having returned at the outbreak of the Russian Revolution of March 1917, he became prime minister of Finland, on November 27. He led the victorious "White" government during the Finnish Civil War of 1918 and secured (with German aid) Finland's independence from Soviet Russia. Being pro-German, he resigned after Germany's defeat in World War I and entered the conservative National Coalition Party. As prime minister from July 5, 1930, to February 16, 1931, and president from March 2, 1931, to February 28, 1937, he aided the rightist Lapua Movement in the suppression of the Communist Party but resisted efforts to turn Finland into an authoritarian, antidemocratic state.

make Finland a monarchy, and in October the German prince Frederick Charles of Hessen was chosen as king. With Germany's defeat in the war, however, General Mannerheim was designated regent, with the task of submitting a proposal for a new constitution. As it was obvious that Finland was to be a republic, the struggle now concerned presidential power. The liberal parties and the reorganized Social Democratic Party wanted power to be invested in Parliament, while the Conservatives wanted the president to have powers independent of Parliament. The strong position held by the Conservatives after the Civil War enabled them to force through their motion that the president should be chosen by popularly elected representatives, independent of Parliament, and also that

he should possess a great deal more authority, especially regarding foreign policy, than at that time was usual for a head of state. After the new constitution had been confirmed on July 17, 1919, the Social Democrats positioned themselves behind the liberal National Progressive Party leader, Kaarlo Juho Ståhlberg, to make him the first president of Finland and to defeat the Conservative candidate Mannerheim, who had not convinced them of his loyalty to republicanism.

AGRARIAN REFORM

During the interwar years Finland, to a much greater extent than the rest of the Nordic countries, was an agrarian country. In 1918, 70 percent of the population was employed in agriculture and forestry, and

KAARLO JUHO STÅHLBERG

The first president of independent Finland was Kaarlo Juho Ståhlberg (born January 28, 1865, Suomussalmi, Oulu county, Finland—died September 22, 1952, Helsinki). Ståhlberg was also the architect of the 1919 Finnish constitution.

Joining the Constitutionalist Party, Ståhlberg was elected to the Diet in 1904 and entered the government of the autonomous Grand Duchy of Finland in 1905 but resigned in 1907. From 1908 to 1918 he was professor of administrative law at the University of Helsinki.

Consistently democratic in outlook, he was among the first Finnish politicians to call for universal suffrage. His draft of a republican constitution (1917) became the basis of the actual constitution of 1919. In the reshuffling of the political parties when national independence was achieved, Ståhlberg joined the National Progressive Party. Elected president of the new republic (1919), he set the pattern for his successors by making full use of his constitutional powers. He did his utmost to narrow the gap between "Reds" and "Whites" after the Civil War. At the end of his term (1925) he did not seek reelection, for he thought that the right wing would become more easily reconciled to the republic if he stood aside. He lost the presidential election of 1931 by two votes and that of 1937 by one vote.

by 1940 the figure was still as high as 57 percent. Paper and wooden articles were Finland's most important export commodities. By the Smallholdings Law of 1918 and by land reform in 1922, which allowed the expropriation of estates of more than 495 acres (200 hectares), an attempt was made to give tenant farmers and landless labourers their own smallholdings. More than 90,000 smallholdings were created, and since then the independent smallholders, who form the majority of the Agrarian Party (now the Centre Party), have been a major factor in Finnish politics.

POLITICAL PARTIES

During Ståhlberg's presidency (1919–25), the right-wing parties and the Agrarian Party held power by means of coalitions. The president tried determinedly to minimize the recriminations of the Civil War, and in the course of time he granted amnesty to those who had received long terms of imprisonment. At the same time, the Social Democratic Party was reorganized under the leadership of Väinö Tanner with an exclusively reformist program. When Tanner in 1926 formed a Social Democratic minority government, which granted a general amnesty, the old differences from the Civil War had been almost eliminated. Lauri Kristian Relander, the Agrarian Party's candidate, was elected president in 1925.

Through the first decade of Finnish independence the Social Democratic

Party remained the largest party in the Parliament. In the early 1920s the leftist wing of the Social Democrats separated from the party to preach Communism and succeeded in winning 27 seats in the 1922 election. It later changed its name from Socialist Labour Party to Labour Party, but this did not stop the police from arresting all of its parliamentary representatives for treason on the grounds of the party's revolutionary intent. The Communists, however, once more reorganized and worked closely with the Finnish Communist Party in the Soviet Union. In the following elections they were able to win about 20 seats in Parliament.

As a reaction to the growing Finnish Communist Party, the Lapua (Lappo) Movement emerged and in the years 1929–32 attempted to force its demands through actions against Communist newspapers, acts of terrorism against individual citizens, and mass demonstrations. These actions, which were supported by the Conservatives and many members of the Agrarian Party, were at first successful. The Communists were prevented from taking part in the 1930 election, and the 66 Social Democrats were one too few in the Parliament to prevent the passage of an anti-Communist law. This law banned the public activities of the Communist Party, forced its members underground, and stripped them of their right to vote, virtually eliminating their influence on Finnish politics. In 1931 Svinhufvud was elected president with the help of the Lapua Movement. When the Lapua Movement shortly afterward turned its activities against

LAPUA MOVEMENT

From 1929 to 1932, a fascist movement in Finland known as the Lapua Movement threatened the young state's democratic institutions and for a time dictated the policies of the government. It was named for the parish of Lapua, where a fascist group disrupted a meeting of communists late in 1929. The movement, engendered by the Great Depression and influenced by Italian fascism, espoused anticommunism and hatred of Russia. Through 1930 the movement gained wide popular support, and in 1930–31 it unofficially dominated the government, forcing it to outlaw the Finnish Communist Party, to curb radical trade unions, and to intimidate the press. The tactics of the movement included mass demonstrations and kidnapping, raids on newspaper offices, and other forms of terror. Military units of the Lapua under Gen. K.M. Wallenius assembled in February 1932 in preparation for a coup d'état. The government took up the challenge, however, and ordered the units to disarm. The rebels complied, Wallenius and others received mild prison sentences, and early in 1932 Parliament banned the Lapua Movement. Financial and popular support soon evaporated, and the movement collapsed.

the Social Democrats and tried to seize power by force in the Mäntsälä coup attempt in 1932, the president intervened and managed in a radio speech to calm the rebellion. Another failure at this time was the law on the total prohibition of alcohol, introduced in 1919. As in the United States, the law resulted in a sharp increase in organized crime and smuggling, and after a referendum in 1932 it was repealed.

THE LANGUAGE QUESTION

The 1919 constitution provided that both Finnish and Swedish should be the national languages. A younger radical generation now raised the demand for the supremacy of Finnish, and the language controversy was a bitterly contested issue during the interwar period. The position of the Swedish language was progressively weakened toward the end of the 1930s, as more Finnish speakers moved into positions of economic and cultural power. The enmity of the language issues was not healed until after the unifying effects of World War II. Following the war, the laws governing language were revised, first in 1947 and again in 1961. The constitution of 2000 guaranteed equal status for Swedish, which remains an official language of the country and a required subject in Finnish schools. For the first time the right of the Roma and Sami to maintain and preserve their cultures was also made explicit and constitutionally binding.

FOREIGN POLICY

After the recognition of Finland as a sovereign state, two problems had to be faced. The first was in connection with the eastern boundary, where influential groups wished to annex eastern Karelia. By the Treaty of Tartu (Dorpat) in 1920, however, the boundary was unchanged except in the north, where Finland acquired the harbour of Petsamo and a route to the Arctic Ocean. The other problem concerned the Åland Islands (Finnish: Ahvenanmaa), which Sweden had temporarily occupied during the Finnish Civil War. The demands of the population of the islands to be united with Sweden were firmly rejected. The League of Nations settled the question in 1921 in accordance with Finland's wishes.

Finland's main security problems resulted from the threat from the Soviet Union. An attempt to solve this by a defense alliance with Estonia, Latvia, and Poland in 1922 failed when Parliament refused to ratify the agreement, and in 1932 a Finnish-Soviet nonaggression pact was signed. Despite this, relations between the two countries did not really improve, and they remained "neighbours against their will." During the second half of the 1930s, a Finnish-Swedish defense association was planned that, among other things, would have brought about the rearming of Åland, but the Soviet Union objected to these plans, and they could not be realized.

FINLAND DURING WORLD WAR II

After Poland's defeat in the autumn of 1939, the Soviet Union, wishing to safeguard Leningrad, demanded from Finland a minor part of the Karelian Isthmus, a naval base at Hanko (Hangö), and some islands in the Gulf of Finland. When Finland rejected the demand, the Soviet Union launched an attack on November 30, 1939, beginning the Russo-Finnish War. Immediately after the attack a coalition government formed under Risto Ryti. Despite courageous resistance and a number of successful defense actions, the defense of the Karelian Isthmus broke down, and Finland had to initiate peace negotiations. By the Treaty of Moscow of March 12, 1940, Finland surrendered a large area of southeastern Finland, including the city of Viipuri (renamed Vyborg), and leased the peninsula of Hanko to the Soviet Union for 30 years.

After the Treaty of Moscow the plan for a Nordic defense union was resumed. The Soviet Union still objected, however, and the plan was thus abandoned. In December 1940 President Kyösti Kallio resigned, and Ryti was elected in his place. When the tension between Germany and the Soviet Union grew in the spring of 1941, Finland approached Germany but did not conclude a formal agreement. Nevertheless, Finland, like Sweden after Norway's capitulation, allowed the transit of German troops. When Germany attacked the Soviet Union on June 22, 1941, therefore, German troops were already on Finnish territory, and Finland was ready for war; its submarines, in fact, were operating in Soviet waters. The "War of Continuation" (1941–44) began with a successful Finnish offensive that led to the capture of large areas of eastern Karelia. Some Finns were reluctant, however, to cross the old border of 1939, and the spirit of the Winter War that had united the Finns began to weaken. From the winter of 1942–43, Germany's defeats gave rise to a growing demand for peace in Finland. After the breakthrough of the Red Army on the Karelian Isthmus in June 1944, President Ryti resigned on August 1. He was succeeded by Marshal Gustaf Mannerheim, who began negotiations for an armistice. This was signed on September 19, 1944, on condition that Finland recognize the Treaty of Moscow of 1940 and that all foreign (German) forces be evacuated. A pledge was given, moreover, to cede Petsamo; to lease an area near Porkkala, southwest of Helsinki, for a period of 50 years (in place of Hanko); and within 6 years to pay the equivalent of $300 million in goods for war reparations. In the meantime, however, the German army refused to leave the country, and, in the series of clashes that followed, it devastated great areas of northern Finland in its retreat. The final peace treaty, signed in Paris on February 10, 1947, reiterated the conditions of the armistice agreement.

MARTTI AHTISAARI

Finnish politician Martti Ahtisaari (born June 23, 1937, Viipuri, Finland [now Vyborg, Russia]) served as president of Finland from 1994 to 2000. Also a noted mediator, he was recognized for his efforts to resolve international conflicts when he was awarded the Nobel Prize for Peace in 2008.

Ahtisaari was displaced along with the rest of his family when the city of Viipuri, Finland, was ceded to the Soviet Union in 1940 after the Russo-Finnish War. The family moved first to Kuopio in south-central Finland and later northwest to Oulu. Ahtisaari graduated from the University of Oulu in 1959 and in the early 1960s worked in Pakistan on an educational project for the Swedish Agency for International Development. He returned to Finland and joined the Foreign Affairs Ministry in 1965; eight years later he was appointed ambassador to Tanzania, a post he held until 1976. He was also an envoy (1975–76) to Zambia, Somalia, and Mozambique. Ahtisaari honed his diplomatic skills as the United Nations (UN) commissioner for Namibia (1977–81), a country torn by internal strife. He continued to represent Namibia during the 1980s while serving in several Finnish Foreign Ministry posts, and he led the UN team that supervised Namibia's transition to independence (1989–90). Ahtisaari was a key figure in the Bosnia and Herzegovina peace talks (1992–93).

In 1994 Ahtisaari ran for the Finnish presidency, and his vision of Finland as an active participant in international affairs helped him win the election. He urged his country's entry into the European Union (EU), and for the first half of 1999, Finland assumed the EU's rotating presidency. In June of that year, Ahtisaari used his diplomatic skills to help end the conflict in Kosovo as he and Russian envoy Viktor Chernomyrdin persuaded Pres. Slobodan Milosevic of Yugoslavia to accept a peace plan as a condition of stopping punitive bombings by the North Atlantic Treaty Organization (NATO). Often encountering resistance from Finland's Parliament, which preferred a more cautious foreign policy, as well as from his party, the Social Democrats, Ahtisaari did not run for reelection in 2000.

After leaving office, Ahtisaari founded the Crisis Management Initiative (CMI) and was selected for a number of diplomatic roles, including acting as an arms inspector in Northern Ireland, heading a UN fact-finding mission into an Israeli army operation in Jenin in the West Bank, and mediating the conflict between the government of Indonesia and the separatist Free Aceh Movement. In 2005 he was named the UN special envoy for the future status of Kosovo, and in 2007 Ahtisaari issued a proposal—accepted by Kosovo's majority Albanian population but rejected by Serbia—that called for UN-administered independence for Kosovo along with self-governance for the region's Serb-dominated municipalities. In 2008 he served as a mediator between Sunni and Shīʿite Muslims in Iraq.

In addition to his Nobel honour, Ahtisaari received the J. William Fulbright Prize for International Understanding in 2000 and the UNESCO Félix Houphouët-Boigny Peace Prize in 2008.

THE POSTWAR PERIOD

After the armistice in 1944 a coalition government was formed under the leadership of Juho Kusti Paasikivi. When conditions had been stabilized, Mannerheim resigned, and Paasikivi was elected president in his place in 1946. In 1956 the leader of the Agrarian Party, Urho Kekkonen, who acted as prime minister a number of times during the period from 1950 to 1956, was elected president. He was reelected three times to the office, with an extension of his third term by the Parliament. When he resigned in 1981 because of ill health, he was succeeded by the Social Democrat Mauno Koivisto, who was reelected in 1988. Koivisto was in turn succeeded in 1994 by another Social Democrat, Martti Ahtisaari.

FOREIGN POLICY

Under the leadership of Paasikivi and Kekkonen, relations with the Soviet Union were stabilized by a consistently friendly policy on the part of Finland. A concrete expression of the new foreign policy—designated the Paasikivi-Kekkonen line—was the Agreement of Friendship, Cooperation, and Mutual Assistance concluded between Finland and the Soviet Union in 1948 and extended in 1955, 1970, and 1983. The agreement included a mutual defense provision and prohibited Finland from joining any organization considered hostile to the U.S.S.R. After

war reparations had been paid in full, trade with the Soviet Union continued, rising to more than 25 percent of Finland's total during the 1980s. Further signs of the détente were evident when the Soviet Union returned its base at Porkkala in 1955.

Relations with the Soviet Union, however, were not entirely without complications. After the elections of 1958, a coalition government under the leadership of the Social Democrat Karl August Fagerholm was formed, in which certain members considered anti-Soviet were included. The Soviet Union responded by recalling its ambassador and canceling credits and orders in Finland. When the Finnish government was reconstructed, relations were again stabilized. During the autumn of 1961, when international relations were severely strained because of the Berlin crisis, the Soviet Union requested consultations in accordance with the 1948 agreement. President Kekkonen succeeded in solving the "Note Crisis" by inducing the Soviet Union to abandon its request. In 1985 the Soviets warned that a split in the Finnish Communist Party between the nationalist-reformist majority and the pro-Moscow minority would jeopardize Soviet-Finnish relations, but the split occurred in 1986 without incident.

Following the demise of the Soviet Union in 1991, Finland moved to end the old mutual defense agreement. A new agreement was reached with Russia in 1992, in which the two countries simply pledged to settle disputes between them peacefully. Finland, now freed from any restrictions, applied for membership to the European Community (from 1993 the European Union [EU]), which it joined in 1995. In 1999 it adopted the euro, the common currency of the EU, phasing out its markka by 2002. Despite shifting much of its foreign trade to EU nations, Finland's relationship with Russia remained pivotal if precarious.

NORDIC COOPERATION

Finland became a member of the United Nations and of the Nordic Council in 1955. Nordic cooperation has led to many legislative and political similarities between Finland, Denmark, Iceland, Norway, and Sweden. These include free movement across the borders of these five countries, the gradual development of a common and free labour market, and other similar measures in the fields of politics, economics, and culture. In 1986 Finland became a full member of the European Free Trade Association. It left that organization in 1995 when it became a member of the EU. Tensions arose within the country when its Baltic Sea neighbours joined the North Atlantic Treaty Organization (NATO) in 1999 (Poland) and 2004 (Estonia, Latvia, and Lithuania). Finland initially resisted pressure from the other Nordic countries to join the international ban on antipersonnel land mines but then declared its intention to join by 2012.

DOMESTIC AFFAIRS

During the early postwar years, Finland's domestic affairs were marked by economic difficulties. After World War II the country was left with the task of absorbing about 300,000 refugees from the areas ceded to the Soviet Union and at the same time paying war reparations. Despite these obstacles, Finland quickly recovered. The war reparations brought about rapid expansion in the metal and shipbuilding industries, and the timber trade soon resumed exporting and quickly exceeded its prewar level. The rebuilding and colonization required to resettle the refugees, however, were such a drain on the country's economic resources that inflation could not be avoided; as a result Finland had to devalue its currency on a number of occasions.

After the armistice, the new Finnish Communist Party held a strong position, which it retained in the subsequent government. When in the spring of 1948 it was alleged that the party had planned a coup, Parliament forced the Communist minister of the interior to resign. After the parliamentary elections in the autumn of 1948, a Social Democratic government came to power under the leadership of Fagerholm. Governments changed rapidly and consisted of various party coalitions during the 1950s, in most cases under the leadership of the Agrarian Party or the Social Democrats. During this period, however, both the Conservative

National Coalition Party and the leftist Finnish People's Democratic League, which included the Finnish Communist Party, were excluded from the government.

Forming and keeping a government in Finland is very difficult because of the proliferation of political parties; no one party, and often no party group, can command a majority in Parliament. As a consequence, there have been many nonpolitical cabinets composed of civil servants appointed by the president. With continuing economic growth and because of internal disputes, Communist Party influence diminished after the 1970s, and after the party's split in the mid-1980s the Communists suffered severe losses in the 1987 election. The Conservatives gained a long-desired victory, and, with a compromise aided by President Koivisto, the Social Democrats and Conservatives, together with some smaller parties, formed a coalition government under Conservative Prime Minister Harri Holkeri. This allowed the Conservatives to return to the cabinet after more than 20 years and forced the Centre Party into opposition for the first time since independence. The Conservative–Social Democratic coalition did not satisfy the traditional constituencies of the two parties, however, and in 1991 the Centre Party reemerged as the largest party.

A new cabinet, formed by major nonsocialist parties and with the Centre's Esko Aho as prime minister, immediately faced Finland's worst peacetime economic recession. During the early 1990s production dropped sharply and unemployment skyrocketed, largely because trade with Russia had shrunk to a fraction of the Soviet-era level. There was also a general policy of privatizing state-owned assets throughout the 1990s, which promoted rationalization in many industries. Recovery came slowly, as export markets shifted toward the EU countries. The government also tried to cut expenditures, notably on social programs. The public expressed its displeasure with the slow pace of recovery by again ousting the Centre from the government in the elections of 1995. Social Democrat Paavo Lipponen formed a cabinet from a broad-based coalition that included, for the first time, members of the environmentalist Green Union.

Economic recovery continued into the 21st century, as did the generally positive benefits of EU membership. Unemployment was brought under control, perhaps in part because of the tremendous success of the high-tech industry, notably the manufacturing of mobile telephones. Food prices and interest rates dropped and even agriculture was not as severely affected as some economists had feared.

Finland's integration into Europe also continued on the political front, as the country assumed the revolving EU presidency at the end of the 1990s. The new constitution, adopted in 2000, reflected both changing concepts

TARJA HALONEN

Finnish politician Tarja Halonen (born December 24, 1943, Helsinki, Finland) was the first woman to be elected president of Finland. She held that office from 2000 to 2012.

As a student at the University of Helsinki, Halonen served (1969–70) as social affairs secretary and general secretary of the National Union of Finnish Students. After earning a degree in law in 1970, she began her professional career as an attorney with the Central Organization of Finnish Trade Unions. Halonen then entered politics, serving in 1974–75 as parliamentary secretary to Prime Minister Kalevi Sorsa. Halonen later became chair of the Finnish National Organization for Sexual Equality. From 1977 to 1996 she was a member of the Helsinki City Council, and in 1979 she was elected to parliament as a candidate of the Social Democratic Party (SDP). In parliament Halonen broadened her experience in domestic and international politics by holding a number of cabinet posts. Before her

Finnish President Tarja Halonen. Frederick Florin/AFP/Getty Images

appointment as foreign affairs minister in 1995, she served as minister of social affairs and health (1987–90), minister for Nordic cooperation (1989–91), and minister of justice (1990–91). In 2000 she was nominated as the SDP candidate for president. After topping the poll in the first round of balloting and winning the required 50 percent threshold to avoid a runoff, she narrowly defeated former prime minister Esko Aho of the Centre Party (51.6 percent to 48.4 percent) on February 6, 2000.

On March 1, 2000, the day of Halonen's inauguration as president, a new constitution for Finland went into effect that reduced the powers of the president and emphasized the position of parliament as the strongest body in the government. The president, however, retained considerable powers in foreign policy, the area of Halonen's greatest strength. As president, Halonen continued Finland's pro-European Union policies, but she opposed the idea of Finnish membership in NATO. She won reelection in 2006 when she narrowly defeated Sauli Niinistö of the National Coalition Party in the second round of balloting. In 2010 Halonen was appointed cochair of the UN Secretary-General's High-level Panel on Global Sustainability, which presented its recommendations two years later. Barred by law from seeking a third term as president, Halonen left office in 2012 and was succeeded by Niinistö.

of sovereignty in light of Finland's membership in the EU and the Finns' cautious approach to internationalization. In 2000 Finland also elected its first female president, Tarja Halonen of the Social Democratic Party. When Anneli Jäätteenmäki, of the Centre Party, was appointed prime minister in April 2003, Finland became the first European country with women as both president and prime minister. However, after Jäätteenmäki was accused of having shared with the press confidential information on Finland's policy toward Iraq, Matti Vanhanen replaced her as prime minister in June. Vanhanen retained his position when the Centre Party won a narrow victory in the 2007 parliamentary elections. The National Coalition Party finished a close second, while the Social Democrats suffered significant losses.

In 2009 a funding scandal tarnished the reputation and popularity of the Centre Party, and Vanhanen was pressured to step down. After first relinquishing the party leadership, he resigned as prime minister in June 2010 and was replaced by Mari Kiviniemi, who had already succeeded him as Centre Party leader. She became the second woman to hold the post of Finnish prime minister. In parliamentary elections in April 2011 the Centre Party dropped from 51 to 35 seats, tumbling to fourth place and out of the government. Its former coalition partner, the National Coalition Party, won the election by capturing 44 seats (a drop of six seats from the 2007 election) but faced the prospect of coalition rule with one of the main opposition parties—either the Social Democrats, who finished second with 42 seats, or the anti-immigrant, "euro-skeptical" True Finn Party, which proved to be the election's biggest surprise as it vaulted from the five seats it won in the 2007 election to 39 seats and third place in 2011.

At the centre of True Finn policy was strong opposition to the EU's bailout of countries such as Greece, Ireland, and Portugal, which were hard-hit by the euro-zone debt crisis that began in 2009. Yet in the first round of voting in January 2012 to replace Halonen (who was constitutionally limited to two terms as president), the True Finn candidate, Timo Soini, and the similarly "euro-skeptical" Centre Party candidate, Paavo Vayrynen, finished fourth and third, respectively. In the runoff election held in February, the National Coalition Party's pro-EU candidate, Sauli Niinistö, a former finance minister, became the first conservative to serve as Finland's head of state in decades. He won the office by defeating the country's first openly gay candidate for the presidency, Pekka Haavisto, of the Green Party.

CHAPTER 11

SWEDEN: THE LAND AND ITS PEOPLE

Sweden is located on the Scandinavian Peninsula in northern Europe. The name Sweden was derived from the Svear, or Suiones, a people mentioned as early as 98 CE by the Roman author Tacitus. The country's ancient name was Svithiod. Sweden has a 1,000-year-long continuous

The national flag of Sweden. Encyclopædia Britannica, Inc.

Political map of Sweden. Encyclopædia Britannica, Inc.

Stockholm. Neil Beer/Getty Images

history as a sovereign state, but its territorial expanse changed often until 1809. Stockholm has been the permanent capital since 1523. Swedish society is ethnically and religiously very homogeneous, although recent immigration has created some social diversity.

Sweden occupies the greater part of the Scandinavian Peninsula, which it shares with Norway. The land slopes gently from the high mountains along the Norwegian frontier eastward to the Baltic Sea. Geologically, it is one of the oldest and most stable parts of the Earth's crust. Its surface formations and soils were altered by the receding glaciers of the Pleistocene Epoch (about 2,600,000 to 11,700 years ago). Lakes dot the fairly flat landscape, and thousands of islands form archipelagoes along more than 1,300 miles (2,100 km) of jagged, rocky coastline. Like all of northwestern Europe, Sweden has a generally favourable climate relative to its northerly latitude owing to moderate southwesterly winds and the warm North Atlantic Current.

Finland lies to the northeast of Sweden; a long coastline forms the country's eastern border, extending along the Gulf of Bothnia and the Baltic Sea; a narrow strait, known as the Sound (Öresund), separates Sweden from Denmark in the south; a shorter coastline along the Skagerrak and Kattegat straits forms Sweden's border to the southwest; and Norway lies to the west. Sweden extends some 1,000 miles (1,600 km) to the north and south and 310 miles (500 km) to the east and west.

The country is traditionally divided into three regions: to the north is Norrland, the vast mountain and forest region; in central Sweden is Svealand, an expanse of lowland in the east and highland in the west; and in the south is Götaland, which includes the Småland highlands and, at the southern extremity, the small but rich plains of Skåne. In the far north, the region of Lappland overlaps Norrland and northern Finland.

RELIEF

Norrland is the largest and most sparsely populated of the regions, covering some three-fifths of the country. The region features an undulating surface of rounded hills and mountains, large lakes, and extensive river valleys. To the west lie the Kölen (Kjølen; Scandinavian) Mountains, through which runs the border demarcating Sweden and Norway. This range is characterized by numerous glaciers, the southernmost of which is on Helags Mountain (Helagsfjället), near the Norwegian border. At the region's far northern edge, north of the Arctic Circle, are Sweden's highest peaks: Mount Kebne (Kebnekaise), which is 6,926 feet (2,111 metres) in elevation, and Mount Sarek (Sarektjåkkå), which rises 6,854 feet (2,089 metres), in the magnificent Sarek National Park.

The interior of southern Sweden, Småland, is a wooded upland with elevations of 980 to 1,300 feet (300 to 400 metres). A region of poor and stony soils, Småland has been cultivated through the ages with some difficulty, as evidenced by the enormous mounds of stone cleared from the land. More recently the area has been characterized by flourishing small factories.

Except for a stretch of scenic "high coast," the Bothnian coastal plain is low-lying and stretches from Norrland into Svealand. Most of the fairly level surface of eastern Svealand and northern Götaland was pressed below sea level by glaciers, leaving a landscape of fragmented bedrock, fertile clayey plains, numerous lakes, and sandy ridges. Today these are intermingled with mixed forests and farmland. Sweden's landscape changes from the hills of Småland to the fertile plains of Skåne, which is physiographically and economically more similar to Denmark than to the rest of Sweden. This is Sweden's oldest settled and most

LAKE VÄNER

With an area of 2,181 square miles (5,650 square km), Lake Väner (Swedish: Vänern) is the largest lake in Sweden. It is located in the southwestern part of the country. Väner is about 90 miles (145 km) long and as much as 348 feet (106 metres) deep, and its surface lies 144 feet (44 metres) above sea level. The lake is fed by numerous rivers (the largest being the Klar), and the lake itself drains westward into the Kattegat (strait) via the Göta River, which is a major source of hydroelectric power. Väner is surrounded by rocky, wooded shores except on the south, where the coast is low and conducive to farming. The lake forms a major link in the Göta Canal, a waterway that crosses Sweden from Gothenburg on Sweden's west coast to Stockholm on the east coast. Improvements on the Trollhätte Canal permit seagoing craft entering from the Kattegat to serve such lake ports as Karlstad, Lidköping, Vänersborg, Kristinehamn, Åmal, Säffle, and Mariestad. These towns have important industries, such as tanneries, ironworks, and paper mills. Väner is the third largest lake in Europe, after Ladoga and Onega (both in Russia).

densely populated agricultural area.

The Swedish coastline is typically rocky, with hundreds of small, sometimes wooded islands. Ground by glacial ice in the same direction, they have a common rounded shape. This type of coast, known as skärgård, is found in both the east and the west, especially around Stockholm and Gothenburg. Off the southern coast in the Baltic, the large, flat islands of Öland and Gotland are outcropping layers of sandstone and limestone.

DRAINAGE

The country's chief rivers originate in the mountains of Norrland, mostly flowing southeastward with many falls and rapids and emptying into the Gulf of Bothnia or the Baltic Sea. The longest, however, is the Klar-Göta River, which rises in Norway and flows 447 miles (719 km), reaching Lake Väner (Vänern) and continuing southward out of the lake's southern end to the North Sea; along its southernmost course are the famous falls of Trollhättan. The Muonio and Torne rivers form the

Log pond on Dal River, Sweden. Bernard Wolf/DPI

frontier with Finland, and in the south the Dal River marks the transition to Svealand. The rivers, except in the far north, where they are protected, are sources of hydroelectric power.

In Svealand are Sweden's largest lakes, including Lakes Väner, 2,181 square miles (5,650 square km); Vätter (Vättern), 738 square miles (1,911 square km); and Mälar (Mälaren), 440 square miles (1,139 square km). The shores of Lakes Siljan and Storsjön and the river valleys support agriculture.

SOILS

The dominant soil of Sweden is till, formed under glacial ice. Till that comes from the archaic bedrock of granites and gneisses forms a poor soil, and forestry and polluted (acid) rain add to its acidification. On the other hand, small areas of clayey till from younger sedimentary limestone, scattered mainly in southern Sweden, form brown earth, providing agricultural soils of high fertility. In addition, vast areas of central Sweden are covered by heavy and fertile sea-bottom clays raised out of the sea by postglacial land uplift. One-fifth of the country, especially in rainy southwestern Sweden and the cold far north, is covered by marshland and peat.

CLIMATE

About 15 percent of the country lies within the Arctic Circle. From about late May until mid-July, sunlight lasts around the clock north of the Arctic Circle, but, even as far south as Stockholm, the nights during this period have only a few hours of semidarkness. In mid-December, on the other hand, Stockholm experiences only about 5.5 hours of daylight; in areas as far north as Lappland, there are nearly 20 hours of total darkness relieved by a mere 4 hours of twilight.

Considering its northerly geographic location (at the latitude of parts of Greenland and Siberia), Sweden enjoys a favourable climate. From the southwest, Atlantic low-pressure winds blow in air warmed by the North Atlantic Current and make the weather mild but changeable. Another type of influence comes from continental high pressures to the east. These create sunny weather, which is hot in summer and cold in winter. The interaction between the Atlantic and continental influences causes periodic shifts in climate.

The north-to-south extension of the country and the higher elevation of the northern part results in great regional differences in winter climate. The northern interior receives heavy snowfall for up to eight months of the year and has severe temperatures that drop as low as –22 to –40 °F (–30 to –40 °C). The average January temperature in Haparanda at the head of the Gulf of Bothnia is 10 °F (–12 °C). Sea ice covers the Gulf of Bothnia from November to May.

In southern Sweden winters vary more from year to year than in the north; snowfall is irregular, and average January temperatures range between 23 and 32 °F (-5 and 0 °C). Coastal waters seldom freeze.

Summer temperatures vary far less, although summer is much shorter in the north. In terms of average daily temperature, "spring" arrives in Skåne during February but not until late May in northernmost Norrland; then it may come virtually overnight. The mean July temperature in Haparanda is 59 °F (15 °C), and in Malmö 63 °F (17 °C).

Late summer and autumn are the rainiest seasons, but precipitation falls throughout the year. Annual precipitation averages about 24 inches (600 mm).

PLANT AND ANIMAL LIFE

Most of Sweden is dominated by forests of fir, pine, and birch. Southern Sweden has more mixed forests, and in the far south deciduous trees such as beech, oak, linden, ash, elm, and maple are common. The forests are rich in berries, lingonberries and blueberries among them, and mushrooms. In Sweden anyone is entitled to hike through the forests and fields and pick berries and mushrooms.

In the high mountains coniferous trees give way to mountain birches, which extend up to the tree line at an elevation of 1,600 to 2,900 feet (480 to 880 metres). The treeless mountains with their heaths, marshes, and boulder fields have Alpine flora. Dwarf birch and willows are typical.

Moose (Alces alces) *with fully developed antlers.* Tom & Pat Leeson—The National Audubon Society Collection/Photo Researchers

Owing to their limestone bedrock and mild climate, Gotland and Öland have a special flora that includes many orchids.

Bears and lynx still inhabit the northern forests, while wolves are making a comeback, having become almost completely extinct in the 20th century. Throughout the country are large numbers of moose, roe deer, foxes, and hares. The moose is a great prize for hunters, but it also constitutes a traffic hazard. Hunting and fishing are closely regulated, and many species of animals are fully protected. Large herds of domesticated reindeer owned by Sami (Lapps) graze the northern mountains and forests.

Winter birdlife is dominated by a few species, but summer brings large numbers of migratory birds from southern Europe and Africa, as, for example, cranes and wild geese. Sweden has a rich variety of aquatic animal life, but environmental pollution has taken its toll. This applies significantly to the Baltic seal. Fish species include the cod and mackerel of the deep, salty Atlantic and the salmon and pike found in the far less saline Baltic and in lakes and rivers. Atlantic herring and its smaller relative, the Baltic herring, are traditional staple foods.

CONSERVATION

Sweden has been in the vanguard of countries seeking to preserve the natural environment. It was the first European country to establish a national park (Sarek National Park was established in 1909), thereby preserving part of Europe's last wilderness. The first Nature Conservancy Act was adopted in 1909, and in 1969 a modern environmental protection act was passed. Since then tens of thousands of square miles have been set aside as national parks and nature reserves. Serious environmental problems persist nevertheless. About one-fifth of the lakes in Sweden have been damaged by acidification, and groundwater, too, is threatened. A chief cause is sulfur fallout (i.e., contamination by what is commonly known as acid rain); most of the sulfur is discharged into the atmosphere by industrial facilities in nearby countries. Pollution in the Baltic Sea and the coastal waters of the Kattegat and Skagerrak also is considered severe.

ETHNIC GROUPS

Although different groups of immigrants have influenced Swedish culture through the centuries, the population has been unusually homogeneous in ethnic stock, language, and religion. It is only since World War II that notable change has occurred in the ethnic pattern. From 1970 to the early 1990s, net immigration accounted for about three-fourths of the population growth. By far, most of the immigrants have come from the neighbouring Nordic countries, with which Sweden shares a common labour market. Immigration from other countries is regulated, but such regulation is relaxed under certain circumstances. Today nearly one in five Swedes has at least one parent who was not born in Sweden.

Sweden has two minority groups of indigenous inhabitants: the Finnish-speaking people of the northeast along the Finnish border, and the Sami (Lapp) population of about 15,000 scattered throughout the northern Swedish interior. Once a hunting and fishing people, the latter group developed a reindeer-herding system that they still operate. Most of the Sami in Sweden have other occupations as well.

LANGUAGES

Swedish, the national language of Sweden and the mother tongue of approximately nine-tenths of the population, is a Nordic language. It belongs to

SAREK NATIONAL PARK

The first national park established in Europe was Sweden's Sarek (also spelled Sarjek) National Park, created in 1909. The park, located in Norrbotten *län* (county) in northwestern Sweden, encompasses most of the Sarek mountain range. It was established with the setting aside of an area of 746 square miles (1,931 square km), and it adjoins two other national parks—Stora Sjöfallet on the north and Padjelanta on the west. The almost inaccessible region, characterized by high peaks, deep valleys, wide plateaus, and glaciers, is drained by Rapa River, which empties into Lake Laitaure. The peaks of several mountains rise above 6,500 feet (2,000 metres). The highest, Mount Sarek (6,854 feet [2,089 metres]), is the second highest in Sweden, after Mount Kebne. Sarek is rich in vegetation and is the habitat of varied wildlife, including bears, wolves, wolverines, and lynxes.

the North Germanic (Scandinavian) subgroup of the Germanic languages and is closely related to the Danish, Norwegian, Icelandic, and Faeroese languages. It has been influenced at times by German, but it has also borrowed some words and syntax from French, English, and Finnish. A common standard language (*rikssvenska*) has been in use more than 100 years. The traditionally varying dialects of the provinces, although homogenized rapidly through the influences of education and the mass media, are still widely spoken. Swedish is also spoken by about 300,000 Finland-Swedes. Swedish law recognizes Sami and Finnish (both of which belong to the Uralic language group), as well as Meänkieli (the Finnish of the Torne Valley), Romani, and Yiddish as national minority languages, along with sign language. About 200 languages are now spoken in Sweden, owing to immigrants and refugees.

RELIGION

Prehistoric archaeological artifacts and sites—including graves and rock carvings—give an indication of the ancient system of religious beliefs practiced in Sweden during the pre-Christian era. The sun and seasons figured largely, in tandem with fertility rites meant to ensure good harvests. These practices were informed by a highly developed mythic cycle, describing a distinctive cosmology and the deeds of the Old Norse gods, giants, and demons. Important gods included Odin, Thor, Freyr, and Freyja. Great sacrificial rites, thought to have taken place every eight years at Old Uppsala, were described by the author Adam of Bremen in the 11th century.

Sweden adopted Christianity in the 11th century, and for nearly 500 years Roman Catholicism was the preeminent

SAMI

The Sami (also spelled Saami or Same) people speak the Sami language and inhabit Lapland and adjacent areas of northern Norway, Sweden, and Finland, as well as the Kola Peninsula of Russia. The Sami people are also called Lapp.

The three Sami languages, which are mutually unintelligible, are sometimes considered dialects of one language. They belong to the Finno-Ugric branch of the Uralic family. Almost all Sami are now bilingual, and many no longer even speak their native language.

The Sami are the descendants of nomadic peoples who had inhabited northern Scandinavia for thousands of years. When the Finns entered Finland, beginning about 100 CE, Sami settlements were probably dispersed over the whole of that country; today they are confined to its northern extremity. In Sweden and Norway they have similarly been pushed north. The origin of the Sami is obscure; some scholars include them among the Paleo-Siberian peoples; others maintain that they were alpine and came from central Europe.

Reindeer herding was the basis of the Sami economy until very recently. Although the Sami hunted reindeer from the earliest times and kept them in small numbers as pack and decoy animals, full-scale nomadism with large herds began only a few centuries ago. The reindeer-herding Sami lived in tents or turf huts and migrated with their herds in units of five or six families, supplementing their diet along the way by hunting and fishing.

Nomadism, however, has virtually disappeared; the remaining herders now accompany their reindeer alone while their families reside in permanent modern housing. While the reindeer of a unit are herded communally, each animal is individually owned. Many Norwegian Sami are coastal fishermen, and those in other areas depend for their livelihoods on farming, forestry, freshwater fishing, and mining or on government, industrial, and commercial employment in cities and towns. Sami increasingly participate in the Scandinavian professional, cultural, and academic world.

The Skolt Sami of Finland (and perhaps also the Russian Sami) belong to the Russian Orthodox faith; most others are Lutheran. The shaman was important in non-Christian Sami society, and some shamanistic healing rites are still performed. There is, at least in most of the northern Sami communities, a strong evangelical congregationalism (Laestadianism), in which local congregations are virtually autonomous.

The Scandinavian countries periodically tried to assimilate the Sami, and the use of the Sami languages in schools and public life was long forbidden. In the second half of the 20th century, however, attention was drawn to the problems of the Sami minority, which became more assertive in efforts to maintain its traditional society and culture through the use of Sami in schools and the protection of reindeer pastures. In each country there are Sami political and cultural societies, and there are a few Sami newspapers and radio programs.

religion. Sweden was the home to Saint Bridget, founder of the Brigittine convent at Vadstena. As the first waves of the Protestant Reformation swept Europe in the mid-1500s, Lutheranism took hold in Sweden, and it remained dominant through the 20th century. The Evangelical Lutheran Church of Sweden was the official state church until 2000; about four-fifths of the population remain members of this church. Since the late 1800s a number of independent churches have emerged; however, their members can also belong to the Church of Sweden. Immigration has brought a steady increase to the membership of the Roman Catholic, Greek Orthodox, and Islamic religions. Judaism is the country's oldest global non-Christian religion, practiced in Sweden since 1776. After Christianity, Islam is the largest religion in Sweden, with about 100,000 active practitioners at the turn of the 21st century, although the number of Swedes of Muslim heritage was nearly three times that number.

Stockholm at dusk. © Digital Vision/Getty Images

STOCKHOLM

Stockholm, the capital and largest city of Sweden, is located at the junction of Lake Mälar (Mälaren) and Salt Bay (Saltsjön), an arm of the Baltic Sea, opposite the Gulf of Finland. The city is built upon numerous islands as well as the mainland of Uppland and Södermanland. By virtue of its location, Stockholm is regarded as one of the most beautiful capital cities in the world.

Stockholm was first mentioned as a town in 1252 and was largely built by the Swedish ruler Birger Jarl. The city came to be officially regarded as the Swedish capital in 1436. Stockholm developed rapidly in the mid-17th century as Sweden temporarily became a great power. By the 18th century, Stockholm had become the cultural centre of Sweden; many of its literary societies and scientific academies date from this time.

Encyclopædia Britannica, Inc.

A new period of development began with industrialization in the 19th century. During this time redevelopment took place in the medieval city nucleus, buildings were reconstructed, boulevards, avenues, and parks were laid out, and many of the city's present-day schools, museums, libraries, and hospitals were built. Many suburbs and satellite towns have subsequently developed.

The original nucleus of the city is the "city between the bridges"—Gamla Stan (Old Town), consisting of Stads Island, Helgeands Island, and Riddar Island. The buildings in this area are mainly from the 16th and 17th centuries. This well-preserved city nucleus, with the original network of streets and many of its buildings dating from the Middle Ages, is legally protected from change. Stads Island contains the Royal Palace; Storkyrkan, also called the Cathedral, or Church, of St. Nicolas; the German Church; the House of Lords; the government offices; the Stock Exchange; and a number of other notable buildings. Riddar Island is dominated by the Riddarholm Church. The House of Parliament and the National Bank are on Helgeands Island.

These islands are connected by old bridges and modern overpasses to city districts occupying the mainland of Uppland to the north and that of Södermanland to the south. The chief northern districts are Norrmalm, Vasastaden, Östermalm, Kungsholmen, and Stadshagen. Of these, Norrmalm is a modern shopping, business, and financial centre, while Kungsholmen has the City Hall and other municipal buildings. East of Gamla Stan lies the island of Djurgården, a cultural-recreational area that has several museums, including the Vasa Museum, which houses a salvaged Swedish warship dating from 1628.

Stockholm is Sweden's leading industrial area. Its major industries include metal and machine manufacturing, paper and printing, foodstuffs, and chemicals. It is also the country's chief wholesale and retail centre and serves as the headquarters of many banks and insurance companies. Stockholm is also the second largest port in Sweden (Göteborg being the first). The national government's many offices are a major employer in the city, as are various educational, scientific, and cultural institutions.

Stockholm is the chief educational centre in Sweden and is home to Stockholm University (1877), the Royal Institute of Technology (1827), and the Caroline Medical Institute. The city's leading cultural institutions include the Royal Theatre (the opera), the Concert Association (Stockholm Philharmonic Orchestra), and the Royal Dramatic Theatre. In 1912 Stockholm hosted the Olympic Games.

SETTLEMENT PATTERNS

The majority of Sweden's population, small in relation to its land area, lives in the southern third of the country, and most of these people live in towns.

Götaland and Svealand, the two southernmost of Sweden's traditional regions, take their names from small prehistoric clans who inhabited central Sweden. The Svear and the Götar (believed by some scholars to be the original Goths) were united into one state about 1000 CE. The Götar lived in Östergötland, Västergötland, and Småland, and the Svear around Lake Mälar. Certain differences remain in the dialects spoken in these two regions. Skåne and the surrounding regions were taken from the Danish crown in the 17th century, and Skåne is still looked upon as a special region in both language and customs, noted for its rich food and hospitality. The vast Norrland was colonized later by Swedes. It is far less populated than the southern and central regions.

Through the course of the 19th century, land reforms gradually dissolved village communities, consolidated farmland, divided commons, and dispersed farms. The reforms favoured modernization of agriculture. Nucleated villages were preserved in Dalarna and on the island of Öland, and a few surviving traditional farm buildings serve as representations of the rural heritage. Settlements grew up along seacoasts and lakeshores, and inland towns arose as markets in old agricultural and mining areas. In the country and in suburban communities, houses are often painted a traditional red with paint made from material produced since the 1700s at the copper mine in Falun. Norrland is thinly populated, with approximately three inhabitants per square kilometre, as compared with about 250 in Stockholm.

Numerous vacation homes dot the coasts and mountains, and castles and manors from the 16th–18th century are located mostly in the far south and around Lake Mälar.

Urban growth in Sweden has followed industrialization. Location of new urban sites was strongly influenced by the development of the railway network and by the exploitation of the natural resources of northern Sweden. At present about 80 percent of the population lives in urban centres. Until 1870 no more than 10 percent of the population was urban. The vast majority of the people live in the Stockholm-Gothenburg-Malmö triangle and along the coast north of Stockholm. In Sweden the average living space is relatively large.

DEMOGRAPHIC TRENDS

The period of rapid economic growth after World War II caused dramatic migration from the countryside and smaller towns throughout Sweden to the large urban centres. Numerous communities suffered depopulation as young and educated people left to improve their lives. This trend brought countermeasures from the state, including subsidies for enterprises in northern and southeastern Sweden and a transfer of state agencies from Stockholm to outlying centres.

CHAPTER 12

THE SWEDISH ECONOMY

Sweden's per capita gross national product (GNP) is among the highest in the world, but so are its taxes. Most enterprises are privately owned and market-oriented, but when transfer payments—such as pensions, sick pay, and child allowances—are included, roughly three-fifths of gross domestic product (GDP) passes through the public sector. Education, health care, and child care costs are primarily met by taxation. Government involvement in the distribution of national income, however, diminished over the last two decades of the 20th century.

With the value of exports amounting to about one-third of its GDP, Sweden is highly dependent on free international trade to maintain its living standard. In 1991 Sweden attached its currency, the krona, to the ecu (European currency unit, replaced in 1999 by the euro), but in 1992 Sweden abandoned its peg to the ecu and allowed the krona valuation to float. Sweden's currency remained independent even after the country became a full member of the European Union (EU) in 1995. In 1999 an executive board of Sweden's Riksbank was established to set monetary policy and sustain price stability. Sweden also has to cope with problems of competitiveness that have caused industry to invest much more abroad than at home. Most of Sweden's large industrial companies are transnational, and some employ more people abroad than in Sweden, where production costs are high.

Farmland stretches along the shore of Lake Vättern in the Götaland region of southern Sweden. Steve Vidler/Leo de Wys Inc.

AGRICULTURE, FORESTRY, AND FISHING

The growing season in Sweden ranges from about 240 days in the south to 120 days in the north. Less than one-tenth of Sweden's land area is under cultivation. Most arable land is found in southern Sweden, but there are arable parcels up to the Arctic Circle. Wheat, barley, sugar beets, oilseeds, potatoes, and staple vegetables dominate in the south, while in the north hay and potatoes are the main crops. In Sweden as a whole, animal agriculture

is more significant than cereal farming. Dairy cows are important in all parts of the country, while pig and poultry raising are concentrated in the extreme south. The yields of Swedish farms are among the highest in the world. Environmental problems, however, have made it necessary to reduce the use of fertilizers.

About half of Swedish forestland is privately owned, about one-fourth company-owned, and about one-fourth publicly owned. Forest work used to be complementary winter employment for small farmers using their horses; today forestry is carried on year-round by a small workforce and large, modern machinery. Nearly three-fourths of all Swedish farms have timberland. The average regrowth and harvest time for spruce and pine is about 50 years in the south and roughly 140 years in the north. Since the late 19th century, forestry in Sweden has been conducted on a sustained-yield basis, which establishes a ratio between cutting and new growth that is strictly enforced. Modern large-scale forestry methods have been subject to severe criticism, and major reforms were implemented in the 1990s. A thorough mapping and inventory of key woodland habitats was undertaken in the mid-1990s to identify areas with high biodiversity values.

Fishing occupies a small sector of the Swedish economy. Through international agreements, Sweden has lost some of its traditional fishing areas in the North Sea. Herring, cod, plaice, mackerel, and salmon are fished, as well as shrimp and lobster. Gothenburg is the leading fishing harbour and fish market.

RESOURCES AND POWER

Wood, metallic ores, and waterpower constitute the historical basis for Sweden's industrial economy. The country is lacking in fossil fuels and must rely on imports for its needs. Hydroelectric power is used to a high degree but provides only about half of the electric energy needed; most of the rest is derived from nuclear power.

Sweden is well endowed with mineral resources. The huge state-owned iron ore deposits at Kiruna in Lappland were opened to export at the end of the 19th century. In the Boliden area of Norrland a wide range of metals, including gold, copper, lead, and zinc, are mined. The copper, silver, and iron ore deposits of central Sweden either have been largely exhausted or are unprofitable to extract.

MANUFACTURING

Manufacturing is export-oriented and produces the bulk of Sweden's export income. Nevertheless, the number of workers employed in private industry is smaller than the number of public employees.

Sweden is a major world exporter of forest products. Timber is transported via a dense road and rail network. Sawmills and pulp and paper factories process the forest products. Swedish manufacturers produce a variety of wood products, including paper, boards, and prefabricated houses and furniture.

BERGSLAGEN

Bergslagen is a major ore-producing region in central Sweden, lying northwest of Stockholm and extending from Lake Vänern (Sweden's largest lake) to the Gulf of Bothnia. It falls predominantly within the *län* (counties) of Dalarna, Örebro, Värmland, and Västmanland.

In the Middle Ages iron was mined in Bergslagen on a large scale and was smelted with charcoal. Metal products were shipped to the south in exchange for cattle. New iron mines opened in the early 18th century. In 1877 an ore export port was constructed on the Baltic coast, at Oxelösund, and was connected by rail to the mines of Grängesberg and Stråssa. The development of Sweden's world-famous steel industry was based on raw materials from Bergslagen.

While iron is the principal ore, Bergslagen has also served as a source of copper (especially at Falun), silver, lead, and zinc. Today the region has many factories producing heavy engineering and metal products. Avesta has important steel works, and Norberg is home to a reconstruction of one of the oldest blast furnaces in Europe. There are also a number of pulp and paper mills in the area.

The pulp and paper industry developed originally at the mouths of rivers along the Gulf of Bothnia and Lake Väner. More recently, plants have been located on the coasts of southern Sweden.

Sweden's metal industry still follows a pattern established during the days when waterpower and forestland (yielding charcoal fuel) determined the location of iron mills. The iron and steel industry is thus still largely found in the Bergslagen region of central Sweden. The iron and steel mills built in the 20th century, at Oxelösund and Luleå, are located on the coast.

Privately owned firms currently produce about nine-tenths of industrial output. Engineering, including the automotive industry, is by far the largest manufacturing industry, producing about half of industrial value added. The automotive and aerospace industries have their main plants in south-central Sweden. Swedish automakers Volvo and Saab enjoyed strong international reputations into the early 21st century.

The electric and electronics industry is concentrated in Stockholm and Västerås. Stockholm is a leading centre for the production of communications equipment. The small metal- and plastic-processing industries, with centres in the forested areas of southern Sweden, have, like the glassware industry, maintained their vitality through flexibility and continued creativity. Stenungsund on the west coast is a centre for the petrochemical industry. The pharmaceutical and biotechnology industries are rapidly expanding fields, located near leading medical research centres. The construction sector and the food-processing industry also play increasingly important roles. Sweden also has an advanced war matériel industry.

FINANCE

The Swedish banking system is dominated by a small number of major commercial banks. The bank of issue is the Swedish Central Bank, and the country's currency is the Swedish krona. There also are savings banks, niche banks, and foreign banks active in Sweden.

TRADE

Exports account for about one-third of Sweden's GDP. The emphasis has shifted from export of raw materials and semi-manufactured products (pulp, steel, sawn wood) to finished goods, dominated by engineering products (cars, telecommunications equipment, hydroelectric power plant equipment) and, increasingly, high technology and chemical- and biotechnology. Together Germany, the United Kingdom, the United States, Norway, Finland, and Denmark account for about half of Sweden's export market.

Imports are more diversified than exports. Before the 1980s petroleum was the single most important import, accounting for more than one-fourth of the total value. In 1990 petroleum accounted for less than 5 percent of the total. Almost half comes from the import of engineering products (including motor vehicles, business machines, and computer equipment). Among the imported foodstuffs are coffee, tea, fruit, and fish. Chemicals and textiles are other groups of imported goods. Germany is the main supplier of Sweden's imports, followed by the United Kingdom, Norway, and Denmark.

SERVICES

More than one-third of actively employed Swedes work in the service sector. Moreover, in the early 21st century, the export of services—including business services and technology consultancy services—was significantly greater than the export of goods. The tourist industry also plays an important role in the Swedish economy.

LABOUR AND TAXATION

Employment in agriculture, forestry, and fishing has declined since the mid-20th century. Employment in industry reached a peak in 1960, but the tertiary sector (including services and administration) has become the main growth area, with the expanding public sector one of its major components. However, an economic downturn in the 1990s resulted in the elimination of many of these jobs. About one-tenth of county and municipal jobs were lost in 1990–97; however, this trend has reversed somewhat in the early years of the 21st century, when more than one-fourth of the Swedish workforce was employed in the public sector. Private-sector production growth during the 1990s and early 2000s was largely due to increased employee hours worked and higher production per employee.

In order to address the problem of unemployment, the government made large investments in education and entrepreneurship. The public sector has played an important role in increasing productivity and participation in the workforce. Since the early 1990s there has been a push to encourage the full workforce participation of parents of preschoolers, by publicly funding preschool and child care resources. Working hours have increased, especially by women, and by the mid-2000s parents of young children had the same number of hours worked per week as other employees.

In Sweden three-fourths of working-age women participate in the workforce, a rate that is among the highest in the world. Sweden has among the lowest wage differentials in the world: women earn on average more than nine-tenths of full-time pay for men. However, only about two-thirds of working women have full-time jobs, while more than nine-tenths of working men do. Only a very small percentage of Swedish women are full-time homemakers.

Sweden is noted for its liberal employee benefit plans. The normal statutory workweek is 40 hours, but 37 hours per week is the de facto norm. The minimum amount of annual paid vacation is five weeks. In addition, there are other legal grounds for paid absence. Sweden is well known for its maternity and parental leave schemes that allow up to 13 months' leave at about four-fifths of their pay. Employers pay additional fees of more than two-fifths of gross wages for statutory social benefits, including pensions. As of 1999, a new general pension system was introduced, which allowed individuals to invest a portion of their contribution while linking payments to general economic growth and cohort life-expectancy.

Sweden is highly unionized, with about four-fifths of all workers belonging to trade unions. Workers are organized into three main groups: the Swedish Trade Union Confederation, the Swedish Confederation of Professional Employees, and the Swedish Confederation of Professional Associations. Most private-sector employers belong to the Confederation of Swedish Enterprise, which was formed in 2001 after the merger of the Swedish Employers Confederation and the Federation of Swedish Industries.

Taxes make up the overwhelming majority of state revenues, which are used to maintain a high level of social services that have virtually eliminated structural poverty in the country. Sweden has a relatively high rate of personal income tax (ranging from about 30 to 60 percent), but taxes for businesses are quite moderate. Since the late 1990s there has been a shift away from tax on personal income and capital gains and toward taxing goods and services and social security contributions. These shifts grew out of policy changes first implemented in the 1990s to stimulate work and savings by cutting the marginal tax rates on earned income. Social insurance policies have been changed to encourage greater participation in the workforce, and pension reforms have been introduced that clearly link the amount paid into the pension system and the amount disbursed with the overall health of the economy.

TRANSPORTATION AND TELECOMMUNICATIONS

Sweden has an extensive network of overland and air transport routes. In earlier centuries sea transport was dominant, land transport being carried on chiefly in winter, over snow and ice. Gothenburg and Stockholm are among the most important of some 20 ports handling foreign trade. The forest industry adjacent to the Norrland coast has its own harbours, which in winter are dependent on icebreaker services.

GÖTA CANAL

The Göta Canal (Swedish: Göta Kanal) is the artificial waterway that crosses southern Sweden to connect Lake Väner with the Baltic Sea. For most of its course, the canal passes through lakes, providing inland navigation from Gothenburg to Stockholm, a distance of 347 miles (558 km) by the canal route and 590 miles (950 km) on the Baltic. The trans-Sweden canal route has 60 miles (97 km) of artificial works and includes 65 locks. The Göta River drains Lake Väner and, with locks to surmount the falls at Trollhättan, is part of the waterway.

Boat on the Göta Canal, in Sweden. Picturepoint, London

The idea of a trans-Sweden waterway has a long history. Gustav I Vasa (king of Sweden, 1523–60) suggested building a canal through the Eskilstuna River, which was completed in 1610, and several other canal sections were built over the next 200 years. A company to connect the Göta River to Lake Väner was formed in 1790, and the first section, the Trollhätte Canal, was completed in 1800, allowing seagoing craft to pass from Gothenburg to Karlstad and other ports on Lake Väner. The Göta Canal proper was opened in 1822. It leads from Sjštorp to Viken on the other major Swedish lake, Vättern, and then to Mem on Slätbaken, an inlet of the Baltic, using two small lakes, Boren and Roxen, on the way.

The Swedish merchant fleet has been drastically reduced by competition from foreign ships charging lower rates. Ferry traffic between Sweden and its neighbours has grown tremendously and increasingly employs larger and more luxurious ferryboats.

In the first half of the 19th century a number of inland waterways, among them the Göta canal, were constructed. They soon became obsolete, however, as the state began in the 1850s to build the national railway network. Sweden soon ranked among the foremost countries in per capita mileage of railroads. Railroads in their turn met competition from the automobile, and since the 1950s many secondary rail lines have been closed. The centuries-old road network was rapidly expanded in the 20th century, and ever-better roads were built. Highways ran between Stockholm, Gothenburg, and Malmö and connected the capital to the northern coastal region. Most households own at least one car. Local public bus transportation is well developed, but only Stockholm has a subway as the backbone of its local transportation system. Gothenburg has developed a tram system.

Air services are dominated by the Scandinavian Airlines System (SAS), which is owned chiefly by the states of Sweden, Denmark, and Norway. The interests of SAS are concentrated on international aviation, but, directly and indirectly, it also dominates domestic service. The most important airports are in Stockholm, Gothenburg, and Malmö.

The interests of the state in transportation and communications are wide. The railways are owned and run by the state, which also maintains bus traffic on a large scale.

As the telecommunications industry has grown in Sweden, so, too, have telecommunications improved, and the country is among the world's leaders in Internet penetration, with a great majority of Swedes having online access.

CHAPTER 13

SWEDISH GOVERNMENT AND SOCIETY

Sweden is a constitutional monarchy. The constitution, dating from 1809 and revised in 1975, is based on the following four fundamental laws: the Instrument of Government, the Act of Succession, the Freedom of the Press Act, and the Riksdag (Parliament) Act. All the laws have been subject to amendment. The constitution is based on the principles of popular sovereignty, representative democracy, and parliamentarism.

The reigning monarch is the head of state but exerts no political power; the responsibilities of the monarch are ceremonial only. Succession is accorded to the firstborn child regardless of sex. The prime minister is nominated by the speaker of the Riksdag after consultations with party leaders and must be approved for office through a vote of the Riksdag. The prime minister appoints the other cabinet members. The cabinet is responsible for all government decisions.

The ministries are small, and they are not concerned with details of administration or implementation of legislation. This is handled by central administrative agencies, whose senior officials are appointed by the cabinet.

In the preparation of important measures to be considered by the government, the responsible minister normally calls upon a commission of inquiry to appraise the measure. The commission may often include politicians from opposition parties, representatives of labour, and scientists and civil servants. They produce a printed report that is sent to various agencies and organizations for official comments before it is presented as background material to government legislation.

The Riksdag, a unicameral parliament elected by the people for four-year terms, is the foundation for the democratic exercise of power through the cabinet. The Riksdag appoints its speaker, deputy speakers, and standing committees, in which parties are represented in proportion to their strength. All bills are referred to committees; the results of their deliberations are reported in printed form to the Riksdag in plenary session.

The Riksdag may call for a consultative (nonbinding) referendum on various issues; decisive (binding) referenda may be held on amendments to the constitution if demanded by one-third of the Riksdag.

LOCAL GOVERNMENT

Local government is allocated to the kommuner (municipalities), each with an elected assembly and the right to levy income taxes and to charge fees for various services. Municipalities have a strong independent position. Streets, sewerage, water supply, schools, public assistance, child welfare, housing, and care for elderly people are among their responsibilities. Elections coincide with parliamentary elections.

Between the national and municipal government is a regional tier of 21 län (counties) headed by a county governor, appointed by the national government. Each county also has an elected council that has the right to levy income tax and that administers health care, certain educational and vocational training, and regional transport.

JUSTICE

The National Law Code of 1734 is still in force, although almost none of its original text remains. In modern times, moreover, a mass of special legislation has grown outside the code to cover new needs. Roman law has had less influence in Sweden than in most European countries. Since the end of the 19th century, much civil law has been prepared in collaboration with the other Nordic countries.

Primary responsibility for the enforcement of law devolves upon the courts and the administrative authorities. Sweden has a three-tiered hierarchy of courts: the district courts (tingsrätter), the intermediate courts of appeal (hovrätter), and the Supreme Court (högsta domstolen). District courts play the dominant role. A peculiar feature of these courts is a panel of lay assessors (nämndemän), who take part in the main hearings, primarily on more serious criminal and family cases. In such cases, the bench consists of a legally trained judge as chairman and three lay assessors. These panels are not to be confused with an Anglo-American or continental type of jury.

Political map of Sweden. Encyclopædia Britannica, Inc.

In the six courts of appeal (the oldest one established in 1614), cases are decided by three or four judges. Appeals against their decisions can be carried to the Supreme Court only if the case is deemed important to the interpretation of law. In the Supreme Court the bench consists of five justices (justitieråd).

Legal aid is provided for anyone who wants it. The general penalties for convictions are fines and imprisonment. Fines are set in proportion to the person's daily income. Offenders under 18 years of age are sentenced to prison only in exceptional cases.

The decisions of administrative authorities, which cannot be appealed to an ordinary court of justice, can be appealed to higher administrative authorities and ultimately to the government or to administrative courts, such as county administrative courts (länsrätter) in matters of taxation. Higher administrative courts of appeal are called kammarrätter. The highest administrative tribunal is the Supreme Administrative Court (regeringsrätten), which tries cases involving such issues as taxation, insanity, alcoholism, and juvenile delinquency.

The Labour Court (Arbetsdomstolen) is a special body that deals with controversies in the interpretation and application of collective bargaining agreements. Of its seven members, two represent labour and two represent management.

The Office of the Parliamentary Ombudsman (Justitieombudsman) is an original Swedish institution, established in 1809; it has become a model for similar offices in other countries. The ombudsman's chief duty is to see that the courts and civil service enforce the laws properly, especially those laws that safeguard the freedom, security, and property of citizens. They have the power to institute prosecutions in court and, in particular, to act

LANDSKAP AND LÄN

Sweden's traditional administrative subdivisions have been the *landskap* (province) and *län* (counties). The 25 *landskap* developed during the pre-Viking and Viking eras and were independent political units with their own laws, judges, and councils. The division was based on geographical and cultural characteristics with which many people continue to identify. Although they no longer have any political or administrative significance, their names remain in common use and appear in official tabulations of data. The *landskap* overlap and occasionally coincide with the 26 *län* (counties) that came into being during the later European Middle Ages. The *län* were established in their modern form in the 17th and early 18th centuries, although through some consolidation their number was reduced to 21 by the end of the 20th century. Län still serve as Sweden's main administrative subdivisions.

against officials who abuse their powers or act illegally. Other ombudsmen are not appointed by the Riksdag but have similar duties of surveillance in other areas. Thus, there are an antitrust ombudsman, a consumer ombudsman, an equal-opportunities ombudsman, and an ethnic-discrimination ombudsman.

The chancellor of justice (justitiekansler) is a government appointee who supervises courts and administrative organs with particular concern for safeguarding the state's interests.

POLITICAL PROCESS

All citizens of Sweden who are 18 years of age or older may vote in elections. Members of the parliament must be Swedish citizens and of voting age. Representation by party is in strict proportion to the national vote. A quota rule excludes parties with less than 4 percent of the national vote or 12 percent of the votes in at least one electoral district. Only in 1919, after decades of work by Elin Wägner and other dedicated suffragettes, were women in Sweden first able to vote in general elections, and not until 1921 could women vote in all elections. Five women entered the Swedish parliament as a result of that election; at the beginning of the 21st century, nearly half of the members of the parliament were women.

Historically, the political party system in Sweden has been relatively stable. Prominent parties include three non-socialist parties—the Moderate Party (formerly the Conservative Party), the Centre Party, and the Liberal Party—and two socialist parties—the Swedish Social Democratic Workers' Party (SAP; commonly called the Social Democratic Labour Party) and the Left Party (former Communist Party). The SAP is closely allied with the trade unions and was in power for a considerable part of the 20th century (1932–76 [except briefly in 1936] and 1982–91). At the end of the century and into the 21st century, power alternated between the Social Democrats and the Moderates.

SECURITY

Sweden has not been under military occupation since the 16th century or been at war since 1814. Until joining the European Union (EU) in 1995, Sweden actively avoided all military alliances through a policy of detachment or neutrality. As a member of the EU, Sweden fully participates in the organization's foreign and security policy.

To safeguard its neutrality and to protect its territory, Sweden maintains a strong military consisting of an army, a navy, and an air force. In 2010 the country ended conscription.

Sweden actively supports international organizations such as the United Nations (UN) and takes an energetic role in resolving security issues through this organ. Together with the other Nordic countries, Sweden has worked to develop and reinforce UN peacekeeping

Police arrest a demonstrator (centre) *in the city of Malmö, outside the building of a Finnish company that supplies rifle scopes to the United States Army, in 2008.* AFP/Getty Images

operations. Since multilateral disarmament negotiations began in Switzerland in 1962, Sweden also has been a key player in international efforts to control and restrict transfers of conventional arms, to enforce the nonproliferation of nuclear weapons, chemical and biological weapons, and missile technology, and to achieve a total ban on antipersonnel mines.

Sweden's national police service is responsible to the Ministry of Justice and includes the National Police Board, the National Security Service, the National Criminal Investigation Department, the National Laboratory of Forensic Science, and the county police authorities. Women make up one-third of all police employees and about one-fifth of police officers.

HEALTH AND WELFARE

In return for high taxes, Swedes are provided with a broad spectrum of public services and social welfare benefits that guarantee a minimum living standard, provide aid in emergencies, and narrow the gap between income groups. All residents are covered by national health insurance administered by the counties.

Health conditions in Sweden are among the best in the world. Infant mortality is low, and the average life expectancy at birth is high. Sweden has one of the world's oldest populations, with a significant slice of the population age 65 or over. The ratio of doctors to population is also relatively high. Primary health care centres are available in every community. For highly specialized health care, Sweden has several major hospitals, which generally have affiliated medical schools. The county councils (and the local authority in the case of Gotland) are responsible for providing health services.

Extremely liberal benefits are available to parents. They are entitled to 13 months of paid family leave from work, which can be shared between them before a child is age 8. They also receive tax-free child allowances, equal for everyone, until a child's 16th birthday. Students who continue their education are entitled to study allowances. At the university level the majority of student funding consists of repayable loans. Municipalities provide an increasing number of day-care and youth activities.

National accident insurance pays all medical costs for on-the-job injuries.

Many working people in Sweden have unemployment insurance through their trade unions, while the unemployed without such coverage can receive a smaller cash benefit from the state. There are extensive government programs for job retraining and sheltered employment (jobs reserved for disabled workers), as well as relocation grants to help the unemployed find work. A basic old-age pension is available to everyone starting at age 65. The state also pays an income-related supplementary pension financed through a payroll plan.

HOUSING

Swedish cities are generally noted for their efficient planning and lack of slums. Up until the 1930s, however, Sweden's housing standards were low compared with those of other European countries. Many dwellings lacked basic sanitation and were overcrowded. In the 1940s the central government addressed these concerns through housing policy by subsidizing rents and instituting rent control. In the post-World War II period, the Swedish government oversaw a new focus on the general improvement of housing standards. Housing subsidies were introduced for the poor and elderly pensioners. From the late 1940s through the 1950s, most municipalities founded their own housing companies. Low-interest loans and interest subsides were provided by the state to these nonprofit companies.

In the 1950s and '60s, as the baby boom began, the "Million Home Program" was instituted to provide a higher standard of housing throughout the country. The goal was to build one million new dwellings, to be occupied by no more than two people per room, not counting the kitchen and living room. This began a policy of state responsibility for the legislation and funding of housing construction, with the municipalities charged with planning and implementation. In the 1970s the construction of single-family houses increased and rent control ended. The housing improvement schemes of the 1980s modernized much of the housing stock, and new projects mushroomed through 1990, a year in which nearly 70,000 units were built.

The economic crisis of the 1990s and the systematic dismantling of many of the iconic features of the welfare state led to a dramatic change in Sweden's housing policy. Construction dwindled at this time as subsidized housing schemes were eliminated in favour of housing allowances or supplements. As the effects of the 1990s depression subsided, the government attempted to address housing problems in the first decade of the 21st century by investing in projects meant to stimulate the construction of new housing, particularly that of smaller apartments. The government also worked with private builders and municipal housing authorities to ensure a sustainable stock of high-quality housing that was both environmentally sensitive and affordable.

In the early 21st century, more than half of Swedish households lived in apartments, while the remainder lived in houses. At the turn of the century, the average Swedish household spent about one-fourth of its disposable income on rent. Housing stock is not evenly distributed throughout the country. In some regions, such as the greater Stockholm area, housing is at a premium, while in other smaller and medium-sized communities, there is a surplus of housing stock.

On average, just over two Swedes live in each dwelling. Approximately two-fifths of the housing stock is owner-occupied; nearly half is rental; and the remainder is owned by cooperative tenant owners. Sweden is the only country where the predominant colour of houses is red.

EDUCATION

The education system is, with few exceptions, public and open to all without fees. Primary schools are run by the municipalities, as are the secondary schools. Universities and colleges are administered by the state, but they have been given far-reaching autonomy in the use of resources. Academic freedom is carefully guarded by faculty and students alike.

All municipalities must provide preschool classes. Parents may choose

UPPSALA UNIVERSITY

The oldest institution of higher learning in Sweden is Uppsala University (Swedish: Uppsala Universitet), the state-sponsored coeducational university at Uppsala. It was founded in 1477 but closed in 1510 owing to the religious disputes of the time. It was reopened in 1595 with faculties of theology and philosophy, and in 1624 King Gustav II Adolf granted it large landed estates, thus providing the school's future financial basis.

The university current faculties include theology, law, medicine, arts, languages, pharmacy, social sciences, educational sciences, mathematics and computer science, physics, technology, biology, earth science, and chemistry. The university's library, the Carolina Rediviva, is one of Sweden's largest and contains the illuminated manuscript *Codex Argenteus,* which is the only extant manuscript of Bishop Ulfilas' 4th-century translation of the Gospels into the Gothic language. The main university building (1887) has a large art collection.

whether or not to send their children, and the great majority does participate. Parents and pupils have the choice of free municipal schools as well as independent schools, which may charge tuition. Only a very small percentage of all Swedish children attend private or independent schools. The comprehensive school (grundskola) is compulsory for nine years. Children are required to attend school between the ages of 7 and 16. Compulsory education is free, and no charge is made for school lunches, transportation, or educational materials. The comprehensive school is divided into three-year stages: lower, middle, and upper. Each school may decide when English and other foreign languages are introduced, but all must meet the same standards by grade 5. About one-third of all schools begin English instruction in grade 1. From the seventh year the curriculum is divided into different lines chosen by the pupils themselves. Special education is given to all pupils suffering from physical or mental handicaps.

Nearly all of the pupils continue from comprehensive school to the upper secondary school. The curriculum in this school (gymnasieskola) is divided between several theoretical programs, which are university-oriented, and a variety of vocationally oriented programs. Certain core subjects are common to all programs.

Marks, or grades, are given in comprehensive school starting in the eighth year. In the upper secondary school grades are given each term. About half of all young people in Sweden go on to higher studies within five years of completing upper secondary school.

Sweden has about a dozen major universities and some 20 university-colleges.

The oldest is the Uppsala University, founded in 1477. Other universities are located in Lund, Stockholm, Gothenburg, Umeå, Linköping, Karlstad, and Växjö. Sweden is also home to other world-renowned institutions, including the Karolinska Institute (medicine) in Stockholm and the Chalmers University of Technology. Education is free of charge; students pay no tuition. Courses are typically taught in Swedish, but course literature is often in English. An increasing number of courses are also offered in English.

Continuing and adult education are important features of the Swedish education system. Adult education outside the public school system is offered at the many folk high schools, a uniquely Scandinavian educational institution. Also characteristic are the nationwide voluntary education associations. About half of Sweden's adult population pursues studies in one form or another. Since 1968 municipalities have offered courses for adults covering the three upper grades of comprehensive school and upper secondary school. University courses also are open to all age groups. Distance learning—including radio and television courses, as well as Internet and correspondence courses—is popular and especially useful for persons who reside far from educational centres.

CHAPTER 14

SWEDISH CULTURAL LIFE

Sweden's cultural heritage is an interweaving of a uniquely Swedish sensibility with ideas and impulses taken from other, larger cultures. As a result, Swedish culture has long been characterized by a push and pull. Swedish art, poetry, literature, music, textiles, dance, and design are deeply infused with a primal relationship with the Nordic landscape and climate, but Swedes also have long been attracted to the greatness of the cultures of such countries as France and Germany, and influences from these and other European cultures have contributed to the development of Swedish literature, fashion, and cultural debate, as well as to the Swedish language itself.

As Swedish political influence grew, particularly in the 17th and 18th centuries, so did a desire among prominent Swedes for their country to take a place at centre stage with other important European cultures. This refusal to be classified as a cultural backwater remains a strong force today. At the same time, simplicity is a hallmark of Swedish culture, as is openness to new thoughts and trends. There is also a sense of wit and playfulness combined with candor and sincerity that is apparent not only in the works of Swedish cultural icons such as Selma Lagerlöf, August Strindberg, Ingmar Bergman, Astrid Lindgren, and Carl Larsson but also in Swedish folk music and folk art.

War-weary and largely nonaligned since the Napoleonic Wars of the early 19th century, Sweden embraced a neutrality and peacefulness that permitted the state in the 20th century to broadly support arts and culture politically, educationally,

AUGUST STRINDBERG

Swedish playwright, novelist, and short-story writer August Strindberg (born Johan August Strindberg, January 22, 1849, Stockholm, Sweden—died May 14, 1912, Stockholm) combined psychology and Naturalism in a new kind of European drama that evolved into Expressionist drama. He is considered by many to be Sweden's greatest writer.

Strindberg's childhood was marred by emotional insecurity, poverty, his grandmother's religious fanaticism, and neglect, as he relates in his remarkable autobiography *Tjänstekvinnans son* (1886–87; *The Son of a Servant,* 1913). He studied intermittently at the University of Uppsala but never earned a degree. To earn his living, he worked as a free-lance journalist in Stockholm, as well as at other jobs that he almost invariably lost. Meanwhile he struggled to complete his first important work, the historical drama *Mäster Olof* (published in 1872), on the theme of the Swedish Reformation. The Royal Theatre's rejection of *Mäster Olof* deepened his pessimism and sharpened his contempt for official institutions and traditions. For several years he

August Strindberg. Encyclopædia Britannica, Inc.

continued revising the play, which was later recognized as the first modern Swedish drama.

In 1874 he became a librarian at the Royal Library, and in 1875 he met the Finno-Swedish Siri von Essen; two years later they married. Their intense but ultimately disastrous relationship ended in divorce in 1891. At first, however, marriage stimulated his writing, and in 1879 he published his first novel, *The Red Room,* a satirical account of abuses and frauds in Stockholm society: this was something new in Swedish fiction and made its author nationally famous. The publication in 1884 of the first volume of his collected stories, *Married,* led to a prosecution for blasphemy. He was acquitted, but the case affected his mind, and he imagined himself persecuted, even by Siri.

He returned to drama with new intensity, and the conflict between the sexes inspired some of the outstanding works written at this time, such as *The Father* (1887), *Miss Julie* (1888), and *The Creditors* (1888). In these bold and concentrated works, he combined the techniques of dramatic Naturalism—including unaffected dialogue, stark rather than luxurious scenery, and the use of stage props as symbols—with his own conception of psychology, thereby inaugurating a new movement in European drama.

After traveling abroad for several years, he returned to Sweden in 1889. Even though revered as a famous writer who had become the voice of modern Sweden, he was by now an alcoholic unable to find steady employment. In 1892 he went abroad again, to Berlin. His second marriage, to a young Austrian journalist, Frida Uhl, followed in 1893; they parted in 1895.

A period of literary sterility, emotional and physical stress, and considerable mental instability culminated in a kind of religious conversion, the crisis that he described in *Inferno* (1898). His new faith, coloured by mysticism, re-created him as a writer. By this time Strindberg had again returned to Sweden, settling first in Lund and then, in 1899, in Stockholm, where he lived until his death. In 1901 he married the young Norwegian actress Harriet Bosse; in 1904 they parted.

Strindberg's last marriage inspired several works, including some plays, the charming autobiography *Ensam* (1903; "Alone"), and some lyrical poems. His *Kammarspel* ("Chamber Plays") embody further developments of his dramatic technique: of these, *The Ghost Sonata* (1907) is the most fantastic, anticipating much in later European drama. His last play, *The Great Highway*, a symbolic presentation of his own life, appeared in 1909.

and economically. During the last half of the 20th century, Sweden welcomed immigrants and refugees who brought with them their own cultural traditions, which have informed the broader Swedish culture. The effects of American popular culture have also been widely felt in Sweden. A rebirth of contemporary Swedish creativity has attracted worldwide attention both in those art forms in which Swedes have traditionally thrived—literature and film—and in design, popular music, photography, fashion, gastronomy, and textiles.

DAILY LIFE AND SOCIAL CUSTOMS

Genuine rural folk traditions are disappearing in urban areas as a result of increasing settlement; however, since the 1990s there has been a resurgence of interest in those traditions among many Swedes who live in towns and cities. Still vital in Gotland, Dalarna, and various other areas are special national costumes, dances, folk music, and the like. Spring is celebrated on the last night of April with bonfires and song across the country. This is a great students' festival in university towns such as Uppsala and Lund. The bright Midsummer's Eve is celebrated around June 21, about the time of the year's longest day. In the ceremony a large pole, decorated with flowers and leaves, is placed into the ground and danced around. Some celebrations have a religious association: Advent, St. Lucia's Day, Christmas, Easter, and Whitsuntide. Pagan elements

A crowd in Edsbro, Sweden, watches as participants dance around the maypole to celebrate the arrival of Midsummer's Eve, the longest day of the year. Pieter Kuiper

are still sometimes evident in these holiday ceremonies.

Immigration, travels abroad, and imports have changed and internationalized the Swedish cuisine. However, the original Swedish buffet of appetizers known as a smörgåsbord remains a national favourite. The typical Swedish kitchen reflects the harsh northern climate, with fresh food available only during the short but intense summer season. In the words of the mother of Swedish cuisine, 18th-century cook Cajsa Warg, "You take what you get." Swedish culinary traditions reflect the importance of being able to preserve and store food for the winter. Lutefisk (dried cod soaked in water and lye so it swells), pickled herring, lingonberries (which keep well without preservatives), knäckebröd (crispbread), and fermented or preserved dairy products such as the yogurtlike fil, the stringy långfil, and cheeses all reflect this need for foods that will keep through the colder parts of the year. Twisted saffron-scented buns called lussekatter and

ST. LUCIA'S DAY

Sweden is among the countries that celebrate a festival of lights on December 13, known as St. Lucia's Day. Also celebrated in Norway and the Swedish-speaking areas of Finland, the holiday honours St. Lucia, one of the earliest Christian martyrs. She was killed by the Romans in 304 CE because of her religious beliefs.

In Scandinavian countries each town elects its own St. Lucia. The festival begins with a procession led by the St. Lucia designee, who is followed by young girls dressed in white and wearing lighted wreaths on their heads and boys dressed in white pajama-like costume singing traditional songs. The festival marks the beginning of the Christmas season in Scandinavia, and it is meant to bring hope and light during the long winter days. Schools generally close around noon on the day of the festival so that families can prepare for the holiday. Families observe St. Lucia's Day in their homes by having one of their daughters (traditionally the eldest) dress in white and serve coffee and baked goods, such as saffron buns (*lussekatter*) and ginger biscuits, to the other members of the family. These traditional foods are also given to visitors during the day.

In earlier centuries the Norse celebrated the winter solstice with large bonfires meant to scare off evil spirits and to alter the course of the sun. After converting to Christianity sometime around 1000, the Norse incorporated the legend of St. Lucia into their celebration. The modern festival of light combines elements of both pagan and Christian traditions.

heart-shaped gingersnaps are served along with coffee in the early morning. Christmas is celebrated on December 24 with the traditional Julskinka ham. Glogg, a mulled, spiced wine, is also enjoyed during this season.

THE ARTS

J.H. Roman, an 18th-century composer, has been called the father of Swedish music, but the Romantic composer Franz Berwald received wider acclaim for his 19th-century symphonies and other works. Notable 20th-century composers include the "Monday group," who were inspired by the antiromantic Hilding Rosenberg in the 1920s and drew also upon leading modern composers from abroad. The vital Swedish folk song has been developed further by a number of musicians. The lively and often moving ballads and "epistles" of Carl Michael Bellman, an 18th-century skald, are still widely performed and enjoyed in contemporary Sweden. A number of Swedish opera singers, among them Jenny Lind, Jussi Björling, and Birgit Nilsson, gained renown throughout the world. Popular music, especially the Europop of the internationally celebrated group ABBA, and music production, editing, and

ABBA

One of the most commercially successful groups in the history of popular music was the Swedish Europop group ABBA. Members included songwriter and keyboard player Benny Andersson (born December 16, 1946, Stockholm, Sweden), songwriter and guitarist Björn Ulvaeus (born April 25, 1945, Gothenburg, Sweden), and vocalists Agnetha Fältskog (born April 5, 1950, Jönköping, Sweden) and Anni-Frid Lyngstad (born November 15, 1945, Narvik, Norway).

In 1969 Andersson and Ulvaeus, who had previously collaborated on a number of folk and pop projects, met Lyngstad and Fältskog. In addition to working together musically, the four paired off romantically, with Andersson becoming involved with Lyngstad and Ulvaeus dating Fältskog. Ulvaeus and Fältskog were married in 1971, and Andersson and Lyngstad followed suit in 1978.

In 1973 the foursome finished third in the Swedish qualifying round of the Eurovision Song Contest with the single "Ring, Ring." Encouraged by that success and dubbed ABBA—an acronym derived from the members' first names—the band returned to Eurovision in 1974 and captured

Members of the music group ABBA perform in 1975. Hulton Archive/Getty Images

the top prize with the song "Waterloo." The resulting single served as the anchor for the album of the same name, released that year.

More than a year after the triumph at Eurovision, *ABBA* (1975) truly established the group as a global pop phenomenon. The singles "Mamma Mia" and "S.O.S." were massive hits in Europe, Australia, and North America, and the band embraced the emerging music video format to capitalize on the quartet's shared charisma. ABBA's 1977 release, *Arrival*, provided the catchy and undeniably club-friendly "Dancing Queen." *The Album* (1978) marked a departure of sorts: although its standout single, "Take a Chance on Me," was a brilliant, if straightforward, pop anthem, other tracks hinted at an art rock influence.

While *The Album* marked an artistic progression for ABBA, personal relations within the band suffered when Ulvaeus and Fältskog divorced prior to the release of *Voulez-Vous* (1979). The pair vowed that their breakup would not affect the band's output, but *Super Trouper* (1980) featured a collection of songs, most notably "The Winner Takes It All" and "Lay All Your Love on Me," that betrayed a melancholic undercurrent that was absent in previous recordings. Andersson and Lyngstad divorced during the recording of *The Visitors* (1981) and this second breakup proved to be too much for the group, which disbanded in 1982.

After the demise of ABBA, Fältskog and Lyngstad embarked on moderately successful solo careers, and Ulvaeus and Andersson collaborated with lyricist Tim Rice to create *Chess* (1984), a concept album and stage musical that produced the surprise radio hit "One Night in Bangkok." Ulvaeus and Andersson later merged their shared love of musical theatre with the ABBA back catalog to produce *Mamma Mia!*, a romantic comedy that debuted on London's West End in 1999 and was subsequently seen by millions of people worldwide. A film version of the play was one of the top global box office draws of 2008. The group was inducted into the Rock and Roll Hall of Fame in 2010.

advertising were major Swedish exports from the late 1970s on. Beginning in the mid-1990s, Swedish songwriter and producer Max Martin played a pivotal role in the success of several American hitmakers, including the Backstreet Boys and Britney Spears. Moreover, in addition to making a national specialty of the heavy metal genre of "death" metal in the late 1980s and early '90s, Sweden also produced a number of other performers and groups who achieved international pop music success in the late 20th and early 21st centuries, among them Ace of Base, the Hives, I'm from Barcelona, Peter Bjorn and John, and the Tallest Man on Earth.

Few names in Swedish literature were well known internationally until the 19th century, when the writings of August Strindberg won worldwide acclaim. He is still generally considered the country's greatest writer. In the early 20th century, novelist Selma Lagerlöf became the first Swedish writer to win the Nobel Prize.

A favourite poet in Sweden is Harry Martinson, who, writing in the 1930s, cultivated themes and motifs ranging from the romantic Swedish countryside to those concerned with global and cosmic visions. Other poets such as Karin Boye and Tomas Tranströmer have international reputations. In contemporary Swedish literature such authors as Kerstin Ekman, P.C. Jersild, Lars Gustafsson, Sara Lidman, Canadian-born Sven Delblanc, Henning Mankell, and Mikael Niemi have found a wide audience. Activist and journalist Stieg Larsson did not start writing fiction until later in his life, and though his literary career was cut short by his death by heart attack in 2004, he dazzled readers worldwide with a series of detective novels that included *Män som hatar kvinnor* (2005; "Men Who Hate Women"; Eng. trans. *The Girl with the Dragon Tattoo*), helping to set the stage for international appreciation of Swedish and Scandinavian crime fiction. One of the most widely published and translated modern Swedish writers is Astrid Lindgren, noted for her children's books, including the famous *Pippi Longstocking* series.

Swedish theatre, opera, and ballet are multifaceted. Birgit Cullberg attained international fame as director of the Swedish Royal Ballet in Stockholm. The Swedish cinema was pioneered in the silent and early sound eras by actor-director Victor Sjöström. Like Sjöström, director Ingmar Bergman moved from the stage to motion pictures, gaining critical acclaim outside Sweden with his film *Wild Strawberries* (1957). Subsequently,

INGMAR BERGMAN

Swedish film writer-director Ingmar Bergman (born Ernst Ingmar Bergman, July 14, 1918, Uppsala, Sweden—died July 30, 2007, Fårö, Sweden) achieved world fame for his films. He is noted for his versatile camera work and for his fragmented narrative style, which contribute to his bleak depiction of human loneliness, vulnerability, and torment.

The rebellious son of a Lutheran pastor, he worked in the theatre before directing his first film, *Crisis* (1945). He won international acclaim for his films *The Seventh Seal* (1957) and *Wild Strawberries* (1957). He assembled a group of actors, including Max von Sydow and Liv Ullmann, and a cinematographer, Sven Nykvist, with whom he made powerful films often marked by bleak depictions of human loneliness, including *Through a Glass Darkly* (1961), *Cries and Whispers* (1972), *Autumn Sonata* (1978), and *Fanny and Alexander* (1982). Bergman later wrote screenplays for *The Best Intentions* (1992) and *Private Confessions* (1996). He directed a number of television movies, most notably *Saraband* (2003), which received a theatrical release. Throughout his career Bergman continued to direct stage productions, usually at Stockholm's Royal Dramatic Theatre.

as many of both his earlier and later films became classics of international cinema, Bergman was hailed as one of the most important filmmakers of all time. Among other Swedes who have made major contributions to the art of filmmaking are actors Greta Garbo, Ingrid Bergman, Bibi Andersson, and Max von Sydow, cinematographer-director Sven Nykvist, and director Lasse Hallström. In the last decades of the 20th century, Lars Norén shouldered the mantle of Sweden's national dramatist.

Modern Swedish visual art was inspired by late 19th-century romantic nationalism, originating with such painters as Carl Larsson, Anders Zorn, and Bruno Liljefors. Carl Milles dominated monumental sculpture in the 1920s. At the Paris World's Fair in 1925, an important connection was established between Swedish industry and designers who had both academic art education and popular handicraft tradition. Superb results have been achieved in ceramics, woodwork, textiles, silver, and stainless steel. Sweden is also renowned for its leadership in glass and furniture design. Many famous glass designers such as Bertil Vallien, Ingegerd Råman, and Ulrica Hydman-Vallien (part of the Orrefors Kosta Boda group) and independent glass artists such as Ulla Forsell, Mårten Medbo, and Frida Fjellman have won international acclaim. Moreover, Sweden has been a world leader in industrial design, blending sound ergonomics, aesthetics, and high functionality. IKEA, perhaps Sweden's best-known company, disseminates design in a thoroughly "Swedish" way all over the world.

CULTURAL INSTITUTIONS

The country's cultural institutions are subsidized through state funding. Cultural activities reach all parts of the country through traveling companies devoted to theatre, concerts, and exhibitions. Despite state support, the majority of these cultural offerings are also dependent on private funding.

Every municipality has a public library where books are loaned free of charge. The libraries are often centres for other cultural events as well. Scientific libraries, including the largest ones, like the University of Uppsala library and the Royal Library, are also open to the public. Sweden has one of the highest library lending rates in the world.

There are about 300 museums and local heritage centres in Sweden. About 20 museums are run by the state; most of them are national museums in Stockholm. Besides the national museums for art, history, natural history, and folklore, the open-air Skansen historical park (founded in 1891) enjoys worldwide interest. In addition, there are county museums with regional responsibility. Sweden has a number of institutional theatres, including Stockholm's Royal Opera and Royal Dramatic Theatre, both of which have held performances since the 1780s.

Several major professional symphony orchestras and chamber orchestras, along with many smaller musical institutions, form the backbone of musical life. The state supports the production of literature, films, and sound recordings, as well as art for public buildings.

Learned societies play an important role as independent promoters of arts and sciences. The Royal Swedish Academy of Sciences, founded in 1739, is engaged in worldwide cooperative programs. It also selects Nobel laureates in chemistry and physics. The Nobel Prize for Literature is awarded by the Swedish Academy, which was inaugurated together with the Royal Swedish Academy of Letters, History and Antiquities by King Gustav III in 1786. The Nobel Prize award ceremony, held on December 10 each year, is the single most heralded annual event held in Sweden. It is arranged by the Nobel Foundation, which administers the funds and other properties from the estate of Alfred Nobel, who died in 1896.

SPORTS AND RECREATION

Swedes are very interested in sports, with nearly one-half of the country's inhabitants belonging to sports clubs. Outdoor recreation is important throughout the year. Facilities for mountain hiking were developed by the Swedish Touring Club about the end of the 19th century. With miles of gently rolling white sand and some of the best windsurfing in the Baltic, the resort town of Ystad draws throngs

of beachgoing Swedes each summer. Sweden is one of the foremost countries in winter sports, and facilities for skiing in particular have developed rapidly. Åre is a major centre of winter sports. Sweden has produced several notable skiing champions, including Ingemar Stenmark (Alpine) and Sixten Jernberg (Nordic), as well as figure skating innovator Gillis Grafström. In competitive sports, other than winter events, football (soccer) and gymnastics are highly developed. Stockholm hosted the highly successful 1912 Olympic Games, which included the legendary performance of American decathlete Jim Thorpe. Swedes have also made international reputations in tennis and golf, most notably Björn Borg and Annika Sörenstam, respectively. Traditional games include kubb, a form of lawn skittles, said to have been played in Sweden since Viking times.

MEDIA AND PUBLISHING

Freedom of the press in Sweden dates back to 1766, and the current Freedom of the Press Act dates from 1949. State censorship of the press as well as other serious restrictions of the publication and distribution of printed matter are forbidden. The law also prohibits the investigation or disclosure of a newspaper reporter's sources except in cases of high treason, espionage, or other related serious crimes.

The principle that every citizen should have access to virtually all documents kept by state or municipal agencies was introduced in 1766. Few other countries have emulated Sweden in providing this guarantee. The right of access is guarded by the parliamentary ombudsman.

In 1969 the office of the press ombudsman was established to supervise adherence to ethical standards in the press. Sweden ranks high among countries in newspaper circulation, although the number of newspapers has declined sharply since the mid-20th century. State subsidies are paid in order to ensure that there will be competitive newspapers to provide balanced news coverage. The major dailies often express the viewpoint of a specific political party. They include *Expressen* (liberal, Stockholm), *Dagens Nyheter* (independent, Stockholm), *Aftonbladet* (social democratic, Stockholm), *Göteborgs-Posten* (liberal, Gothenburg), *Svenska Dagbladet* (independent moderate, Stockholm), *Sydsvenska Dagbladet* (independent liberal, Malmö), and *Arbetet* (social democratic, Malmö). Sweden is also home to the oldest continuously published newspaper in the world, the *Post-och Inrikes Tidningar*; although published only on the Internet since the early 2000s, it has been available daily since 1645.

Radio and television broadcasting is monopolized under public supervision. A government-appointed Broadcasting Commission reviews program activities to ensure that standards of objectivity and impartiality are met. Radio and television programming is financed from license revenues. Regular radio broadcasting began in 1925 and television in 1956.

CHAPTER 15

SWEDEN: PAST AND PRESENT

The thick ice cap that covered Sweden during the last glacial period began to recede in the southern region about 14,000 years ago. About 12,000 years later the earliest hunters in the region began following migratory paths behind the retreating ice field. The stratified clay deposits that were left annually by the melting ice have been studied systematically by Swedish geologists, who have developed a dependable system of geochronology that verifies the dates of the thaw. The first traces of human life in Sweden, dating from about 9000 BCE, were found at Segebro outside Malmö in the extreme southern reaches of Sweden. Finds from the peat at Ageröd in Skåne dated to 6500 BCE reveal a typical food-gathering culture with tools of flint and primitive hunting and fishing equipment, such as the bow and arrow and the fishing spear. New tribes, practicing agriculture and cattle raising, made their appearance about 2500 BCE, and soon afterward a peasant culture with good continental communications was flourishing in what are now the provinces of Skåne, Halland, Bohuslän, and Västergötland. The so-called Boat-Ax culture (an outlier of the European Battle-Ax cultures) arrived about 2000 BCE and spread rapidly. During the Neolithic Period, southern and central Sweden displayed the aspects of a homogeneous culture, with central European trade links; in northern Sweden the hunting culture persisted throughout the Stone and Bronze ages.

Settlers became familiar with copper and bronze around 1500 BCE. Information about Sweden's Bronze Age has been obtained by studying rock carvings and relics of the period, as, for example, the ornate weapons of chieftains and other decorative items preserved in the earth. The early Bronze Age (c. 1500–1000 BCE) was also characterized by strong continental trade links, notably with the Danube River basin. Stone Age burial customs (skeleton sepulture, megalithic monuments) were gradually replaced by cremation. Rock carvings suggest a sun cult and fertility rites. Upheavals on the continent, combined with Celtic expansion, seem to have interrupted (c. 500 BCE) bronze imports to Scandinavia, and a striking poverty of finds characterizes the next few centuries. The climate, comparatively mild since the Neolithic Period, deteriorated, necessitating new farming methods. At this time, iron reached the north.

For the early Iron Age (c. 400 BCE–c. 1 CE) the finds are also relatively scanty, showing only sporadic contacts with the La Tène culture, but they become more abundant from the Roman Iron Age (c. 1–400 CE) onward. The material from this period shows that Sweden had developed a culture of its own, although naturally reflecting external influences.

Trade links between the Roman Empire and Scandinavia gave Rome some knowledge of Sweden. The *Germania* (written 98 CE) of Tacitus gives the first description of the Svear, or Suiones (Swedes), stated to be powerful in men, weapons, and fleets. Other ancient writers who mention Scandinavia are Ptolemy, Jordanes, and Procopius.

THE VIKING AGE

At the beginning of this period a number of independent tribes were settled in what is now Sweden, and their districts are still partly indicated by the present divisions of the country. The Swedes were centred in Uppland, around Uppsala. Farther south the Götar lived in the agricultural lands of Östergötland and Västergötland. The absence of historical sources makes it impossible to trace the long process by which these provinces were formed into a united and independent state. The historical events leading to unification are reflected darkly in the Anglo-Saxon epic poem *Beowulf*—which gives the earliest known version of the word sveorice, svearike, sverige (Sweden)—and also in the Old Norse epic *Ynglingatal*, contained in the *Heimskringla* of Snorri Sturluson.

TRADE

As a result of Arab expansion in the Mediterranean area in the 8th and 9th centuries, the trade routes along the Russian rivers to the Baltic Sea acquired enhanced importance. In the second half of the 9th century, Swedish peasant chieftains secured a firm foothold in what is now western Russia and Ukraine and ruthlessly exploited the Slav population. From their strongholds, which included the river towns of Novgorod and Kiev, they controlled the trade routes along the Dnieper to the Black Sea and Constantinople (now Istanbul) and along

BIRKA

The medieval city of Birka in southeastern Sweden, on the Lake Mälar island of Björkö, was Sweden's first major urban centre. It served as a thriving international trade centre between western and eastern Europe.

Founded in the 9th century and thus one of the earliest urban settlements in Scandinavia, Birka was the Baltic link in the river and portage route through Russia to the Byzantine Empire. A major part of the city's commerce involved Russian, Byzantine, and Arabic goods, in addition to western European articles. Birka declined and disappeared after 975 because the Baltic island of Gotland was in a better strategic position for receiving Russian-Byzantine trade and perhaps also because the water level around Björkö had dropped. Birka's activity was taken over by Gotland and by a new Mälaren site, Sigtuna.

Model depicting the Swedish medieval city of Birka, one of the earliest settlements in Scandinavia. Anders Blomqvist/Lonely Planet Images/Getty Images

the Volga to the Caspian Sea and the East. Trade in slaves and furs was particularly lucrative, as the rich finds of Arab silver coins in Swedish soil demonstrate. Swedish Vikings also controlled trade across the Baltic; and it was for this activity that Birka, generally regarded as Sweden's oldest town, was founded (*c.* 800). Swedish Vikings took part in raids against western Europe as well.

From the 10th century, however, control of the Russian market began to slip from Swedish hands into those of Frisian, German, and Gotland merchants.

CHRISTIANIZATION

The first attempt to Christianize Sweden was made by the Frankish monk Ansgar in 830. He was allowed to preach and set up a church in Birka, but the Swedes showed little interest. A second Frankish missionary was forced to flee. In the 930s another archbishop of Hamburg, Unni, undertook a new mission, with as little success as his predecessors. In Västergötland to the southwest, Christianity, introduced mainly by English missionaries, was more generally accepted during the 11th century. In central Sweden, however, the temple at Uppsala provided a stronghold for pagan resistance, and it was not until the temple was pulled down at the end of the 11th century that Sweden was successfully Christianized.

The struggle between the old and new religions strongly affected the political life of Sweden in the 11th century. Olaf (Olof Skötkonung), who came from Västergötland but proclaimed himself ruler of all Sweden during the early 11th century, was baptized in Skara about the year 1000. He supported the new religion, as did his sons Anund Jakob (reigned c. 1022–c. 1050) and Edmund (c. 1050–60). The missionaries from Norway, Denmark, and even Russia and France, as well as from Hamburg, won converts, especially in Götaland, the area where the royal dynasty made its home and where early English missionaries had prepared the ground. Many pagans refused to abandon their old faith, however, and civil wars and feuds continued. Claimants vied for the throne until the mid-13th century, when a stable monarchy was finally achieved.

THE 12TH, 13TH, AND 14TH CENTURIES

When and where Sweden originated have long been matters of debate. Some historians contend that the cradle of Sweden is located in Västergötland and Östergötland—i.e., in the southwestern and southeastern parts of the country. Others maintain that Sweden was founded in the Lake Mälar region in Uppland by the Svear, who subjugated the central provinces and eventually conquered the provinces of Götaland. Evidence indicates, however, that, at the end of the Viking era in the 11th century, Sweden remained a loose federation of provinces. The local chieftains from time to time proclaimed themselves rulers over all Sweden, when in reality each formally exerted power only over his own province. It appears that the Swedish provinces were first united in the 12th century. The oldest document in which Sweden is referred to as a united and independent kingdom is a papal decree, by which Sweden in 1164 became a diocese with its own archbishop in Uppsala.

Sweden in the 12th century consisted of Svealand and Götaland, which were united into a single kingdom during the first half of that century, while the provinces of Skåne, Halland, and Blekinge in the south belonged to Denmark; Bohuslän in the west, along with Jämtland and Härjedalen in the north, were part of Norway. About 1130 Sverker, a member of a magnate family from Östergötland, was acknowledged as king, and this province now became the political centre of Sweden. Sverker sided with the church and established several cloisters staffed by French monks; he was murdered about 1156. During the later years of Sverker's reign, a pretender named Erik Jedvardsson was proclaimed king in Svealand; little is known about Erik, but according to legend he undertook a crusade to Finland, died violently about 1160, and was later canonized as the patron saint of Sweden.

CIVIL WARS

Erik's son Knut killed Sverker's son (1167) and was accepted as king of the entire country. Knut organized the currency system, worked for the organization of the church, and established a fortress on the site of Stockholm. After his death in 1196, members of the families of Erik and Sverker succeeded each other on the throne for half a century. While the families were battling for the throne, the archbishopric at Uppsala was established, and the country was organized into five bishoprics. The church received the right to administer justice according to canon law and a separate system

of taxation, protected by royal privileges, and the pretenders sought the church's sanction for their candidacies. The first known coronation by the archbishop was that of Erik Knutsson in 1210. The church also gave its sanction to the "crusades" against Finland and the eastern Baltic coast; the action combined an attempt at Christianization with an attempt at conquering the areas.

By the mid-13th century the civil wars were drawing to an end. The most important figure in Sweden at that time was Birger Jarl, a magnate of the Folkung family. The jarls (earls) organized the military affairs of the eastern provinces and commanded the expeditions abroad. Birger was appointed jarl in 1248 by the last member of the family of St. Erik, Erik Eriksson, to whose sister he was married. Birger's eldest son, Valdemar, was elected king when Erik died (1250). After Birger defeated the rebellious magnates, he assisted his son in the government of the country and gave fiefs to his younger sons. Birger was in fact ruler of the country until he died in 1266. During this time central power was strengthened by royal acts that were binding throughout Sweden, in spite of the existence of local laws in the provinces. The acts promulgated included those giving increased protection to women, the church, and the thing ("courts") and improving the inheritance rights of women. By a treaty with Lübeck in 1252, Birger promoted the growth of the newly founded city of Stockholm. At the same time, the Hanseatic merchants received privileges in Sweden, and the establishment of towns blossomed.

In 1275 Valdemar was overthrown by his brother Magnus I (Magnus Ladulås) with the help of a Danish army. In 1280 a law was accepted establishing freedom from taxes for magnates who served as members of the king's cavalry, creating a hereditary nobility; the following year Magnus Ladulås exempted the property of the church from all taxes. Under Magnus's reign the position of jarl disappeared and was replaced by the drots (a kind of vice king) and the marsk (marshall), together with the established kansler (chancellor). The export of silver, copper, and iron from Sweden increased trade relations with Europe, especially with the Hanseatic cities.

Magnus died in 1290 and was succeeded by his 10-year-old son, Birger. The regency was dominated by the magnates, especially by the marsk, Torgils Knutsson; even after Birger's coronation in 1302, Torgils retained much of his power. The king's younger brothers Erik and Valdemar, who were made dukes, attempted to establish their own policies and were forced to flee to Norway (1304), where they received support from the Norwegian king; the following year the three brothers were reconciled. A new political faction was created by the leaders of the church, whom Torgils had repressed, together with a group of nobles and the dukes, and in 1306 the marsk was executed. Birger then issued a new letter of privileges for the church, but his brothers captured and imprisoned him. Two years

later the kings of Denmark and Norway attacked Sweden on his behalf. Birger was again recognized king of Sweden at a peace concluded in 1310 with Denmark and Norway, but he was forced to transfer half of the kingdom to his brothers as fiefs. Erik's territory, together with his earlier acquisitions, then consisted of western Sweden, northern Halland, southern Bohuslän, and the area around Kalmar and stretched across the borders of the three Scandinavian kingdoms. In 1312 the dukes married two Norwegian princesses, increasing their power and dynastic position; but in December of 1317 the dukes were imprisoned by their brother following a family dinner, and they died in prison. The nobility rebelled against Birger, who was forced to flee to Denmark in 1318, and the king's son was executed.

CODE OF LAW

The magnates now seized control of Sweden and reasserted their power to elect a king. They chose Magnus, the three-year-old son of Duke Erik, who had shortly before inherited the crown of Norway. In connection with the election, the privileges of the church and the nobility were confirmed, and the king was not to be allowed to raise taxes without the approval of the council and the provincial assemblies. The magnates now revised the laws of Svealand and, by the Treaty of Nöteborg (1323), established the Finnish border with Russia. The Danish province of Skåne was bought and put under the Swedish king; by 1335 Magnus ruled over Sweden, including Skåne and Blekinge, Finland, and Norway, to which he soon added Halland. During Magnus's reign a national law code was established (c. 1350), providing for the election of the king, preferably from among the royal sons, and a new town law code was written that gave the German merchants considerable privileges. In 1344 Magnus's elder son Erik was elected heir to the Swedish throne, one year after his younger brother Haakon received the crown of Norway. Erik made common cause with the nobility and his uncle, Albert of Mecklenburg, against his father; and in 1356 Magnus was forced to share the kingdom with his son, who received Finland and Götaland. Two years later Erik died, and the kingdom was again united under Magnus's rule.

In his struggles with the nobles, Magnus received the support of the Danish king, Valdemar Atterdag, and in 1359 Magnus's son Haakon of Norway was engaged to Valdemar's daughter Margaret. The following year Valdemar attacked Skåne, and Magnus relinquished Skåne, Blekinge, and Halland in return for Valdemar's promise of help against Magnus's Swedish enemies. In 1361 Valdemar attacked Gotland and captured Visby, an important Baltic trading centre. Haakon, who had been made king of Sweden in 1362, and Margaret were married in 1363. Magnus's opponents among the nobility went to Mecklenburg and persuaded Duke Albert's son, also named Albert, to attack Sweden; Magnus was forced to flee to Haakon's

territory in western Sweden. In 1364 the Folkung dynasty was replaced by Albert of Mecklenburg (1363–89). Albert joined in a coalition of Sweden, Mecklenburg, and Holstein against Denmark and succeeded in forcing Valdemar Atterdag from his throne for several years. Albert was not as weak as the nobles had hoped, and they forced him to sign two royal charters stripping him of his powers (1371 and 1383). At the end of the 1380s Albert had plans to reassert his power, primarily by recalling the royal lands that had been given to the nobles; in 1388 the Swedish nobles called upon Margaret, now regent of Denmark and Norway, for help. In 1389 her troops defeated and captured Albert, and she was hailed as Sweden's ruler. Albert's allies harried the Baltic and continued to hold out in Stockholm, and it was only in 1398 that Margaret finally won the Swedish capital. In 1396 her greatnephew Erik of Pomerania, then about age 16, became nominal king of Sweden, and the following year he was hailed and crowned king of Sweden, Denmark, and Norway, marking the beginning of the Kalmar Union.

THE KALMAR UNION

Sweden had entered the Kalmar Union on the initiative of the noble opponents of Albert of Mecklenburg. After Margaret's victory over Albert and his allies, the national council announced its willingness to return those royal estates that had been given to its members during Albert's reign, and Margaret succeeded in carrying out the recall of this property. She remained popular with the Swedes throughout her reign, but her successor, Erik, who took real power after her death in 1412, appointed a number of Danes and Germans to administrative posts in Sweden and interfered in the affairs of the church. His bellicose foreign policy caused him to extract taxes and soldiers from Sweden, arousing the peasants' anger. His war with Holstein resulted in a Hanseatic blockade of the Scandinavian states in 1426, cutting off the import of salt and other necessities and the export of ore from Sweden, and led to a revolt by Bergslagen peasants and miners in 1434. The rebel leader, Engelbrekt Engelbrektsson, formed a coalition with the national council; in 1435 a national meeting in Arboga named Engelbrekt captain of the realm. Erik agreed to change his policies and was again acknowledged as king of Sweden by the council. Erik's agreement was not fulfilled to the Swedes' satisfaction, however, and in 1436 a new meeting at Arboga renounced allegiance to Erik and made the nobleman Charles (Karl) Knutsson captain of the realm along with Engelbrekt. Soon after, Engelbrekt was murdered by a nobleman; Charles Knutsson became the Swedish regent, and in 1438 the Danish council deposed Erik, followed in 1439 by the Swedish council.

The Danish council elected Christopher of Bavaria as king in 1440, and Karl Knutsson gave up his regency, receiving, in return, Finland as a fief,

whereupon the Swedish council also accepted Christopher. He died in 1448 without heirs, and Charles Knutsson was elected king of Sweden as Charles VIII of Sweden. It was hoped that he would be accepted as the union king, but the Danes elected Christian of Oldenburg. The Norwegians chose Charles as king, but a meeting of the Danish and Swedish councils in 1450 agreed to give up Charles's claims on Norway, while the councils agreed that the survivor of Charles and Christian would become the union king or, if this was unacceptable, that a new joint king would be elected when both were dead. Charles refused to accept this compromise, and war broke out between the two countries. In 1457 the noble opposition, led by Archbishop Jöns Bengtsson Oxenstierna, rebelled against Charles, who fled to Danzig. Oxenstierna and Erik Axelsson Tott, a Danish noble, became the regents, and Christian was hailed as king of Sweden. Christian increased taxes, and in 1463 the peasants in Uppland refused to pay and were supported by Oxenstierna, whom Christian then imprisoned. The bishop of Linköping, a member of the Vasa family, led a rebellion to free the archbishop, and Christian's army was defeated. Charles was recalled from Danzig (now Gdansk, Poland) and again became king, but within six months difficulties between him and the nobles, especially Oxenstierna and the bishop of Linköping, forced him to leave the kingdom. Oxenstierna served as regent from 1465 to 1466 and was succeeded by Tott;

Portrait of Christian II, king of Denmark, who usurped the Swedish crown in 1520. Christian II executed many Swedish citizens who had opposed him, giving rise to the Stockholm Bloodbath. © SuperStock

the battles between the two families led to the recall of Charles, who ruled from 1467 to his death in 1470.

POLITICAL CONFLICT

After Charles's death, Sten Sture the Elder was elected regent by the council; his army, including the Totts and their sympathizers, burghers, and men from Bergslagen, defeated Christian's troops in the Battle of Brunkeberg on the outskirts of Stockholm (1471). During Sten's rule, Uppsala University was founded (1477). When Christian I died in 1481, the matter of the union again arose, and in 1483 John, Christian's son, was accepted as king of Sweden; Sten, however, managed to delay his coronation until 1497. In 1493 a new element entered Nordic affairs: John formed an alliance with the Muscovite Ivan III Vasilyevich directed against Sweden, which led to an unsuccessful Russian attack on Finland in 1495. The council became discontented with Sten's acquisition of power and in 1497 called on John, whose army defeated Sten's. John was crowned and Sten returned to Finland. By 1501 John's supporters were discontented with his rule, and Sten was recalled as regent. He died in 1503, and Svante Nilsson Sture became regent. In 1506 a new war with Denmark began, in which Lübeck supported the Swedes. Svante died in 1512, and the council now attempted a reconciliation with Denmark under the regency of Erik Trolle, whose family supported the union. Svante's son, Sten Sture the Younger, led a coup, however, and was elected regent. Peace with Denmark was concluded in 1513.

The final years of the Kalmar Union were marked in Sweden by the struggle between the archbishop, Gustav Trolle (inaugurated 1516), and Sten Sture the Younger. The archbishop was head of the council, and he took over the leadership of the pro-union party. A civil war broke out, and in 1517 a meeting of the estates in Stockholm declared Trolle removed from his position. Despite military assistance from Christian II, Trolle was imprisoned. After a defeat by the Swedes, Christian began negotiations and took six noblemen, among them Gustav Vasa, to Denmark as hostages. The Swedish treatment of Trolle brought a papal interdict of Sweden, and Christian could now act as executor. In 1520 a Danish army of mercenaries attacked Sweden, and Sten Sture was mortally wounded in a battle won by the Danes. Christian was acknowledged as king in return for a promise of mercy and constitutional government. The peasants, led by Sten's widow, refused to abandon the war, however, and it was several months before Stockholm capitulated. Christian was then crowned by the archbishop as hereditary monarch, breaking his promises to the council; and, despite promises of amnesty, 82 people, noblemen and clergy who had supported the Stures, were executed for heresy in the Stockholm Bloodbath. The responsibility for this execution has aroused considerable discussion among Swedish and Danish historians; the large part played by Gustav Trolle is now generally accepted.

END OF THE UNION

Christian II now appeared to have Sweden under his control, but not all his opponents were dead or in prison. The nephew of Sten's widow, Gustav Vasa, had escaped from his Danish prison and returned to Sweden in 1520.

STOCKHOLM BLOODBATH

On November 8–9, 1520, the Danish king Christian II (reigned 1513–23) ordered the mass execution of Swedish nobles in an event that came to be known as the Stockholm Bloodbath. This incident led to the final phase of the Swedish war of secession from the Kalmar Union of the three Scandinavian kingdoms under Danish paramountcy.

With the support of the pope, Christian invaded Sweden in 1519 at the head of a large mercenary army after an antiunion Swedish faction led by Sten Sture the Younger had imprisoned the unionist archbishop Gustav Trolle. After defeating the Sture forces and taking Stockholm (September 1520), Christian, at the instigation of Trolle, had more than 80 Swedish nobles executed for heresy on November 8 and 9. Further executions followed, spreading throughout Sweden and Finland. The Kalmar Union seemed secured, but the outrage of the bloodbath alienated virtually all Swedish factions from support of the union. By 1522 Gustav I Vasa (reigned 1523–60) was able, with the help of the peasants of the Dalarna region and the Hanseatic League, to drive the Danes out of Sweden and finally to dissolve the Kalmar Union.

After the Stockholm Bloodbath he went to Dalarna, where the Stures had their staunchest support, and soon a rebellion there was under way, followed by others around the country. By the spring of 1521 the army of men from Dalarna had won its first battle with the Danes, and soon noblemen were allying themselves with Gustav, who was chosen regent in August. In 1522 he persuaded Lübeck to aid the Swedish rebels; in 1523 the Danish nobility forced Christian to give up the Danish throne and elected Frederick of Holstein-Gottorp as king. Three months later Gustav Vasa was elected Sweden's king by a meeting of the estates, and the Kalmar Union was dissolved.

The balance of power in Sweden shifted during the union from the monarchy to the nobility, who took over the government of the country while the union kings were resident in the other kingdoms. The monarchs' attempts to control the administration by appointing their own supporters from Denmark aroused protests and rebellion from the Swedes. During the later half of the union, a split developed within the nobility between a pro-union and an antiunion faction. The pro-unionists generally owned estates in Denmark or Norway as well as in Sweden and believed that a union monarch would enable the nobility to exercise greater influence; the antiunion nobles preferred a strong national monarchy supported by a strong national nobility. The king and regents elected in Sweden during the union period came from within the ranks of the antiunion nobility.

An important new class in society was composed of the commercial men and miners from Bergslagen, who were interested in the unimpeded export of Sweden's iron and copper. When the Danish interests conflicted with their own, most notably during the wars with the Germans, these men rebelled and supported a strong national monarchy, as did the burghers, who were also interested in the growth of trade. The church, on the other hand, preferred a weak monarch and supported the union.

The great majority of Swedes continued to be peasants, and agriculture was the basic occupation of more than 90 percent of the people. From the Viking period through the 12th and 13th centuries, the cultivation of land expanded. The plains in the centre of Svealand around Lake Mälar, as well as in Västergötland and Östergötland, were all cultivated by the end of that period, and the wooded areas in the adjacent provinces of Småland, Värmland, and Dalarna were being brought under cultivation. In the first half of the 14th century, the expansion ceased, and, during the rest of that century and the beginning of the 15th, a recession set in that gave rise to extensive wasteland, reduced production, and increased the cost of living. The Black Death, which struck Sweden in 1349–50, was one of the reasons for this crisis in the late Middle Ages; it was not confined to Sweden but spread through most of Europe. In the latter half of the 15th century, a recovery occurred, and the wasteland began to be reclaimed. The major surplus product of Sweden was butter; from the mid-14th century, a fourth of Sweden's export consisted of this product. As the lands exempt from taxation owned by the nobility and the clergy increased, the burden of taxation on the peasants grew; from the Engelbrekt rebellion in the 1430s through the remaining decades of the union, the peasants fought on the side of the antiunion forces.

THE EARLY VASA KINGS (1523–1611)

After Gustav I Vasa was elected to the throne in 1523, he began to restore the power of the Swedish king and to organize a central administration under his own direct leadership. On the one hand, this task was facilitated by the elimination of a great part of the high nobility by the Stockholm Bloodbath. On the other hand, the influence of the king was limited by the economic dependence of Lübeck and the Hanseatic League. In connection with the war against Denmark and the liberation of Stockholm in 1523, Gustav Vasa had been forced to make great concessions to Lübeck, which had given him both economic and military support. In exchange, the merchants of Lübeck and the Hanseatic League were given privileges that created a monopoly of Swedish foreign trade and even had considerable influence on domestic trade and industry. The concessions also included a large payment and left Sweden heavily in debt to Lübeck. Under the mediation of Lübeck, the war with Denmark was brought to an end by a treaty concluded in Malmö in 1524.

After the death of the Danish king Frederick I, his son Christian III became king in 1534. When Lübeck attempted at this time to restore the exiled Christian II as king in Denmark, Gustav Vasa gave the young Christian III strong military support in a war against Lübeck. The Hanseatic army was beaten in 1535, and by the terms of a truce in 1536 the Swedish debt to Lübeck was wiped out and the privileges of Lübeck traders were abolished. By this action Hanseatic hegemony was destroyed, other foreign traders were allowed to enter Sweden, and Swedish traders could now move freely beyond the Baltic. Sweden's relations with Denmark remained peaceful for the rest of Gustav Vasa's reign.

Gustav Vasa devoted the major part of his rule to domestic politics, and he is credited with establishing Sweden as a sovereign state. His initial goal as king was to stabilize the nation's financial situation. Through stern acts passed by the Diet at Västerås in 1527, he was able to confiscate all the properties of the Roman Catholic Church. The church at that time held 21 percent of Sweden's land, as opposed to only 6 percent held by the crown. The appropriation of the possessions of the church thus added enormously to the wealth of the state. To some degree the king could justify his actions on the basis of the doctrines of Martin Luther, which were being accepted nationwide with royal encouragement. The Swedish and Roman Catholic

HANSEATIC LEAGUE

The Hanseatic League (also called Hansa; German: Hanse) was founded by north German towns and German merchant communities abroad to protect their mutual trading interests. The league dominated commercial activity in northern Europe from the 13th to the 15th century. (*Hanse* was a medieval German word for "guild," or "association," derived from a Gothic word for "troop," or "company.")

The Hanseatic League attempted to protect its ship convoys and caravans by quelling pirates and brigands, and it fostered safe navigation by building lighthouses and training pilots. Most importantly, it sought to organize and control trade throughout northern Europe by winning commercial privileges and monopolies and by establishing trading bases overseas. The league established permanent commercial enclaves (*Kontore*) in a number of foreign towns, notably Bruges in Flanders, Bergen in Norway, Novgorod in Russia, and the Steel Yard in London. The league's principal trade consisted of grain, timber, furs, tar, honey, and flax traded from Russia and Poland to Flanders and England, which in turn sent cloth and other manufactured goods eastward to the Slavs. Swedish copper and iron ore were traded westward, and herring caught off the southern tip of Sweden was traded throughout Germany southward to the Alps.

The Hanseatic League's aggressively protectionist trading practices often aroused opposition from foreign merchants. The league typically used gifts and loans to foreign political leaders to protect its commercial privileges, and when this proved inadequate, it threatened to withdraw its trade and occasionally became involved in embargoes and blockades. Only in extreme cases did the league engage in organized warfare, as in the 1360s, when it faced a serious challenge from the Danish king Valdemar IV, who was trying to master the southwestern Baltic and end the league's economic control there. The league's members raised an armed force that defeated the Danes decisively in 1368, and in the Peace of Stralsund (1370) Denmark was forced to recognize the league's supremacy in the Baltic.

The Hanseatic League declined partly because it lacked any centralized power with which to withstand the new and more powerful nation-states forming on its borders. Lithuania and Poland were united in 1386; Denmark, Sweden, and Norway formed a union in 1397; and Ivan III of Moscow closed the Hanseatic trading settlement at Novgorod in 1494. The Hanseatic League Dutch were growing in mercantile and industrial strength, and in the 15th century they were able to oust German traders from Dutch domestic markets and the North Sea region as a whole. New maritime connections between the Baltic and Mediterranean seas and between the Old World and the Americas caused a gradual diversion of trade westward to the great Atlantic ports. By the mid-16th century, Dutch ships had even won control of the carrying trade from the Baltic to the west, dealing a serious blow to Lübeck. The league died slowly as England contested with the Netherlands for dominance in northern European commerce and Sweden emerged as the chief commercial power in the Baltic Sea region. The Hanseatic League's diet met for the last time in 1669.

churches separated as the Reformation spread, and the Lutheran Swedish church was eventually adopted as the state church. The establishment of the new religious order occurred simultaneously with a reorganization of government, which was accomplished with the assistance of German administrators brought in by Gustav. The new, highly centralized administration attained an unprecedented degree of efficiency.

During the latter part of his reign Gustav achieved absolute power and ruled Sweden in accordance with his own precepts. In 1544 the king established a hereditary monarchy in Sweden and accelerated the annexations of land, which finally gave the crown direct possession of about 60 percent of Swedish soil before he died. Gustav Vasa has been compared to a landowner in his behaviour toward the crown properties and the state incomes. He personally took part in developing their administration, and he continuously inspected the crown servants. He nominated county governors himself and reserved the most important charges for members of his own family. Money economy had barely come to Sweden, and many state incomes were therefore paid in kind; some of the goods exchanged were used directly to feed and clothe public servants and soldiers, while others were sold to foreign merchants. Gustav took great pleasure in literally filling the treasury, in which condition it was handed over to his son. The nobility was allowed no part in state affairs, and the Diet was convened only for

royal propaganda, of which Gustav was a master. Not surprisingly, Gustav's new system was not universally accepted. In such regions as Västergötland, Dalarna, and Småland, there was considerable resentment over the imposition of state control. In the 1530s and '40s the farmers grumbled over taxes, and the clergymen complained about interference in church matters. Gustav met opposition from his former friends—e.g., the farmer-miners of Dalarna—with the same ruthlessness as that from other dissenters. Gustav led a careful foreign policy; nevertheless, a considerable army and a strong navy were created during his reign. Sweden also advanced culturally under Gustav's rule: among the notable literary accomplishments of the period were a complete translation of the New Testament and the publication of the hymns and theological writings of Olaus Petri, who played an important role in the Swedish Reformation.

Following the death of Gustav Vasa, his oldest son, Erik XIV, became king. In his will Gustav had, however, appointed his younger sons dukes and given them part of the realm as duchies with great power in domestic affairs. One of the first steps taken by Erik XIV was to strip his brothers of all power by a treaty that he forced them to sign at Arboga in 1561. The main interest of Erik XIV was, however, devoted to foreign policy. One of his goals was to gain control of Russian trade through the Baltic ports. As a first step he negotiated with the Estonian nobility, which agreed to Swedish rule in 1561 and thereby laid the foundation for a Swedish Baltic empire. His aspirations led to conflicts with Denmark and Lübeck, which, up to the 16th century, had been the leading powers in this region. Control of the Baltic Sea became a central issue. In the 16th and 17th centuries the Baltic region, Europe's main source of grain, iron, copper, timber, tar, hemp, and furs, was as important as either the Mediterranean or the Atlantic. The Swedish effort to gain control over trade in the Baltic resulted in war with Denmark, Lübeck, and Poland in 1563. After seven bloody years, during which the southern parts of Sweden were ravaged, a peace was signed at Stettin (now Szczecin, Poland) in 1570, without change to any of the borders. Sweden was forced, however, to pay a large ransom to retrieve the fortress of Älvsborg, its only stronghold in the west. Before the peace was concluded, Erik XIV, accused of lunacy after having murdered some of the leading aristocrats by his own hand, was deposed in 1568 by his brother John, who was supported by the high nobility. Erik later died in prison, probably poisoned on the order of his brother.

With the support of the high nobility, John III ascended to the throne in 1568. His reign (1568–92) was characterized by conflict between the king and the high nobility, who asked for a constitutional government and greater influence for the council. At the same time, John tried to reintroduce Roman Catholic customs into the Swedish church, which led to conflict with the clergy. His religious policy was a consequence of his marriage to a Polish princess and the subsequent close political alliance between Sweden and Poland. Their son, Sigismund III Vasa, was elected king of Poland in 1587 before inheriting the throne of Sweden in 1592. Opposition to Sigismund developed because of his Roman Catholicism and his extensive stays in Poland. At a meeting in Uppsala in 1593 the clergy adopted a declaration that became the definitive confirmation of Sweden as a Lutheran country. The strong feelings against Sigismund were also exploited by his uncle Charles, who organized all conceivable Swedish opposition against the recognition of Sigismund. By doing so, Charles made the Diet (and of course the clergy) a political force against the high nobility. The final outcome was the resignation of Sigismund in 1599.

Charles IX was an administrator very much like his father. His foreign policy aimed at dominating the Russian trade routes toward the Kola Peninsula and the White Sea and at grasping as much as possible of the territory (Russian and other) south of the Gulf of Finland. Sweden thus was susceptible to Danish attack, which came in 1611 and began the so-called Kalmar War, a conflict that ended with the Peace of Knäred in 1613. By the terms of the peace, Sweden had to renounce its claim on the territories in the far north of Scandinavia and pay a new large ransom for the fortress of Älvsborg, taken by the Danes during the war. Charles

IX, however, did not live to experience the defeat.

THE AGE OF GREATNESS

The early Vasa kings created the Swedish state. Its chief characteristic was a strong monarchy in a rather rustic and backward economy (with the mining industry a noteworthy exception). Its chief weaknesses were opposition from the high nobility and a thirst for revenge on Denmark. In the following decades Sweden relegated Denmark to second place in the north and became a most aggressive great power.

THE REIGN OF GUSTAV II ADOLF

Gustav II Adolf (Gustavus II Adolphus; ruled 1611–32) was only 16 years old when his father, Charles IX, died, so the actual leadership passed to the aristocrat Axel Oxenstierna and the council. The regency period lasted only a few months, however, before Gustav Adolf took full power. After the Kalmar War the king joined in organizing the Swedes for the next war. Civil servants and officers were selected exclusively from among the nobility. A standing army was organized. The infantry was conscripted among the peasants and regularly trained by officers who lived on the king's farms among their soldiers; only the cavalry and the navy were professional. Swedish copper and iron were made into the best firearms of the period. The Swedish field artillery proved especially mobile and effective. The central administration was professionalized and became a model of efficiency; directing it were members of the high nobility, working together in collegiate bodies. The new organization of the Swedish administration, parts of which still exist, was confirmed by the constitution adopted in 1634.

When Gustav II Adolf ascended the throne, the country was already embroiled in wars with Denmark, Russia, and Poland. As noted above, the war with Denmark was concluded by the Peace of Knäred with some losses for Sweden. The war with Russia was fought more successfully, however, with Swedish armies even reaching Moscow. Russia was thereby forced to agree to the Treaty of Stolbovo in 1617, by the terms of which Sweden acquired the provinces of Ingria and Kexholm. The war with Poland continued into the 1620s, and after several campaigns in the Baltic States it was successfully concluded in 1629 by the Truce of Altmark, by which Sweden received Livonia and the right to the customs of key Baltic harbours. At about the same time, Gustav Adolf negotiated with France for its support against the German emperor, whose armies threatened the south shores of the Baltic. In 1630 Gustav Adolf with his Swedish army landed in northern Germany, joining in the Thirty Years' War. In 1631 Sweden concluded its treaty with France, and,

THIRTY YEARS' WAR

From 1618 to 1648, a series of intermittent conflicts in Europe were fought for various reasons, including religious, dynastic, territorial, and commercial rivalries. The overall war was mainly a struggle between the Habsburg-controlled Holy Roman Empire and the Protestant principalities that relied on the chief anti-Catholic powers of Sweden and the Netherlands. It also involved the rivalry of France with the Habsburg powers, which formed anti-French alliances. The conflicts began in 1618 when the future Emperor Ferdinand II tried to impose Roman Catholicism on his domains and the Protestant nobles rebelled; the war was sparked by the Defenestration of Prague. The battlefield centred on the principalities in Germany, which suffered severely from plundering armies. Early successes by the Catholic League were countered by military gains by Sweden. When the bloodshed ended with the Peace of Westphalia (1648), the balance of power in Europe had been radically changed. France emerged as the chief Western power, and states of the Holy Roman Empire were granted full sovereignty, establishing a framework for a modern Europe of sovereign states.

at Breitenfeld in that same year, the Swedish army practically annihilated the imperial forces under the famous Bavarian general the Count von Tilly.

Gustav Adolf's German campaign swept southward, and by late 1631 he had taken Mainz and Frankfurt am Main. By the spring and summer of 1632, he had marched through Bavaria, where Nürnberg, Augsburg, and Munich also fell. At Lützen on November 6, Gustav Adolf's Swedish forces engaged the imperial army led by Albrecht von Wallenstein, and a fierce battle ensued. The encounter resulted in an important tactical victory for Sweden but at great cost: Gustav Adolf was killed in battle.

Gustav Adolf's only heir, his daughter Christina, had not reached her sixth birthday at the time of her father's death. A council of the high nobility led by

the chancellor Axel Oxenstierna controlled the regency during her minority. The council resolved to carry on the war against Germany despite its great cost and a diminishing German threat.

WARFARE THROUGH THE MID-17TH CENTURY

For 16 more years the war continued with varying success. The Swedish armies, which at the beginning of the war were composed largely of Swedish peasants, consisted during its later stages mostly of mercenaries from Germany, Scotland, and England. Many foreign officers took up permanent residence in Sweden and were ennobled. At the Peace of Westphalia, which in 1648 ended the war, Sweden was granted most of Pomerania and other territorial concessions along the Baltic and the North Sea coasts, but the Polish ports had to be relinquished.

Sweden's strategic position was now entirely changed, and in a short war with Denmark (1643–45) Sweden

The Swedish empire in 1660. Encyclopædia Britannica, Inc.

demonstrated its military superiority and established its position as the dominant power in the Baltic region. During the reign of Queen Christina (ruled 1644–54), the transfer of crown property to the nobility, which had begun as an instrument to finance the wars, continued on an increasing scale. The queen, however, proved to have a remarkably independent will. She refused to marry, and she used the Diet and the threat of the Reduction (return of crown properties) to have her first cousin, Charles Gustav of the Palatinate, recognized as her heir to the throne. Then Christina, the daughter of the "saviour of Protestantism," abdicated, converted publicly to Catholicism, and went to Rome, where she lived the rest of her life.

In 1655 Charles X Gustav (ruled 1654–60) initiated a campaign (known as the First Northern War) in Poland and conquered most of the country. When in 1657 the resistance grew stronger, Denmark used the opportunity to declare war. Charles Gustav then turned his forces toward Denmark. In one of the most daring exploits in military history, he led his troops over the straits called the Belts, which only rarely freeze over, and scored a quick victory over the Danes. In the Peace of Roskilde that followed in February 1658, Sweden acquired the provinces of Skåne, Halland, Blekinge, and Bohuslän, thus establishing the country's modern-day boundaries. In addition, Sweden received Trondheim and the island of Bornholm, both of which were lost two years later when Charles Gustav,

in a second war against Denmark, tried to take the entire country and achieve his goal of unifying Scandinavia. The king suddenly died after failing to capture Copenhagen.

Charles XI, only four years old at his father's death, became king. During the long regency that followed, the influence of the high nobility under the chancellor Magnus Gabriel De la Gardie grew to a degree that threatened the freedom of the peasants and the finances of the crown. In 1672, at age 17, Charles XI led a difficult offensive against Denmark for possession of the southern provinces. Peace was finally agreed to in 1679 with no advantage for either side; Charles was then faced with the enormous problem of reorganizing the economy and the administration of the country.

IMPACT OF CONTINUOUS WARFARE

A generation of continuous warfare had had a profound impact on Swedish society. The Swedish nobility had gained about two-thirds of Swedish and Finnish soil through the transfer of crown property and of royal ground taxes. The nobles wanted to perpetuate this process and to introduce the same feudal structure that they had seen and used in their annexations in the Baltic area.

This danger to Swedish and Finnish peasants was not finally averted until the 1680s, when the noble possessions were greatly reduced. The reduction had started in the 1650s as a means of leverage to get the high nobles to pay their taxes and agree to various acts. Faced with this threat, the high nobility agreed to pay, and even agreed to minor reductions in their possessions. While Charles XI was still a minor during the 1660s, the high nobles were able to retain their advantages for yet another generation.

With the reduction of the holdings of the nobility in the 1680s, Sweden returned to the political structure of the early Vasa kings. The income of public properties recaptured from the nobility was permanently allotted to public servants, officers, and soldiers. This system, which remained in force throughout the 18th century and far into the 19th, made the crown less dependent on the Diet in matters of finance. The years 1680–1700 were a period of consolidation. It has been called the Carolingian absolutism because it occurred during the reign of Charles XI (ruled 1672–97). But, because of the precariousness of the Swedish annexations in the Baltic, the Carolingian absolutism involved a continuous preparation for war.

THE REIGN OF CHARLES XII

Charles XII acceded to the throne at age 15 at a time when, in the hinterland of the Baltic coast, dominated by the Swedes, new states were being formed. Brandenburg and Russia, together with such older states as Denmark and Poland, were natural enemies of Sweden. Denmark, Poland, and Russia made a treaty in 1699, while Prussia preferred to wait and see. The Second Northern War (also known as the Great Northern War) began when the three allies attacked the Swedish provinces in February 1700, prompting a swift retaliatory attack on Denmark by Swedish forces. The strike by Sweden forced Denmark to leave the alliance and conclude peace. The Russian army, which had invaded Sweden's Baltic provinces, was shortly afterward overwhelmingly beaten by Charles's troops at the Battle of Narva. Charles then turned toward Poland (1702–06). In so doing, he gave the Russian tsar, Peter I (the Great), sufficient time to found St. Petersburg and a Baltic fleet and to reorganize the Russian army. Charles XII began his Russian offensive in 1707. The Russians for the first time used a scorched-earth strategy, thus diverting the Swedish armies from Moscow to Ukraine, where the Swedes suffered a crushing defeat at Poltava in June 1709.

Charles spent the next five years in Bender (now Bendery, Moldova), then under Turkish rule, attempting in vain to persuade the Turks to attack Russia. The sultan clearly had no reason to do so because Peter had turned his attention toward the Baltic. In the years following Poltava, Russia occupied all the Swedish annexations on the Baltic coast and even Finland; Hannover occupied Bremen and Verden; Denmark took Holstein-Gottorp; and Prussia lay waiting for the Swedish part of Pomerania.

Astonishingly, Charles governed Sweden from his residence in Bender during this catastrophe. In 1715 he returned to Sweden (he had left in 1700). He then decided to attack Norway in order to obtain a western alliance against the Baltic powers. On November 30, 1718, during a siege of the fortress of Fredriksten east of the Oslo fjord, Charles was killed by a bullet of either Norwegian or Swedish origin. His death ended the so-called Age of Greatness. By the Peace of Nystad (1721), Sweden formally resigned the Baltic provinces, part of Karelia, and the city of Vyborg (near St. Petersburg) to Russia.

SOCIAL AND ECONOMIC CONDITIONS

As in most of Europe, agriculture was the main preoccupation in the Scandinavian countries in the 16th and 17th centuries. But increasing economic activity in these centuries stimulated a more specialized and commercial exploitation of their natural resources.

Because of the growing demand for cereals and meat in western Europe, Denmark underwent the same change as did the countries east of the Elbe—the domanial system was introduced for commercial agriculture and cattle raising. Sweden and Norway had other resources. Their forests were still virgin, thus providing the indispensable raw materials for European shipbuilding and overseas expansion. Because the trees grew slowly, the wood became hard and well suited also for furniture and tools.

The mining industry in Sweden was founded in the 13th century. In the 16th and 17th centuries copper and iron were the most important exports from Sweden. But Sweden also had its own metallurgical industry, producing weapons especially.

The Scandinavian countries had very little active foreign trade of their own. Only Dutch and British—and to a certain extent German—merchants had sufficient capital and the foreign ties to organize the export.

The landlordship in Sweden sprang less from economic than from political causes. The Swedish nobility had a vested interest in lifting Sweden from its underdog position of the 16th century. As noted, the nobles acquired strong positions as commanders and administrators in the conquered areas. Thus, in Sweden, they were able to introduce the domanial system on the soil transferred to them during the Age of Greatness. But, in great contrast to Denmark or the conquered areas, serfdom never came to Sweden; Swedish farmers remained free. Sweden was the only European country in which peasants formed the fourth estate in the Diet. Since the Middle Ages royal propaganda had been designed to influence the opinion of the peasants in political matters.

Because Swedish industry was adapted to Sweden's aggressive foreign policy and because exports were in foreign hands, there was little room for an independent bourgeoisie in this period. Social mobility was primarily influenced by the state. Individual careers and personal fortunes could best be made as soldiers, purveyors to the crown, officers, and public servants. In the 16th and 17th centuries the social structure of Sweden also spread to the formerly completely agrarian Finland.

Swedish society had a considerable capacity for assimilation. Although Denmark-Norway did not until 1720 give up hope of recapturing the provinces that had been lost to Sweden around the middle of the 17th century, it could not count on active support from the populations of these provinces.

THE 18TH CENTURY

Charles XII had no successor. In 1718 his sister Ulrika Eleonora had to convene the Diet in order to be elected. In 1720 she abdicated in favour of her husband, Frederick of Hessen (ruled 1720–51).

THE AGE OF FREEDOM (1718–72)

This period saw a transition from absolutism to a parliamentary form of government. The real reason for the change was the complete failure of the policy of "greatness" connected with the Carolingian absolutism. According to the constitutional laws of 1720–23, the power now rested with the estates. The estates met regularly in the Diet, which designated the council. There the king was accorded a double vote but had no right to make decisions. In the Diet, decision making took place in the "Secret Committee," from which the peasants, or the fourth estate, were excluded. The public sessions of the estates in the Diet were reserved for speeches and debates. The three upper estates consisted mainly of state servants. Thus, the so-called Age of Freedom, which lasted until 1772, was also an age of bureaucracy.

During this period a dual-party system evolved; the parties were known by the nicknames "Nightcaps" (or "Caps") and "Hats." Both parties were mercantilist, but the Nightcaps were the more prudent. Up to 1738 the Nightcaps were in power. They led a most careful foreign policy so as not to provoke Russia. From 1738 to 1765 power passed to the Hats, who made treaties with France in order to obtain subsidies and support against Russia. War with Russia in 1741–43 led to a temporary Russian occupation of Finland and to a further loss of Finnish provinces northwest of St. Petersburg. A war with Prussia in 1757–62 was very expensive. The Hats attempted to make Sweden a great economic power, but their economic policy and the war costs led to inflation and financial collapse, and their regime came to an end in 1765.

For some years political confusion reigned in Sweden. The Nightcaps received subsidies from Russia, and their negotiations with Prussia and Denmark intensified party struggles in Sweden. Economic chaos, territorial losses, foreign infiltration, and famine in the countryside undermined the parliamentary system. Historians have sometimes stressed these failures too strongly, however, in glorifying the past Carolingian age and the future Gustavian epoch. It has become increasingly clear that during the period the Swedish heritage of freedom was significantly shaped. A true parliamentary system gradually developed, which, although hampered by cumbersome procedures, is a notable parallel to the contemporary English system. The political changes that marked the period are especially significant because of their influence on the Swedish constitution. Despite the turmoil that prevailed, the period was notable for its social and cultural advancements. Ideas about land reform were formulated; progress in science was encouraged; and the Swedish press was initiated. Noteworthy individual achievements include the thermometer scale of Anders Celsius, the botanical classification system of Carolus Linnaeus (Carl von Linné), and the religious philosophical postulations of Emanuel Swedenborg. During the Age of Freedom, Sweden reached a level of scholarly and cultural attainment equal to that of the most advanced nations of western Europe. By the last years of this period, however, numerous problems beset the country, and Sweden was ripe for a change of government.

THE ERA OF GUSTAV III

When Frederick of Hessen died in 1751, he was succeeded by Adolf Frederick, who ruled until his death in 1771. While visiting Paris, Gustav III (ruled 1771–92) acceded to the throne. Before returning, he concluded another treaty with France. In 1772 he used the royal guard and officers of the Finnish army to seize control of the government from the parliament in a bloodless coup d'état. Gustav tried to exploit the Vasa and Carolingian traditions of personal royal power. He could rely on no class of the Swedish society nor on the political institutions of the 18th century, so he had to make the most of royal propaganda to the public. In this he was not without success; the traditional picture of Gustav is that of "King Charming," the promoter of the arts and sciences.

But Gustav's politics were unstable. Until 1786 he put into effect social reforms that belonged to enlightened despotism, thus enmeshing himself in its traditional dilemma: alienating the "haves" without satisfying the "have nots." Even his solution to the dilemma was a traditional one—war. After Turkey attacked Russia in 1787, Gustav went to war against Russia in 1788 to recapture the Finnish provinces. The Swedish attack failed, partly because of a conspiracy by noble Swedish officers—the Anjala League—who, during the war, sent a letter to Catherine II (the Great) of Russia, proposing negotiations. Gustav used the treason of the Anjala League to provoke an outburst of genuine patriotism in Sweden, hoping to channel popular opinion through the Diet, which he convened in 1789. At this Diet the king called the four estates to a joint meeting, where he, with the support of the members of the three lower estates, overruled the nobility and stripped the council of all its authority, giving the king absolute power. At the same time, however, the three lower estates, against Gustav's will, abolished practically all the privileges of the nobility (e.g., the nobility no longer had special rights to any posts in the administration or to any category of Swedish land). On March 16, 1792, the king was mortally wounded by a nobleman and former officer of the royal guards. The last years of the king and especially the days between the shooting and his death (March 29) made him a martyr in the minds of his people, perhaps undeservedly.

Viewed in its entirety, the 18th century in Sweden was a golden age of trade and commerce. In 1731 the Swedish East India Company was founded, which was extremely successful until it was forced out of business during the Napoleonic Wars. The capital produced by the East India Company and other commercial enterprises formed the basis for a rapid growth of manufacturing enterprises, such as shipbuilding and textile production. But the most important manufacturing industry in Sweden was

Scene depicting the assassination of Gustav III in 1792.© Pantheon/SuperStock

ironworking, which expanded rapidly during the 18th century. Iron was also the most important export commodity, and the production of pig iron in Sweden increased to more than one-third of world production by 1750.

The 18th century was also characterized by great social changes. Farmers obtained the right to purchase clear title to crown lands, and so most of the peasants came to own their farms. At the same time, the prices of their products were increased and profits grew. This development coincided with the growth of a large rural proletariat. The burghers' wealth and influence grew rapidly, as did trade and industry. A consequence of the social changes was that commoners were allowed to own exempt land and were admitted to high government posts previously held only by nobles. The nobility became less exclusive, and social mobility increased.

THE NAPOLEONIC WARS AND THE 19TH CENTURY

A fear of the influence of revolutionary France dominated the Swedish government during the last decade of the 18th century and the first of the 19th. These fears were reflected in major economies in public finances, the legislation of land reforms, and the censoring of French literature.

ROYALIST REACTION

Gustav IV (ruled 1792–1809), unlike his father, Gustav III, was pious and superstitious. He considered events in France to be insults to moral order. A deep aversion toward the revolutionaries and toward Napoleon characterized his foreign policy. Of decisive importance was his resolution in 1805 to join the coalition

ANJALA LEAGUE

The Swedish war effort in the Russo-Swedish War (1788–90) was undermined by the Anjala League, a group of Swedish army officers who felt that the war was illegal. Shortly after the outbreak of war, 113 officers in the Finnish town of Anjala dispatched a letter to Empress Catherine II the Great of Russia calling for peace on the basis of the pre-1743 status quo—one favourable to Sweden. Although this condition made Catherine's acceptance unlikely, it did not lessen the letter's treasonable nature. In another document the officers demanded the abdication of the king. When King Gustav III of Sweden learned of these documents, he called upon the officers to repudiate it in return for a full pardon. The officers, however, answered that the war was unjust and therefore Swedes could not be inspired to fight to victory; they denied that their act had been treasonable, noting that they would consider a refusal by Catherine to negotiate as a personal attack on them. Unmoved by this explanation, Gustav III, after first dealing successfully with an attack in the west by Denmark, punished the Anjala group in 1789: one officer was executed, and many were imprisoned.

against France. When France and Russia signed the Treaty of Tilsit in 1807, Gustav stubbornly accepted war, even with Russia. Denmark, which had sided with France in October 1807, declared war against Sweden in 1808. England, at the moment busy in Spain, could offer little help. Sweden thus became politically isolated, with enemies in the east, south, and west. The Swedish army defended Finland poorly, with that defense reaching its nadir when the strong fortress of Sveaborg near Helsingfors was handed over to the Russians by treason. The Russians advanced as far as Umeå in Sweden.

In March 1809 Gustav IV was deposed by a group of high officials and officers. More than anything else, a widespread longing for a quick and cheap peace brought the men of 1809 to power, but they were unable to save Finland. In September 1809 a bitter peace was made at Fredrikshamn, in which Sweden surrendered Finland and the Åland Islands (northeast of Stockholm) to Russia. A new constitution was promulgated, embodying the principle of separation of powers. The division of the Diet into four estates remained. Charles XIII (ruled 1809–18), the uncle of Gustav IV, was elected king. The fact that he was senile and childless opened the question of succession to the throne.

With the consent of Denmark, the commander in chief of the Norwegian army, Christian August (at the moment waging war against Sweden), was elected crown prince and took the name Charles August. Behind this decision were thoughts of a Scandinavian confederation. This solution was cherished by Denmark and even by Napoleon.

In 1810 Charles August died, and the question of the succession to the throne was reopened. The old king, Charles XIII, and the majority of the council wanted to elect the brother of the deceased, the Danish prince Frederick Christian of Augustenborg. However, the younger officers and civil servants, who were great admirers of Napoleon and wanted Sweden to join France, worked for another solution. A Swedish lieutenant, Baron Carl Otto Mörner, was sent to Paris as their envoy to offer one of Napoleon's marshals the throne of Sweden. The choice fell on the prince of Pontecorvo, the marshal Jean-Baptiste Bernadotte. This choice pleased Napoleon, though he may have preferred the Swedish throne to be taken over by his ally King Frederick VI of Denmark-Norway. Meanwhile, the French consul in Gothenburg and the Francophile Swedish foreign minister, Lars Engeström, managed to persuade the Diet to set aside the Danish alternative and to name Bernadotte as crown prince of Sweden in August 1810.

BERNADOTTE

From his arrival in Sweden in October 1810, Bernadotte, who took the name Charles John, became the real leader of Swedish politics. In designating him for the crown, the Swedes hoped that he would somehow reconquer Finland and the Åland Islands. Charles John, however, who was well aware of the weakness of the Napoleonic empire, initiated a completely different policy. Rather than fight for Finland, he sought alliances with Napoleon's enemies that would permit Sweden to take Norway from Denmark. He approached Tsar Alexander I of Russia, and in April 1812 Sweden entered a treaty by which it promised to support Russia against Napoleon. According to the treaty, Finland would remain a Russian possession, but in compensation Sweden would be allowed to acquire Norway. When Napoleon began his Russian campaign shortly thereafter, Charles John sided with Tsar Alexander. A meeting between Charles John and Alexander in August 1812 further strengthened the alliance, and the tsar apparently promised to support Charles John's plan to play a major political role in France after the fall of Napoleon.

Charles John then turned to the West. In March 1813 he negotiated a treaty with England by which, for participating in the final offensive against Napoleon, England also agreed to let Charles John take Norway. Thus, Charles John became commander in chief of the northern allied army, consisting of Prussian, Russian, and Swedish soldiers. He used this army sparingly, especially the Swedish contingent, even at the Battle of Leipzig

in October 1813, because he cherished a hope of succeeding Napoleon and also because he needed troops to attack Denmark. After Leipzig, Charles John refused to cross the Rhine; instead he led the northern army against Denmark. The result was the Treaty of Kiel, whereby Norway was surrendered.

By accepting a constitution in Norway, Charles John became heir, peacefully, to his second throne in four years and consequently gained a more independent position in Sweden. He hoped, moreover, to impress liberal circles in France favourably. The cession of Finland to Russia was a bitter loss for Sweden; but, in the words of the Swedish historian Sten Carlsson in 1969, "The loss of Finland was the price of the long and still unbroken period of peace that was to begin in 1814."

SOCIETY AND POLITICS (1815–1900)

The population of Sweden, which in 1815 was barely 2.5 million, reached 3.5 million by 1850 and 5.1 million by 1900. During the period 1815 to 1900, therefore, the country's population had more than doubled, despite a loss of 850,000 emigrants (mainly to North America) during the period 1840 to 1900.

POPULATION AND THE ECONOMY

Until the last quarter of the 19th century, Sweden was a predominantly agricultural country. In 1850, 90 percent of the population lived off the land. By 1900 the figure was still as high as 75 percent. At the beginning of the 19th century, rural dwellings were clustered together in the villages, and the fields were cultivated under an old open-field system. The basis for an agricultural modernization was laid down by a statute of 1827 on enclosures (laga skifte), which stated that, when possible, the fields of the individual farm should be assembled together in a compact area. Enclosures of lands, which took place throughout the 19th century, changed the face of the countryside. Villages were split up, and scattered farms became the predominant type of dwelling in Sweden. The move away from the village system brought about a widespread reclamation of wasteland and the modernization of agriculture, which accounted in part for the increase in population.

During the first half of the 19th century, trade and industry were still restricted by regulations and guild rules. The middle of the 19th century witnessed the beginning of industrial organization, primarily in the timber trade, and in the last quarter of the 19th century the industrial revolution began in earnest with the advent of new methods in iron and steel production and the birth of a number of specialized industries, such as those of machines and machine tools. During the greater part of the 19th century, however, Sweden was a poor and overpopulated country.

THE CONSERVATIVE ERA (1815–40)

At the conclusion of the Napoleonic Wars, Sweden was hard hit by an economic slump that lasted until 1830, characterized by abortive attempts to reestablish the value of the currency. After devaluation in 1834, the currency was finally stabilized. Charles John, who became king under the name of Charles XIV John (ruled 1818–44), pursued a strictly conservative policy. The king's power, invested in him by the constitution, was exploited to the limit; and the ministers were recruited from his henchmen without regard to the wishes of parliament. In the 1820s the liberal opposition steadily increased its demands for reforms, and 1830 was the year in which liberal opinion made a breakthrough. In Sweden this was indicated by the establishing of a newspaper, *Aftonbladet*, which, with Lars Johan Hierta as editor, became the leading journal of the liberal opposition. Simultaneously, the king's one-man rule, which was exercised through his powerful favourite Magnus Brahe, became even more emphatic. The struggle against the growing liberal opposition, which reached its climax at the end of the 1830s, was characterized by actions against the freedom of the press and indictments of high treason and countered by the liberals with sharp criticism, demonstrations, and street riots.

LARS JOHAN HIERTA

Lars Johan Hierta (born January 23, 1801, Uppsala, Sweden—died November 20, 1872, Stockholm) was a journalist and politician. He is known for being a leading agitator for Swedish political and social reform.

Hierta's work as a clerk for the noble estate of the Riksdag (estates assembly) in the 1820s acquainted him with the operation of the increasingly conservative Swedish regime and made him its critic. He established the *Aftonbladet* ("Evening Press") in 1830, remaining its owner-editor until 1851. Under him the newspaper gained a large and loyal following for its wide-ranging liberal opposition to the regime (causing conservatives to refer to Hierta as "King Lars"). In the 1830s he countered numerous attempts of the government to suppress the paper by reissuing it under such slightly different names as Second *Aftonbladet*, Fourth *Aftonbladet*, etc., until censorship was ended in 1844.

The main issues Hierta fought for were extension of the franchise, a modern parliament, mass public education, and free choice of occupation. He was elected to the third (middle-class) chamber of the Riksdag in 1859, and, as a leader in that body, he continued to press for reform, which culminated in the establishment of a modern two-chamber parliament (still called the Riksdag) in 1865. From 1866 to 1872 he served as president (*ålderspresident*) of the lower chamber.

THE LIBERAL REFORM PERIOD

The pressure of the opposition, however, at last forced the king to yield, and the 1840 parliament, in which the liberal opposition had attained a majority, forced through the "departmental reform," which meant that the ministers actually became the heads of their own ministries. Another reform of great significance was the introduction in 1842 of compulsory school education. When Charles XIV John died in 1844 and was succeeded by his son Oscar I (ruled 1844–59), the liberal reform period had already gained momentum.

PRINCIPAL REFORMS

Among the most important of the reforms was the introduction of free enterprise in 1846, which meant the abolition of the guilds. They were now replaced by free industrial and trade associations. Simultaneously, the monopoly of trade that the towns had held since the Middle Ages was also abolished. Finally, by the introduction of a statute in 1864, complete freedom of enterprise became a reality. The lifting of almost all bans on exports and imports in 1847, together with a reduction in customs duties, was the first step toward free trade. A number of other liberal reforms were introduced: equal rights of inheritance for men and women (1845), unmarried women's rights (1858), a more humane penal code through a number of reforms (1855–64), religious freedom (1860), and local self-government (1862). Another significant step was the decision in 1854 that the state should be responsible for the building and management of main-line railroads.

PARLIAMENTARY REFORM

Oscar I, who took the initiative himself in many of these reforms, became more conservative after the disturbances in Stockholm in 1848. When he was succeeded by his son, Charles XV (ruled 1859–72), the power had in reality gradually passed into the hands of the privy council, which, under the leadership of the minister of finance, Baron Johan August Gripenstedt, and the minister of justice, Baron Louis De Geer, completed the reforms. From the beginning of the 19th century, the most important of the liberal demands had been for a reform of the system of representation. It was not until 1865–66 that agreement was reached to replace the old Riksdag—with its four estates of nobility, clergy, burghers, and peasantry—with a parliament consisting of two chambers with equal rights. The members of the first were chosen by indirect vote and with such a high eligibility qualification that it bore the stamp of an upper chamber representing great landowners and commercial and industrial entrepreneurs. The members of the

BARON JOHAN AUGUST GRIPENSTEDT

Baron Johan August Gripenstedt (born August 11, 1813, Holstein [now in Germany]—died July 13, 1874, Stockholm, Sweden) initiated and guided Sweden's transition to a capitalist economy. He also played a decisive part in turning Sweden away from a Pan-Scandinavian foreign policy in the 1860s.

After a career as an artillery officer in the Swedish army, Gripenstedt entered the upper chamber of the Riksdag (estates assembly; after 1865, the modern Swedish Parliament), in which he became the country's leading advocate of economic liberalism. While serving as minister without portfolio from 1848 to 1850 and from 1852 to 1855 and as finance minister in 1851 and again from 1856 to 1866, he emphasized the need to adopt a free-trade policy. After bringing about partial tariff reductions in the 1850s, he negotiated a trade agreement with France in 1865 embodying the principle of free trade. After ratification by the Riksdag, the agreement initiated a national policy of minimal trade restrictions. In 1863 Gripenstedt played a major role in Sweden's foreign policy by dissuading the government from entering a defense alliance with Denmark that would have embroiled Sweden in Denmark's war against Prussia and Austria (1864). His action led to the decline of the Pan-Scandinavian movement.

second were chosen by direct popular vote, which was limited, however, by a property qualification and therefore gave the farmers an advantage.

POLITICAL STAGNATION (1866–1900)

The reform of the representative system marked the end of the liberal reform period. During the following 20 years, Swedish politics were dominated by two issues: the demand for an abolition of ground tax, which had been levied from ancient times, and the defense question, where the demand was for an abolition of the military system of indelningsverket—i.e., an army organization in which the soldiers were given small holdings to live on. The defense system was to be modernized by an increase in conscription. The first chamber's demand for rearmament, however, was impossible in view of the second chamber's demand for the abolition of the ground tax. As these issues had been linked together in the 1873 compromise, they were not resolved until 1892, when it was decided to abolish the ground tax and to replace the old army organization with a larger and better-trained conscripted army. The latter was completed through the defense reform of 1901, which introduced a conscripted army with a 240-day period of service.

The falling prices of wheat on the world market in the 1880s gave rise to a serious agricultural crisis. In 1888 a moderate tariff was introduced that was gradually raised in the following years. The second chamber, which since the electoral reform had been dominated by the Farmers' Party, was at this time split into a protectionist faction and a free-trade faction. In this era the parties that still dominate Swedish politics today came into being: the Swedish Social Democratic Workers' Party (SAP; commonly called the Swedish Social Democratic Party) was founded in 1889; liberal factions in the Riksdag merged into the Liberal Union in 1900; and conservatives united under the banner of the Conservative (later Moderate) Party in 1904.

FOREIGN POLICY

Until the end of the 19th century, foreign policy was still regarded as the monarch's personal province. Already, as crown prince, Charles John had concluded an alliance with Russia against almost unanimous opposition and by so doing initiated the Russia-oriented policy that characterized the whole of his reign. The succession of Oscar I to the throne in 1844 brought no immediate alteration. The only deviation was in his somewhat carefully demonstrated sympathy for the growing Pan-Scandinavian movement. When the German nationals rebelled against the Danish king in 1848, Oscar I aligned himself with Frederick VII and contributed, together with the tsar, to a cease-fire and armistice.

CHANGE IN ALLIANCE POLICY

During the negotiations on Schleswig-Holstein, Oscar I was still on the side of Tsar Nicholas I of Russia, aligned more or less against the radical nationalism in Germany. But in reality he endeavoured to extricate Sweden from the conservative Russia-oriented policy that Charles John had initiated in 1812. The opportunity came during the Crimean War (1853–56), when Oscar I adopted a friendly attitude to the Western powers and, among other things, opened Swedish harbours to English and French warships and tried to induce the Western powers, with the help of Swedish troops, to attack St. Petersburg. With this intention, he signed the November Treaty with the Western powers in 1855. The peace treaty that was concluded in Paris shortly afterward, however, ended the hopes cherished in Sweden of winning Finland, or at least Åland, back again. All that was gained was the Åland Convention, which forbade Russia to build fortifications or to have other military installations on Åland.

PAN-SCANDINAVIANISM

During the 1840s and '50s the idea of a united Scandinavia had won great support among students and intellectuals. Crown Prince Charles had spoken out enthusiastically in favour of this ideal, and, after his succession to the throne in 1859, he assured the Danish king of Sweden's solidarity, promising Swedish support to defend the frontier at the Eider—the southern boundary of Schleswig. Encouraged by these promises, Denmark embarked upon the policy that led to the Danish-Prussian War of 1864. The Swedish government, however, reluctantly refused to honour the king's pledge. Scandinavian unity subsequently suffered a decisive defeat and ceased to be the guiding light of Swedish foreign policy.

NEUTRALITY AND FRIENDSHIP WITH GERMANY

In the wars between Prussia and Austria in 1866 and between Germany and France in 1870–71, Sweden was officially neutral, even if in the latter the king's personal sympathies were with France. Oscar II (ruled 1872–1907) reoriented the country's foreign policy. The new German Empire, under the leadership of Otto von Bismarck, excited his admiration. At the same time, connections with Germany became much closer, and from the mid-1870s Swedish politics were influenced by a close friendship with Germany, which was emphasized during the last years of the 19th century by the growing fear of Russia.

THE SWEDISH-NORWEGIAN UNION

From the Swedish viewpoint, the union with Norway was a disappointment.

Instead of an alliance of the two countries, the incompatibilities grew, and the union was actually confined to a joint monarchy and foreign policy. One of the few positive results of the union was an 1825 statute that abolished or greatly reduced tariffs between the countries. The union also had an important influence on Sweden's domestic affairs, and Norway served as a model for Swedish radicals who demanded parliamentary democracy.

As crown prince in the 1850s, Charles XV had promised the Norwegians that on his succession to the throne he would abolish the post of governor-general, which in Norway was regarded as a sign of the country's subordinate position in the union. In reality, the post of governor-general had not been occupied by a Swede since 1829 and had been vacant since 1855. When Charles XV succeeded to the throne, however, and tried to honour his pledge to abolish the post, the Swedish parliament and the government headed by the powerful minister of finance, Baron J.A. Gripenstedt, opposed the resolution. Charles XV was forced to give way. The government, with support from parliament, had thus strengthened its position over the king. The governor-general question marked the beginning of the struggle for power between king and parliament that characterized Sweden's internal politics for the rest of the 19th century. With the dissolution of the union in 1905, the king's power was again usurped, and a government chosen by the majority parties in parliament and headed by the right-wing leader Christian Lundeberg was appointed to negotiate with Norway. Thus, the dissolution of the union led to the first real parliamentary government in Sweden.

THE 20TH CENTURY

The economic expansion that started in the early 19th century laid the foundations for internal developments in Sweden during the 20th century. The turning point came during and immediately after World War I. There was suddenly a worldwide demand for Swedish products such as steel and pulp, matches and ball bearings, telephones and vacuum cleaners. The composition of the population underwent a decisive change, and Sweden was transformed from an agricultural to a modern industrial country.

POLITICAL REFORM

Politically, the economic development meant that a universal and equal franchise was more and more vociferously demanded. The issue was solved in 1907 by a compromise submitted by a Conservative government under the leadership of Arvid Lindman. The motion granted a universal and equal franchise for the second chamber, a certain democratization of the first chamber, and proportional representation for elections to both chambers of the Riksdag. The elections to the second chamber in 1911 produced a landslide victory for the Liberal Party, which had grown out of the Liberal Union of 1902, and Gustav V (ruled 1907–50) was forced to ask Karl Staaff to form a Liberal government.

DEFENSE POLICY

One of the most important points of Liberal policy in 1911 was a decrease in military expenditure. The realization of this demand led to sharp conflicts between Gustav V and Staaff. As the tension between the Great Powers grew, a farmers' rally was organized, and 30,000 farmers from all over the country sought out the king and demanded that the country's defenses be strengthened. In his reply (Borggårdstalet, the Courtyard Speech) the king promised to reinforce the military defenses. As he had given this pledge without having consulted the government, it resigned, and the king appointed a civil-servant government with Hjalmar Hammarskjöld as prime minister.

POLICY DURING WORLD WAR I

During World War I, Sweden attempted to remain neutral and to assert its right to trade with the belligerent countries. For Great Britain, the blockade was an important weapon, and Sweden's demand to import freely favoured Germany exclusively. As a result, the Allies stopped a large percentage of Sweden's trade. This, however, not only affected Sweden's exports to Germany but also from 1916 caused a severe shortage of food in Sweden. The situation was worsened by unrestricted submarine warfare and by the entry of the United States into the war in 1917. Hammarskjöld was forced to resign; he was followed by a Conservative government and shortly afterward by a Liberal one, both of which conducted a more-diplomatic trading policy with the Allies. In May 1918 an agreement was reached with Great Britain and the United States that allowed Sweden again to import produce from the West, on condition that exports to Germany be limited and that a large part of Sweden's merchant fleet be put at the Allies' disposal.

THE LIBERAL–SOCIAL DEMOCRATIC COALITION

In the general election of 1917, the left-wing parties (the Social Democrats and Liberals) secured a further increase in their majority in the second chamber, and the king was obliged to choose a Liberal–Social Democratic government. Under Nils Edén, the new government, as one of its first measures, amended the constitution. The main issues were suffrage for women and the introduction of a universal and equal franchise for elections to the first chamber and for local elections.

DOMESTIC POLICY (1918–45)

From 1920 onward a line was drawn between the socialist parties on one side and the Liberals and Conservatives on the other. From 1920 to 1932 the parties held power alternately, but no government

NILS EDÉN

Nils Edén (born August 25, 1871, Piteå, Sweden—died June 16, 1945, Stockholm) was a Swedish historian and politician. He led what is generally regarded as the first parliamentary government in Swedish history.

A historian of early modern Sweden and a professor at the University of Uppsala (1903–20), Edén was elected to the Riksdag (parliament) in 1908 and quickly rose to prominence in the Liberal coalition party of Karl Staaff. Serving before and during World War I on the important defense and constitution committees, he became chairman of his party on Staaff's death in 1915.

The royal request that Edén form a government in 1917 after the Liberal and Social Democratic election victory is considered the first clear acknowledgment of the principle of parliamentary government in Swedish history. As head of the coalition government, he brought about better trade relations with the Allied powers and procured a constitutional amendment providing for woman suffrage and universal suffrage in local and lower chamber parliamentary elections. Leaving office in 1920, he served as governor of Stockholm province (1920–38) and returned to historical research. His scholarly writings include *1809 års revolution* (1911; "The Revolution of 1809") and *Den svenska riksdagen under femhundra år* (1935; "The Swedish Riksdag for 500 Years").

had any chance of gaining firm support for its policy in the Riksdag. From a political viewpoint the 1920s were a period of stagnation.

From an economic point of view, however, the picture was quite different. The 1920s were marked by steadily improving trade conditions, and in this boom period Sweden was one of the countries that prospered significantly.

Sweden suffered severely during the early years of the Great Depression. In the early 1930s unemployment rose, and reductions in wages caused a series of harsh labour conflicts. The election of 1932 brought a considerable advance to the Social Democratic Party, and to some extent to the Farmers' Party as well, and led to a Social Democratic administration under the leadership of Per Albin Hansson. It offered a comprehensive policy to fight the crisis, including extensive public works and a number of moves in support of agriculture. This policy was subjected to scathing criticism by the right-wing parties, but an agreement reached with the Farmers' Party in 1933 made it possible to implement the program. The economic crisis of the '30s was overcome more rapidly in Sweden than in most other countries. As early as 1936, wages had reached their old level, and by the end of the decade unemployment had become insignificant.

From a political point of view, the '30s were a time of preparation, when a series of bills for radical reforms were worked out. The whole program could be summarized in the term *folkhemmet*, in which society is viewed as a "home" for the people, taking care of their needs in unemployment, sickness, and old age; but, with the advent of World War II in 1939, reforms were postponed because of rising military expenditure and supply difficulties.

FOREIGN POLICY (1918–45)

When World War I ended, Russia and Germany were among the defeated nations, and Sweden thus found itself in an unusually good position regarding external security. In 1925 military expenditure was considerably reduced. Problems regarding foreign policy were confined to Sweden's application for membership in the League of Nations, which was granted in 1920, and to its relationship with Finland.

When the Finnish Civil War ended in 1918, the problem of Åland reemerged. The inhabitants of the Åland Islands (Finnish: Ahvenanmaa) were purely Swedish-speaking, and a plebiscite revealed that almost all were in favour of affiliation with Sweden. The League of Nations, however, decided in 1921 to award Finland sovereignty over the islands, though with certain conditions pertaining to internal self-government and limiting the right to fortify or otherwise utilize the islands for military purposes.

Adolf Hitler's rise to power in Germany resulted in a reexamination of Sweden's defense policy, which in 1936 was amended to strengthen the country's defenses. Sweden followed a strictly neutral course, in close collaboration with the other Scandinavian countries and the Netherlands, Belgium, and Switzerland. As a consequence, Hitler's proposal in the spring of 1939 for a nonaggression pact was rejected. Sweden's attempt to form a Nordic defense union or, failing that, a Swedish-Finnish alliance led to nothing, primarily because the Soviet Union objected.

On the outbreak of war in 1939, Sweden declared itself neutral. When the Soviet Union shortly afterward launched an attack on Finland, Sweden gave Finland aid in the form of vast matériel and a volunteer corps. On the other hand, Sweden, in common with Norway, refused the Allies' request to march through its territory in order to intervene in the war. After the German occupation of Denmark and Norway in 1940, however, Sweden was forced by German military superiority to allow the transit of German troops through Sweden to Norway. Many Norwegians and Danes sought refuge in Sweden, the majority of them with the intention of fleeing to England. When Germany attacked the Soviet Union in June 1941, transit facilities were demanded for a division of German troops from Norway to Finland, and Sweden acquiesced under threat of military reprisals. In 1943 the agreement concerning the transit of German troops was revoked. Toward the end of the war, Norwegian and Danish police were trained and equipped in Sweden. Immediately after the war, Sweden was

RAOUL WALLENBERG

Swedish businessman and diplomat Raoul Wallenberg became legendary through his efforts to rescue Hungarian Jews during World War II. His mysterious disappearance while a prisoner in the Soviet Union also fueled his notoriety.

Born August 4, 1912, in Stockholm, Sweden, Wallenberg was a descendant of a wealthy and prestigious family of bankers, industrialists, and diplomats. He studied architecture in the United States and in 1936 became the foreign representative for a central European trading company, whose president was a Hungarian Jew. After the Germans sent troops and SS (Nazi paramilitary corps) units into Hungary in March 1944 to round up "subversives" and Jews, Wallenberg, with the help of Jewish and refugee organizations from Sweden and the United States, persuaded the Swedish Foreign Ministry to send him to Budapest on July 9 with a diplomatic passport. There, several thousand Jews (estimates vary from 4,000 to 35,000) were enlisted and sheltered by Wallenberg in "protected houses" flying the flags of Sweden and other neutral countries. By this time, some 438,000 Hungarian Jews had already been deported to the Nazi extermination camps—Wallenberg arrived just after the deportations came to a halt. He also dogged the Germans at deportation trains and on "death marches," distributing food and clothing to the Jewish prisoners and trying to rescue some of them with papers and money for their passage out of the country. In the process, he was threatened more than once by Adolf Eichmann.

Photograph of Swedish diplomat Raoul Wallenberg, who saved the lives of thousands of Hungarian Jews during World War II. Keystone/Hulton Archive/Getty Images

Soon after Soviet troops reached Budapest, Wallenberg reported to the occupying authority on January 17, 1945, but was immediately arrested for espionage—his money, radio, and dubious diplomatic status making him suspect. According to Swedish authorities, the Soviets later privately admitted that his arrest had been a mistake, during a confused period at war's end, but that their only information was that Wallenberg had died of a heart attack in a Moscow prison cell in 1947. There were unconfirmed reports from freed Soviet prisoners, however, that he had been seen alive in prison, notably in 1951, 1959, and 1975.

On September 22, 1981, the U.S. Congress, under the leadership of Representative Tom Lantos—who had himself been rescued by Wallenberg—granted honorary citizenship to the missing Wallenberg. Such honorary citizenship had been granted only once before, to Sir Winston Churchill.

granted membership in the United Nations, without having relinquished its principally neutral foreign policy.

THE WELFARE STATE

The coalition government that was formed in 1939 was replaced shortly after the end of the war in 1945 by a Social Democratic government under the leadership of Per Albin Hansson. After his death in 1946, Tage Erlander became prime minister, a post that he held until his resignation in 1969. He was succeeded by Olof Palme, who took over the leadership of the government without any other changes being made in its composition.

THE PERIOD OF SOCIAL REFORM

The period 1946 to 1950 may justly be called the great period of reform, during which new, comprehensive laws were adopted concerning old-age pensions, child allowances, health insurance, rent allowances, educational reforms, and the expansion of institutions of higher education and research. Those parts of the Social Democrats' postwar program that aimed at nationalization

of industry were not carried through. By tax reorganization the government tried, however, to achieve wider distribution of wealth.

Surprisingly, the years after World War II had been marked by stable trading conditions and a scarcity of labour. During the Korean War, the boom reached its climax, entailing large price increases and rapid inflation. A recession followed at the end of 1951. In Sweden this meant that the upward movement of prices and incomes was interrupted, and for the first time since World War II there was a rise in unemployment. Even though the crisis of 1951–52 was neither serious nor long, it drew attention to the problems of economic stability. The Social Democrats now became primarily preoccupied with securing the advances already achieved. They began to collaborate with the Farmers' Party, and in the autumn of 1951 the Social Democratic government was replaced by a coalition government consisting of Social Democrats and Farmers, which lasted until 1957.

In the late 1950s the question of a compulsory pension for all employees

OLOF PALME

Olof Palme (born Sven Olof Joachim Palme, January 30, 1927, Stockholm, Sweden—died February 28, 1986, Stockholm) is arguably Sweden's best-known international politician. He served as prime minister of Sweden (1969–76, 1982–86), was a prominent leader of the Swedish Social Democratic Workers' Party (Sveriges Socialdemokratiska Arbetar Partiet), and held various international leadership positions.

Born into a wealthy Stockholm family, Palme studied at Kenyon College, Ohio, U.S. (B.A., 1948), and obtained a law degree from Stockholm University in 1951. An active member of the Social Democrats from the early 1950s, Palme became Prime Minister Tage Erlander's personal secretary in 1953 and entered the Swedish Parliament in 1958. Palme joined the Social Democratic government in 1963 as minister without portfolio. In 1965 he advanced to the post of minister of communication and in 1967 to the dual post of minister of education and ecclesiastical affairs. He succeeded Erlander as party secretary and as prime minister in 1969. Soon afterward his attacks on U.S. war policy in Vietnam and his acceptance of U.S. Army deserters who sought refuge in Sweden led to strained relations between his country and the United States. (He denied the deserters official political refugee status, however, saying that one could not be a refugee from a free country.)

The 1976 general election resulted in the defeat of the Social Democrats after 44 years in power. Between terms in office Palme continued to be active in his party and maintained his strong pacifist stance. He also had close personal relations with European Social Democratic politicians such as Bruno Kreisky of Austria and Willy Brandt of West Germany. He served as president of the Nordic Council from 1979 to 1980, chaired the Independent Commission on Disarmament and Security in Geneva, and acted as UN special envoy to mediate in the war between Iran and Iraq.

The nuclear accident in 1979 at Three Mile Island in the United States had a great impact in Sweden, and Palme contributed to a referendum (passed in 1980) to remove all nuclear reactors in Sweden. After being elected prime minister again in 1982, Palme tried to reinstate socialist economic policies in Sweden, and he continued to be outspoken on matters of European security. He was assassinated by a gunman in 1986; his murder remains unsolved.

became a principal political issue. The opposition fought it energetically, mainly because it was feared that control of the pension fund would create a latent risk of complete socialism; the government finally enacted the bill in 1959.

NEW CONSTITUTION

In 1955 a committee to review the constitution of 1809 (the Instrument of Government) was appointed. On its recommendations, the old two-chamber

Riksdag was replaced in 1971 by a one-chamber Riksdag composed of 350 members elected by proportional representation. The new Instrument of Government, which entered into force on January 1, 1975, reduced the membership of the Riksdag to 349 (to minimize the risk of evenly divided votes) and the voting age to 18. It also further curtailed the powers and duties of the king to a point merely ceremonial. King Carl XVI Gustaf, who succeeded Gustav VI Adolf in 1973, was the first king to serve under the new constitution.

FOREIGN POLICY INTO THE 1990s

Sweden's foreign policy since 1945 has remained strictly neutral. When the international situation became tense in 1948 during the Berlin blockade and airlift, the Swedish government took the initiative in negotiations on a defense alliance between Sweden, Norway, and Denmark. Sweden insisted that the alliance should be truly independent of the Great Powers, while Norway wanted cooperation with the Western powers; as a result, negotiations came to nothing. In accordance with its policy of neutrality, Sweden did not apply for membership in the European Economic Community (EEC), although it did pursue its policy of liberalizing trade by participating in the establishment of the European Free Trade Association (EFTA) in 1959. In addition, Scandinavian collaboration

was intensified by the Nordic Council, which was formally inaugurated in 1952. Among the important results of the council's work were the dropping of passport requirements between the Scandinavian countries, the creation of a free-labour market, and the establishment of a far-reaching coordination of economic and social legislation. On the other hand, plans for a Nordic customs union, which were discussed during the 1960s and which aimed at more extensive cooperation than already existed within the framework of EFTA, produced no result. The so-called Nordek plan, submitted in 1969, which also aimed at far-reaching economic cooperation between the Nordic countries, met with opposition, primarily from Finland, and was abandoned in 1970. During negotiations for entry into the European Communities (EC, later European Community; the successor of the EEC), in which Denmark and Norway took part in 1971, Sweden repeated its declaration that it did not intend to seek membership, on the grounds of neutrality. But the expansion of the EC and the plans for a closer integration of the EC nations made it more and more difficult for Sweden to carry out its policy. Finally, after the dissolution of the U.S.S.R. made the Swedish policy of neutrality obsolete, Sweden applied for membership in the EC in 1991, joining in 1995 after it had been reorganized and embedded in the newly formed European Union (EU).

NORDIC COUNCIL OF MINISTERS

The Nordic Council of Ministers was established in February 1971 under an amendment to the Helsinki Convention (1962) between the Nordic countries of Denmark, Finland, Iceland, Norway, and Sweden for the purpose of consultation and cooperation on matters of common interest. It consists of the ministers of state of the member countries, as well as other ministers with responsibility for the subject under discussion. Formal decisions are usually binding on the member governments. The Council of Ministers provides funds for a large number of joint Nordic institutions and projects in such fields as investment finance, scientific research and development, culture, education, and social welfare and health. A related organization, the Nordic Council, serves as an advisory body.

DOMESTIC AFFAIRS INTO THE 21ST CENTURY

In the election of 1970 the Social Democrats lost the absolute majority they had held since 1968. But in spite of this the Social Democratic government of Palme, with the support of the Communists, continued in office until the election of 1976, when the nonsocialist parties won a majority. Palme's resignation brought an end to 44 years of Social Democratic domination.

Nonsocialists formed governments from 1976 to 1982, the first coalition being led by Thorbjörn Fälldin (Centre Party). His government felt repercussions of the international economic crisis of the 1970s, manifested in unemployment and adverse effects on the standard of living. Political discussion, however, focused above all on the question of nuclear power. Fälldin, who had campaigned for the cessation of building nuclear power plants, was forced to compromise on this

issue. As a result, he resigned in October 1978. Ola Ullsten, leader of the People's Party (widely known as the Liberal Party and officially the Liberal People's Party from 1990), succeeded him as prime minister, forming a minority government in which one-third of the ministers were women. Following a general election in 1979, the nonsocialist coalition led by Fälldin was returned to office.

The development of nuclear power continued to be a hotly debated issue. A national referendum on the issue was held in 1980, with the government considering gradually discontinuing its nuclear power plants. Since then, public opinion generally has been supportive of the continued use of nuclear power, even though the government has decommissioned some plants.

Throughout the 1980s, political debate focused on economic problems, particularly those related to escalating inflation, an unfavourable international trade balance, and unemployment. These problems grew more severe as a result of worldwide changes in the methods of processing raw materials and in industrial production that developed from the beginning of the 1970s. Changes of this kind created economic difficulties throughout Sweden's industrial complex, including such major sectors as textile manufacturing, iron- and steel-making, shipbuilding, and mining. Escalating unemployment generated by the economic downturn was especially significant during 1980–83 and at the beginning of the 1990s.

Unemployment became a central issue of the 1982 parliamentary elections, along with the deficit and a proposal by the Social Democrats to establish a wage-earner investment fund. The Social Democrats won a resounding victory in the elections, and a new government was formed by Palme. The elections signaled a new polarization of Swedish politics, with the Moderate Party (as the Conservative Party had been known since 1969) gaining a significant number of new seats in the Riksdag, while the Liberals lost almost half of their representation.

The new government quickly took strong steps to alleviate the country's economic stagnation, including an increase in the value-added tax (VAT) and a sharp decrease in the value of the national currency, the krona. Simultaneously, pressures were brought to bear on employers to resist workers' demands for higher wages to offset the resulting price increases. Signs of recovery began to appear in response to the government's measures and also as a result of the improving international economic scene in 1983–84. Taxation rose to a very high level, however, as a result of the large budget deficit and rapidly growing employment in the public sector. At the same time, a controversial issue developed over the legislation for the wage-earner investment fund that the Social Democrats and the Communists had managed to push through the Riksdag in late 1983, in spite of unified resistance from the nonsocialist parties and the business community. The opposing groups feared that the legislation would move Sweden too heavily in the direction of socialism. After their implementation the employee funds appeared not to affect the economic system in any appreciable way. Although they suffered some losses, the socialist parties continued to hold a majority of the seats in the Riksdag after the 1985 election. The most significant outcome of the election was a strong advance by the Liberal Party, which had come under new leadership.

On February 28, 1986, Prime Minister Palme was assassinated, shocking a country unused to political violence (this was the first political assassination in modern Swedish history). He was replaced by Ingvar Carlsson, the deputy prime minister, who, although a less-dynamic figure, shared Palme's political philosophy. Without Palme, however, Sweden's role in the arena of international politics, where it had championed human rights and promoted peace and disarmament, diminished.

The 1988 election did not change the political picture greatly. Nonetheless, the Green Ecology Party garnered 5.5 percent of the vote, exceeding the 4 percent minimum required to enter the parliament. The domestic policy of the Social Democratic government was characterized by concessions to a more liberal program carried through with the support of the Liberal Party. For example, there was a considerable reduction in direct taxes on income, and a program for an energy policy for the future was developed.

The September 1991 election, on the other hand, resulted in a major change in Swedish politics. With the country mired in a recession, the Social Democrats were swept from office. The main victor in this election was the Moderate Party, under the leadership of Carl Bildt. The Moderates received 22.1 percent of the vote and took 80 seats in the Riksdag, while the Social Democrats lost 18 seats. As a result, the nonsocialist parties controlled 170 seats (not a majority) against only a combined 154 for the Social Democrats and the Left Party (the former Communist Party). Prime Minister Carlsson immediately resigned, and a nonsocialist coalition government was formed by Bildt. He had campaigned on a platform of directing Sweden's economy away from socialism and toward a free-market system. His centre-right coalition immediately proposed privatizing state-owned companies, cutting taxes and government spending, and lifting restrictions on foreign ownership of Swedish companies.

With the recession continuing, the Social Democrats returned to office in September 1994 again under Carlsson's leadership. He attempted to reduce both Sweden's enormous budget deficit—which had reached 13 percent of gross domestic product—and its 13 percent unemployment rate. With the Soviet Union's collapse having rendered Sweden's traditional neutrality obsolete, Carlsson also pursued membership in the EU, despite opposition from within his own party and from environmentalists. On November 13, 1994, 52 percent of voters backed EU membership, and Sweden officially joined in 1995. However, notwithstanding the favourable recommendation of a government commission, Prime Minister Göran Persson (who succeeded Carlsson in 1996 after his retirement) cited public opposition and rejected adoption of the euro, Europe's single currency, when it went into effect in 1999.

By the end of 1999, Sweden had emerged from its economic crisis. A number of economic changes occurred in the late 1990s, reflecting a profound change in the concept of folkhemmet and shifting more economic responsibility from the central government to the provinces and municipalities and from the state to the individual. Although the Social Democratic Party's share of the vote dropped from 45.3 percent in 1994 to 39.8 percent in 2002, Persson was able to continue as prime minister. While still

Sweden's largest political party, it was increasingly divided on such important issues as the September 2003 referendum on the replacement of the krona with the euro, which voters overwhelmingly rejected. That same month the public stabbing of Anna Lindh, the popular minister of foreign affairs, shocked Swedes and again raised questions about the price of an open and egalitarian society.

Despite a thriving economy, growing concerns about Sweden's ability to maintain its strong social welfare programs while remaining competitive in the globalized economy contributed to the victory of the Moderate Party, under the leadership of Frederik Reinfeldt, in a tightly contested election in 2006. Among the policy changes of the new government was retreat from the Social Democrats' commitment to end the use of nuclear power by 2010. Initially Reinfeldt's government pledged to plan no new nuclear plants during its first term, but then in 2009 it rescinded that

FREDRIK REINFELDT

Swedish politician Fredrik Reinfeldt became prime minister of Sweden in 2006. He also served as leader of the Moderate Party from 2003.

Though born in Stockholm (on August 4, 1965), Reinfeldt spent part of his early childhood in London, where his father worked as a consultant for Shell Oil Company. The family returned to Sweden in the late 1960s. While completing his compulsory military service, Reinfeldt was elected deputy chair of the Swedish Central Conscripts Council (1985–86). He studied business administration and economics at Stockholm University, where he was a board member for the Swedish National Union of Students before graduating with a bachelor's degree in 1990.

In 1991 Reinfeldt was elected to the Riksdag, Sweden's parliament. He held a number of posts on the board of the youth wing of the Moderate Party, including chairman of its executive committee (1992–95). In the wake of the Moderate Party's 1994 electoral loss, Reinfeldt publicly denounced the leadership and allies of former prime minister and Moderate Party leader Carl Bildt. As a result, Reinfeldt was kept out of significant political posts until 1999, when Bildt ceded party leadership to Bo Lundgren.

By the time Lundgren resigned in 2002, Reinfeldt was the most likely contender for succession, and in 2003 he was elected leader of the Moderate Party. In addition to emphasizing tax cuts (a party touchstone), Reinfeldt turned his attention toward lessening the Swedish people's dependence on the welfare state by proposing various reforms, such as reducing jobless benefits, that were designed to lower the unemployment rate. For the 2006 parliamentary election, the Moderate Party formed an alliance with the Christian Democrats, the Liberals, and the Centre Party. It won a majority of seats in the tightly contested race, and Reinfeldt succeeded Göran Persson as prime minister, ending the Social Democrats' 12 years in power.

During Reinfeldt's first year in office, the country's jobless rate fell, and his administration oversaw cuts in both taxes and unemployment benefits. In 2009 he began his six-month term as the rotating president of the European Council, the European Union's chief decision-making body, and his tenure was widely considered a success. The following year he earned additional praise for his handling of the Swedish economy, which experienced a strong rebound after struggling in the wake of the global financial crisis of 2008. In the September 2010 election, the Moderate Party captured 30 percent of the vote, though his centre-right coalition fell short of a majority. Reinfeldt subsequently formed a minority government the following month.

restriction and looked forward to a long-term future that would continue to include nuclear power.

The Swedish economy was hard-hit by the global financial crisis and economic downturn of 2008–09, with gross domestic product (GDP) growth at a virtual stand-still in 2008 and declining by more than 5 percent in 2009, arguably the most difficult year for the country's economy since World War II. During this period unemployment climbed to more than 8 percent, an unheard-of level for a country in which the pursuit of full employment was a source of national pride. Partly as a result of government stimulus-spending efforts, however, the economy bounced back quickly, with GDP growth back in the black by more than 4 percent in 2010.

Seemingly rewarding the government for its assured handling of the economic downturn, Swedish voters again showed strong support for the four-party centre-right alliance led by Reinfeldt, though the coalition came up three seats short of a majority in the September 2010 parliamentary election and chose to form a minority government, with Reinfeldt remaining as prime minister. The election marked the first time that a nonsocialist government had won reelection. It was also notable for the success of the anti-immigrant Sweden Democrats, who broke through the 4 percent threshold necessary for representation and became the first far-right party to enter the Swedish parliament, capturing 20 seats.

Notwithstanding the Riksdag's approval in 2008 of the Lisbon Treaty, which sought to restructure some of the institutions of the EU, Sweden remained outside the euro zone. Nevertheless, because of Sweden's extensive trade with other EU countries, its recently bright economic prospects dimmed somewhat in response to the euro-zone debt crisis that afflicted Greece, Portugal, and Ireland (as well as European states with larger economies, such as Spain and Italy).

The Scandinavian countries of Denmark, Finland, and Sweden have affinities with one another and a distinctness from the rest of continental Europe, evident in their history and culture. Indeed, these three countries have been linked together for centuries, and in spite of the remoteness of their location, they have made an impact on the rest of the world.

From the 9th century to the 11th century, Danes and other Scandinavians revamped European society when the Vikings undertook marauding, trading, and colonizing expeditions. Finland was a part of Sweden from the 12th century until the early 19th century, and Denmark and Sweden were part of the Kalmar Union, which dominated northwestern Europe for a time during the Middle Ages. Philological and archaeological discoveries of the late 18th and 19th centuries—which pointed to an earlier unity among Denmark, Finland, and Sweden—helped fuel a Pan-Scandinavian sentiment in the 19th century. The latter part of the 20th century saw a resurgence of Pan-Scandinavian sentiment, yet this did not interfere with any of the three countries opting to join the broader international organization of the European Union.

GLOSSARY

ABSOLUTISM A political theory that absolute power should be vested in one or more rulers.

APOGEE The furtherest and highest part of something.

ARCHIPELAGO A body of water dotted with many scattered islands.

AUTONOMOUS Having the right or power of self-government.

BURGHER A prosperous member of a town's middle class.

CONSCRIPTION Mandatory enrollment in a country's armed forces; a military draft.

DEBACLE A violent disruption or complete and utter failure.

DEPREDATION The state of being ruined, plundered, or laid to waste.

DOWRY Traditionally, the money, goods, or estate that a woman brings to her husband in marriage.

FEUDALISM An medieval political system wherein homage and service are given by vassals to lords in exchange for living on a noble's land.

FJORD A narrow inlet of the sea between cliffs or steep slopes.

GLACIER A large body of ice moving slowly down a slope or valley or spreading outward on a land surface.

HOMOGENEOUS Of the same or a similar kind or nature; uniform.

MEGALITH A very large, usually rough stone used in prehistoric cultures as a monument or building block.

MUNICIPALITY A mostly urban political unit that holds corporate status and is usually self-governing.

NOMADIC Roaming from place to place frequently or without a fixed pattern of movement.

OMBUDSMAN In government, an official appointed to receive and investigate complaints made against abuses by public officials.

PAGAN Someone who has little or no religion and who delights in sensual pleasures and material goods.

PHYSIOCRAT Someone who believes that government policy should not interfere with the operation of natural economic laws, and that land is the source of all wealth.

PRELATE A religious leader of great rank.

REPARATIONS The payment of damages, specifically paid by a defeated nation for damages to or expenditures sustained by another nation as a result of hostilities.

SUBSIDY A monetary grant or gift.

TITULAR Existing in title only.

UNICAMERAL Having or consisting of a single legislative chamber.

BIBLIOGRAPHY

DENMARK

GEOGRAPHY

Kenneth E. Miller (compiler), *Denmark* (1987), contains an annotated bibliography of various 19th- and 20th-century publications. Judith Friedman Hansen, *We Are a Little Land: Cultural Assumptions in Danish Everyday Life* (1980), describes the social and cultural values that characterize the Danish lifestyle as a distinctive variant of modern Euro-American civilization. Robert T. Anderson and Barbara Gallatin Anderson, *The Vanishing Village: A Danish Maritime Community* (1964), is an easy-to-read study of Danish life in a village as it changed from that of a small inner-focused community to that of a mid-20th-century suburb of Copenhagen. Clemens Pedersen (ed.), *The Danish Co-operative Movement*, trans. from Danish (1977), offers an authoritative history of how Danish cooperatives first became influential in shaping the modernization of agriculture in Denmark. Thomas Rørdam, *The Danish Folk High Schools*, 2nd rev. ed., trans. from Danish (1980), describes historically the movement initiated by N.S.F. Grundtvig that culminated in the folk high school movement as a means of putting education to the service of defining national goals of equality and self-respect for a peasant ancestry. Eric S. Einhorn and John Logue, *Modern Welfare States: Politics and Policies in Social Democratic Scandinavia* (1989), extensively describes and analyzes the expansion of the public sector in developing and managing the social welfare system that characterizes Denmark, Norway, and Sweden. John L. Campbell, John A. Hall, and Ove K. Pedersen (eds.), *National Identity and the Varieties of Capitalism: The Danish Experience* (2006), analyzes Denmark's political economy. Mary Hilson, *The Nordic Model: Scandinavia Since 1945* (2007); David Arter, *Scandinavian Politics Today*, 2nd ed. (2008); and Erik Allardt et al., *Nordic Democracy* (1981), consider politics and political institutions in Scandinavia. Stanley V. Anderson, *The Nordic Council: A Study of Scandinavian Regionalism* (1967), a rather technical account from the perspective of political science and international law, studies how Danish communal values find expression through international cooperation with other Scandinavian nations. Christine Ingebritsen, *Scandinavia in World Politics* (2006), examines Scandinavian politics in a post-World War II global context.

HISTORY

General works include Knud J.V. Jespersen, *A History of Denmark*, trans.

by Ivan Hill and Christopher Wade, 2nd ed. (2011); *Palle Lauring, A History of Denmark*, trans. by David Hohnen, 3rd ed. (2009); W. Glyn Jones, *Denmark: A Modern History*, rev. ed. (1986), a well-written survey; and Bent Rying, *Denmark: History* (1988), and *Danish in the South and the North*, vol. 2 (1988), which collectively deal with Denmark from the Stone Age to the 20th century and beyond.

Danish prehistory and archaeology are examined in Palle Lauring, *Land of the Tollund Man* (1957; originally published in Danish, 1954), covering the first settlers of hunting nomads to the Vikings; P.V. Glob, *Denmark: An Archaeological History from the Stone Age to the Vikings* (also published as *Danish Prehistoric Monuments*, 1971; originally published in Danish, 1942), a scholarly survey, *The Mound People: Danish Bronze-Age Man Preserved* (1974, reissued 1983; originally published in Danish, 1970), a thoroughly illustrated technical monograph, and *The Bog People: Iron Age Man Preserved* (1969, reissued 1988; originally published in Danish, 1965); Else Roesdahl, *The Vikings*, trans. by Susan M. Margeson and Kirsten Williams, 2nd ed. (1998), and *Viking Age Denmark* (1982; originally published in Danish, 1980), providing an extensive description of Viking activities; and James Graham-Campbell (ed.), *Cultural Atlas of the Viking World* (1994), an admirable coverage of Viking geography. Jenny Jochens, *Women in Old Norse Society* (1995), goes further in uncovering the history of Viking women.

Brian Patrick McGuire, *The Cistercians in Denmark: Their Attitudes, Roles, and Functions in Medieval Society* (1982), presents a good example of the role of monasticism in medieval Denmark. Ruth Mazo Karras, *Slavery and Society in Medieval Scandinavia* (1988), draws on a wide variety of primary sources and archaeological data about the social, legal, and economic aspects of slavery. John Robert Christianson, *On Tycho's Island: Tycho Brahe and His Assistants, 1570–1601* (2000), gives a detailed look at intellectual life in Christian IV's time. Fridlev Skrubbeltrang, *Agricultural Development and Rural Reform in Denmark* (1953); and Jens Christensen, *Rural Denmark, 1750–1980*, ed. by Claus Bjorn (1983), concern agriculture. Jørgen Hæstrup, *Secret Alliance: A Study of the Danish Resistance Movement, 1940–1945*, 3 vol. (1976–77; originally published in Danish, 1954), analyzes the movement in detail, based on "illegal" documents and personal accounts by leading members of the resistance; and Erik Kjersgaard, *Besættelsen 1940–45*, 2 vol. (1980–81), describes the lives of ordinary people during the occupation. For current research, three journals are useful: *The Scandinavian Economic History Review* (3/yr.); *Scandinavian Journal of History* (5/yr.); and *Scandinavian Political Studies* (quarterly).

FINLAND

GENERAL WORKS

Overviews are provided in Laura Kolbe (ed.), *Portraying Finland: Facts and Insights*, trans. by Malcom Hicks and William Moore, 2nd rev. ed (2008); Päivi Elovainio, *Facts About Finland*, 3rd ed. (2002); Max Engman and David Kirby (eds.), *Finland: People, Nation, State* (1989); Eric Solsten and Sandra W. Meditz (eds.), *Finland: A Country Study*, 2nd ed. (1990); and *Finland Handbook* (annual), published by the Finnish Tourist Board.

GEOGRAPHY

W.R. Mead, *An Historical Geography of Scandinavia* (1981); and Kalevi Rikkinen, *A Geography of Finland*, trans. from Finnish (1992), provide comprehensive surveys. A broad interpretive treatment, with a look at the social customs of Finland, is found in Philip Ward, *Finnish Cities: Travels in Helsinki, Turku, Tampere, and Lapland* (1987).

Ethnological studies include Aurélien Sauvageot, *Les Anciens Finnois* (1961); and William A. Wilson, *Folklore and Nationalism in Modern Finland* (1976). Social life and customs are explored in Aini Rajanen, *Of Finnish Ways* (1981); Caj Bremer and Antero Raevuori, *The World of the Sauna* (1986; originally published in Finnish, 1985);

Antti Tuuri, *The Face of Finland*, ed. by Pauli Kojo, trans. from Finnish (1983); and Anneke Lipsanen, *The Finnish Folk Year: A Perpetual Diary & Book of Days, Ways, and Customs* (1987).

Finland's economy is discussed in Fred Singleton, *The Economy of Finland in the Twentieth Century* (1986); Riitta Hjerppe, *The Finnish Economy, 1860–1985: Growth and Structural Change* (1989; originally published in Finnish, 1988); *Organisation for Economic Co-operation and Development, Reviews of National Science and Technology Policy: Finland* (1987); *Environmental High-Technology from Finland* (1986), published by the Ministry of the Environment; *Economic Survey* (annual), published by the Ministry of Finance; and *Finnish Industry*, rev. ed. (1982), an overview of developments, published by the Bank of Finland.

Government and politics are analyzed in D.G. Kirby, *Finland in the Twentieth Century* (1979); Anthony F. Upton, Peter P. Rohoe, and A. Sparring, *Communism in Scandinavia and Finland* (also published as *The Communist Parties of Scandinavia and Finland*, 1973); Juhani Mylly and R. Michael Berry (eds.), *Political Parties in Finland* (1984); *David Arter, Politics and Policy-Making in Finland* (1987); Risto Alapuro, *State and Revolution in Finland* (1988); Max Jakobson, *Finland in the New Europe* (1998); and Jorma selovuori, *Power and Bureaucracy in Finland, 1809–1998*, trans. from Finnish

(1999). David Arter, *Scandinavian Politics Today*, 2nd ed. (2008), describes and analyzes the politics of Finland and its Scandinavian neighbours.

Finnish architecture and design are discussed in J.M. Richards, *800 Years of Finnish Architecture* (1978); Erik Kruskopf, *Finnish Design, 1875–1975: 100 Years of Finnish Industrial Design* (1975); Elizabeth Gaynor, *Finland, Living Design* (1984, reissued 1995); Jaakko Lintinen et al., *Finnish Vision: Modern Art, Architecture, and Design*, trans. from Finnish (1983); Marianne Aav and Nina Stritzler-Levine (eds.), *Finnish Modern Design: Utopian Ideals and Everyday Realities, 1930–1997* (1998); and Kenneth Frampton, "The Legacy of Alvar Aalto: Evolution and Influence," in Peter Reed (ed.), *Alvar Aalto: Between Humanism and Materialism* (1998). Other studies of national art and culture include John Boulton Smith, *The Golden Age of Finnish Art: Art Nouveau and the National Spirit*, 2nd rev. ed. (1985); Marianne Aav and Kaj Kalin, *Form Finland*, trans. from Finnish (1986), on decorative arts; Jaakko Ahokas, *A History of Finnish Literature* (1973); Matti Kuusi, Keith Bosley, and Michael Branch (eds. and trans.), *Finnish Folk Poetry: Epic: An Anthology in Finnish and English* (1977); Bo Carpelan, Veijo Meri, and Matti Suurpää (eds.), *A Way to Measure Time: Contemporary Finnish Literature*, trans. from Finnish (1992); Kai Laitinen, *Literature of Finland: An Outline*, 2nd ed., trans. from Finnish (1994); *Kalevala*, ed. by Aivi Gallen-Kallela and trans. by W.F. Kirby (1986), a jubilee edition of the national epic, illustrated by Akseli Gallen-Kallela; *The Kalevala: Epic of the Finnish People*, trans. by Eino Friberg and ed. by George C. Schoolfield (1988); Antony Hodgson, *Scandinavian Music: Finland & Sweden* (1984); Paavo Helistö, *Music in Finland* (1980); Maija Savutie, *Finnish Theatre: A Northern Part of World Theatre*, trans. from Finnish (1980); and Rauno Endén, *Yleisradio, 1926–1949: A History of Broadcasting in Finland*, trans. from Finnish (1996). Jan Sjåvik, *Historical Dictionary of Scandinavian Literature and Theater* (2006); and Arnold L. Weinstein, *Northern Arts: The Breakthrough of Scandinavian Literature and Art, from Ibsen to Bergman* (2008), both include coverage of Finnish art and literature.

HISTORY

General works on Finnish history include Henrik Meinander, *A History of Finland*, trans. by Tom Geddes (2011); John H. Wuorinen, *A History of Finland* (1965); Eino Jutikkala and Kauko Pirinen, *A History of Finland*, trans. by Paul Sjöblom, 6th rev. ed. (2003; originally published in Finnish, 1966); Eino Jutikkala, *Atlas of Finnish History*, 2nd rev. ed. (1959); Byron J. Nordstrom (ed.), *Dictionary of Scandinavian History* (1986); Fred Singleton, *A Short History of Finland*, revised and updated by A.F.

Upton (2005); and Matti Klinge, *A Brief History of Finland*, trans. from Finnish, 10th ed. (1997).

More detailed discussions of events in the 19th and 20th centuries are available in Juhani Paasivirta, *Finland and Europe: International Crises in the Period of Autonomy, 1808–1914*, ed. and abridged by D.G. Kirby (1981; originally published in Finnish, 1978); L.A. Puntila, *The Political History of Finland, 1809–1966* (1974; originally published in Finnish, 5th rev. and improved ed., 1971); Anthony F. Upton, *The Finnish Revolution, 1917–1918* (1980), a comprehensive analysis, and *Finland, 1939–1940* (1974); Max Jakobson, *Finland Survived: An Account of the Finnish-Soviet Winter War, 1939–1940*, 2nd enlarged ed. (1984); Philip Jowett, *Finland at War, 1939–45*; and Henrik O. Lunde, *Finland's War of Choice: The Troubled German-Finnish Coalition in World War II* (2011).

Foreign relations are the main topic of Tuomo Polvinen, *Between East and West: Finland in International Politics, 1944–1947*, ed. and trans. by D.G. Kirby and Peter Herring (1986; originally published in Finnish, 3 vol., 1979–81); Roy Allison, *Finland's Relations with the Soviet Union, 1944–1984* (1985); R. Michael Berry, *American Foreign Policy and the Finnish Exception* (1987); and Max Jakobson, *Finland: Myth and Reality* (1987). The *Yearbook of Finnish Foreign Policy*, published by the Finnish Institute of International Affairs, is another helpful source.

SWEDEN

GENERAL WORKS

Axel Sømme (ed.), *A Geography of Norden: Denmark, Finland, Iceland, Norway, Sweden*, new rev. ed. (1968), is a broad survey written by local geographers. Michael Jones and Kenneth Olwig (eds.), *Nordic Landscapes: Region and Belonging on the Northern Edge of Europe* (2008), is a consideration of the political, geographical, cultural, and artistic landscapes of the Nordic region by a diverse group of scholars including geographers, archaeologists, ethnologists, and anthropologists. Information specifically on Sweden is available from the Swedish Institute, the Swedish government's official information portal, which offers *Fact Sheets on Sweden* and *Sweden in Brief*.

ECONOMY

Daniel Viklund, *Sweden and the European Community: Trade, Cooperation, and Policy Issues*, trans. from Swedish (1989); and Gunnar Sjöstedt, *Sweden's Free Trade Policy: Balancing Economic Growth and Security* (1987), were published by the Swedish Institute. More comprehensive and detailed analyses include Barry P. Bosworth et al., *The Swedish Economy* (1987); Mary Hilson, *The Nordic Model: Scandinavia Since 1945* (2007); and

Staffan Marklund, *Paradise Lost?: The Nordic Welfare States and the Recession, 1975–1985* (1988).

GOVERNMENT AND SOCIAL CONDITIONS

The government system is described and analyzed in Peter Esaiasson and Sören Holmberg, *Representation from Above: Members of Parliament and Representative Democracy in Sweden*, trans. from Swedish (1996); Eric Lindström, *The Swedish Parliamentary System: How Responsibilities Are Divided and Decisions Are Made*, 2nd ed. (1983; originally published in Swedish, 1981); Ibrahim Ismail Wahab, *The Swedish Institution of Ombudsman: An Instrument of Human Rights* (1979); and Agne Gustafsson, *Local Government in Sweden*, trans. from Swedish, new ed. (1988). The dynamics of political background are explored in Gunnar Boalt and Ulla Bergryd, *Political Value Patterns and Parties in Sweden* (1981); and Mona Rosendahl, *Conflict and Compliance: Class Consciousness Among Swedish Workers* (1985). Concise surveys of particular political and social issues include Krister Wahlbäck, *The Roots of Swedish Neutrality* (1986); Walter Korpi, *The Development of the Swedish Welfare State in a Comparative Perspective* (1990); Britta Stenholm, *The Swedish School System* (1984; originally published in Swedish, 1984); and *National Board of Health and Welfare, The Swedish Health Services in the 1990s* (1985). Books dealing with the law include Stig Strömholm, *An Introduction to Swedish Law*, 2nd ed. (1988); *National Council for Crime Prevention, Crime and Criminal Policy in Sweden* (1990); and Ruth Bader Ginsburg and Anders Bruzelius, *Civil Procedure in Sweden* (1965).

CULTURE

Central Board of National Antiquities, The Cultural Heritage in Sweden, trans. from Swedish (1981), surveys conservation and restoration work on historic sites and buildings. Informative studies include Mereth Lindgren et al., *A History of Swedish Art*, trans. from Swedish (1987); Mariah Larsson and Anders Marklund (eds.), *Swedish Film: An Introduction and Reader* (2010); Andrew K. Nestingen, *Crime and Fantasy in Scandinavia: Fiction, Film, and Social Change* (2008); Ingemar Algulin, *A History of Swedish Literature* (1989); and Arnold Weinstein, *Northern Arts: The Breakthrough of Scandinavian Literature and Art, from Ibsen to Bergman* (2008). Other publications of the Swedish Institute cover numerous aspects of cultural life, including Ingemar Algulin, *Contemporary Swedish Prose* (1983); Ingemar Liman, *Traditional Festivities in Sweden* (1983); Henrik Sjögren, *Stage and Society in Sweden: Aspects of Swedish Theatre Since 1945*, trans. from Swedish (1979);

Peter Cowie, *Swedish Cinema, from Ingeborg Holm to Fanny and Alexander* (1985); Monica Boman and Bertil Lundgren (eds.), *Design in Sweden* (1985; originally published in Swedish, 1985); Nils K. Ståhle, *Alfred Nobel and the Nobel Prizes*, 3rd rev. ed. (1989); and *Claes Caldenby*, Olof Hultin, Gunilla Linde Bjur, Johan Mårtelius, and Rasmus Wærn, *A Guide to Swedish Architecture* (2001).

GENERAL HISTORY WORKS

Broad surveys spanning the centuries include Martina Sprague, *Sweden: An Illustrated History* (2005); Ingvar Andersson, *A History of Sweden*, 2nd ed. (1970; originally published in Swedish, 1944); Byron J. Nordstrom, *The History of Sweden* (2002); Franklin D. Scott, *Sweden, the Nation's History*, enlarged ed. (1988); Lars Magnusson, *An Economic History of Sweden* (2000); and H. Arnold Barton, *Essays on Scandinavian History* (2009).

EARLY PERIODS

Interpretations of runic inscriptions provide a glimpse of the early periods of history in Sven B.F. Jansson, *The Runes of Sweden*, trans. from Swedish (1962). Also informative is Mats Widgren, *Settlement and Farming Systems in the Early Iron Age: A Study of Fossil Agrarian Landscapes in Östergötland, Sweden* (1983). Medieval times are studied in P.H. Sawyer, *Kings and Vikings: Scandinavia and Europe, ad 700–1100* (1982); and Svend Gissel et al., *Desertion and Land Colonization in the Nordic Countries c. 1300–1600* (1981).

MODERN HISTORY

Other period histories are Michael Roberts, *The Early Vasas: A History of Sweden, 1523–1611* (1968, reprinted 1986), and *Gustavus Adolphus: A History of Sweden, 1611–1631*, 2 vol. (1953–1958); Curt Weibull, *Christina of Sweden*, trans. from Swedish (1966); Michael Roberts (ed.), *Sweden's Age of Greatness, 1632–1718* (1973); and R.M. Hatton, *Charles XII of Sweden* (1968).

Focus on the 19th century is provided in Roger Miller and Torvald Gerger, *Social Change in 19th-Century Swedish Agrarian Society* (1985); and Raymond E. Lindgren, *Norway-Sweden: Union, Disunion, and Scandinavian Integration* (1959, reprinted 1979). Broad topical analyses provide views ranging into the 20th century: Steven Koblik (ed.), *Sweden's Development from Poverty to Affluence, 1750–1970* (1975; originally published in Swedish, 1973); Kurt Samuelsson, *From Great Power to Welfare State: 300 Years of Swedish Social Development* (1968; originally published in Swedish, 1968); Lennart Jörberg, *Growth and Fluctuations of Swedish Industry, 1869–1912: Studies in the Process of Industrialisation*, trans. from Swedish (1961); W.M. Carlgren, *Swedish Foreign Policy During the Second*

World War (1977; originally published in Swedish, 1973); O. Fritiof Ander, *The Building of Modern Sweden: The Reign of Gustav V, 1907–1950* (1958); Allan Pred, *Even in Sweden: Racisms, Racialized Spaces, and the Popular Geographical Imagination* (2000); Mauricio Rojas, *Beyond the Welfare State: Sweden and the Quest for a Post-industrial Welfare Model* (2001); Lene Hansen & Ole Wæver (eds.), *European Integration and National Identity: The Challenge of the Nordic States* (2002); and Francis Sejersted, *The Age of Social Democracy: Norway and Sweden in the Twentieth Century*, trans. by Richard Daly (2011).